&Canada &the American Revolution
1774 1783

By GUSTAVE LANCTOT
of the Royal Society

Translated by MARGARET M. CAMERON

HARVARD UNIVERSITY PRESS
CAMBRIDGE, MASSACHUSETTS
1967

Printed in Canada

To Mr. Henry Allen Moe,
former President of
the John Simon Guggenheim Memorial Foundation

ACKNOWLEDGEMENTS

The author desires to express his deep gratitude to the John Simon Guggenheim Memorial Foundation which provided him with the means to complete the research for this work. He also wishes to thank the Humanities Research Council which, with the support of the Canada Council, helped to defray the expense of publication.

CONTENTS

ILLUSTRATIONS

MAPS

FOREWORD

The American invasion of 1775, an important event in Canada's brief history, gave rise to a political and a religious crisis. The political crisis found expression in aid to the rebels to the south, refusal of militiamen to bear arms, the struggle between loyalist and pro-rebel Canadians, and a project for union with the American Colonies. The religious crisis manifested itself in repudiation of loyalist directives from the clergy, insults to the Bishop and to priests, the capture of priests and their removal to American camps, and excommunication of pro-rebels by the Bishop. By drawing Church and State within range of an impending upheaval, the invasion came within an ace of making Canada American territory and creating schism in the Canadian Church. But even as it exposed the country to these dangers, the American Revolution, through the letters of the Continental Congress and the propaganda of its partisans, revealed to Canadians the rudiments of constitutional law. In short, it was the instrument of Quebec's political initiation. Neither at that time nor today, however, have historians brought out the important social impact of the event. The present work, based on a study of contemporary correspondence, memoirs, and files, proposes to describe this aspect of the past, and to present to the reader a virtually unknown page of Canadian history.

Rather than an interpretative synthesis of the period, this study seeks to present a documentary and chronological narrative of events with their accompaniment of opposing complexes and collective psychological reactions. The narrative form makes it possible to follow the day-by-day progress of the politico-religious drama which, unsettling minds and troubling consciences, determined the ideas and the behaviour of leaders and parties. It also makes it plain that, although popular history must so represent it, the past cannot be divided into neat, self-contained units. On the contrary, the past is revealed as a tangle of public and private interests, of political and economic conditions, of social and religious influences, a complex of inseparable elements which overlap and react upon one another.

For a monograph, this method appears to offer the advantage of a closer, more vital contact with the whole past, its succession of events, and its individual and collective reactions. By throwing more light on the picture, it leads the reader to a keener appreciation of the facts of history and the men who created its great moments.

Concluding this exploratory journey into the life of an age, the final chapter will also formulate a number of ideas which emerge from the narrative and which are basic to it.

CANADA
AND
THE AMERICAN REVOLUTION
1774–1783

1

CANADA UNDER ENGLISH DOMINATION

*Character of the Canadian people. Military govern-
ment. Treaty of Paris. Political administration. No general
exodus from the country. Loyalty of the clergy. Demand for
French laws. Redemption of paper money. British immigration.
Petition of British-American settlers for a representative system
of government. Opposition of Canadians. Murray replaced by
Carleton. Carleton inclined to favour Canadians' ideas rather
than those of British settlers.*

AFTER Montcalm's death, Vaudreuil had shown himself incapable
of defending New France, and on September 8, 1760 he surrendered to General Amherst, whose three armies surrounded
Montreal. The terms of surrender guaranteed neither military
honours to the army nor political security to the country. With
one blow the capitulation demolished the barrier which for two
centuries had confined the English colonies to the Atlantic sea-
board, and the France in America which had struck fear into the
hearts of Shirley and Franklin passed under the English flag.[1]
Canada's population now numbered 75,000. Moreover, the
Canadians were a fertile race, deeply attached to their traditions
and to the soil of their hard northern land. With the surrender
of its country, this French-Catholic population found itself
suddenly confronted with an extremely grave problem: what
fate did the future hold in store for it, exile or subjection,
assimilation or survival?

Already, under the influence of a new environment, the
Canadian had developed characteristics quite different from

3

those of the Frenchman in France. In military, religious, and social spheres, ideas and customs were becoming increasingly different from those of the mother country. With the exaggeration of youth, Bougainville, a witness of bitter quarrels between French and Canadian officers, went so far as to say: "We seem to belong to another, almost an enemy, nation."[2] The same rivalry existed between Canadian priests and French members of the higher clergy,[3] and the subservience of the French vassal to his lord[4] was unknown in Canada, where the tenant farmer seized every opportunity to display "a sort of independence."[5] Accustomed to "liberty,"[6] and "naturally indocile,"[7] Canadians were inclined to recognize "neither rule nor regulation."[8] This tendency to insubordination had its counterpart in a rooted social egalitarianism, remarkable in a country with an aristocratic form of government and well-defined social classes. "Here, everyone is *monsieur* or *madame*, the peasant as well as the gentleman, the peasant woman as well as the greatest lady";[9] and the countrymen "haven't the rough rustic air of our French peasants." This spirit of equality, which surprised both newcomers from France and travellers from other lands, was the result of certain factors in the environment: the habit of self-sufficiency, the autonomy of militia companies, the absence of privileged classes, the comparative poverty of seigneurs and the contrasting prosperity of the "very well-to-do peasants, living like minor noblemen in France."[10] An intendant, Raudot, found the typical Canadian: "intelligent, proud, conceited, lively, bold, industrious, and able to endure the most extreme fatigue."[11] Montcalm's opinion of Canadians was that they were endowed with "intelligence and courage."[12]

Under British rule, more liberal than that of the Bourbons, Canadian individualism became even more marked. "Since they have experienced the blessings of an English government," wrote one officer, "they are become insolent and overbearing."[13] Members of the seigniorial class were conscious of this tendency in their humbler compatriots, and their opinion was reported by the Lieutenant-Governor: "The Canadian *noblesse* often alleges that from the freedom enjoyed under their present government, the middling and lower sort of people daily lose of that deference and respect which they used formerly upon all occasions to show their superiors."[14] Even Governor Carleton had to admit that the habitants had "in a manner emancipated themselves,"[15] whereas earlier their first British Governor, who had seen them at work and on the field of battle, had been high in his praise of the "peasantry, . . . a strong and healthy race, plain in their dress, virtuous in their morals, and temperate in their living";[16] and of Canadians in general, "perhaps the bravest and best race upon the globe."[17]

With few exceptions, probably less than a hundred, all Canadians were Catholics, although it was sometimes observed that their religion made no deep mark on their everyday lives. Kalm commented that "religion here appears to consist solely in exterior practices,"[18] and Mgr. Briand was distressed at the lack of fervour displayed by his flock. "How little faith there is in Canada," he exclaimed, "although the outer shell of religion still remains!"[19] Moreover, these practising Catholics did not hestitate, on occasion, to display a spirit of independence, and even of insubordination towards the clergy. As early as 1691 Mgr. de Saint-Vallier considered that he had "reason to complain of the lack of respect shown by members of certain parishes";[20] while at the end of the French régime discord reigned in the parish of Cap Saint-Ignace, and Mgr. Briand was insulted by parishioners at Sainte-Anne-de-Beaupré.[21]

The blow struck by the capitulation of Montreal fell then on a sturdy little people, constant in courage and inclined to a certain independence of attitude in the face of established authority. Pending the final settlement of a peace treaty, General Amherst established a military type of administration. He maintained the three districts into which the country was divided, and appointed three army officers as lieutenant-governors: Murray in Quebec, Gage in Montreal, and Burton in Three Rivers. The former captains of militia companies, who carried out the functions of administration, applied French

5

law in all cases. There were no restrictions on the practice of the Catholic religion.[22]

This régime, a surprisingly generous one for the time, ended on February 10, 1763 with the signing of the Treaty of Paris. The treaty ceded all New France to England. It also granted religious freedom to the people of Canada, but with the disturbing provision, "as far as the laws of Great Britain permit." A time limit of eighteen months was set for those who preferred not to remain in the country. Within that limit, they were free to leave and to take their possessions with them. Soon the new rulers set about the task of establishing a civil administration.[23] A royal proclamation of October 7, 1763 created the province of Quebec and defined its limits. Shorn of a vast hinterland which extended from Labrador to the great Northwest, the new province was reduced to a narrow parallelogram stretching from the head of the River St. John to Lake St. John and thence to Lake Nipissing. From Lake Nipissing the line ran towards the St. Lawrence and Lake Champlain, then back to the Baie de Chaleur and Gaspé, across the St. Lawrence and up the River St. John to its starting point. The province was to be administered by a governor-general, James Murray, who would govern with the advice of a council of higher officials and members chosen by him until such time as he could convoke an elective assembly. Membership in the assembly would be restricted to Protestant British subjects. While suggesting that the people of Canada might "by degrees be induced to embrace the Protestant religion," the King's instructions to Murray conceded their freedom in this regard, but, in conformity with British statutes, denied any jurisdiction to the "see of Rome." Canadians were to swear allegiance to George III, on pain, in case of refusal, of expulsion from the country. The formula of abjuration, which recognized the Protestant succession, became obligatory for all persons occupying public charges; thus Catholics were effectively excluded from all such charges. Courts of justice, instituted by an ordinance of September 17, 1764, completed the administrative structure. The courts recognized English law

6

only, although later, in exceptional cases, Canadians were granted the privilege of serving on juries.[24]

Informed of the terms of the Treaty of Paris, Canadians had no choice; they had to accept their fate and resign themselves to life under the British flag. Apart from officials who had come from France and Canadian officers commanding French army units, almost no one, either among the country's leaders or among the lower classes, thought of emigrating to France. Descended as they were from generations of forbears who had created for themselves a free and satisfying life, Canadians, at the time of the conquest, did not for a moment consider the possibility of leaving a country which for them represented home, the family, worldly goods, land, and all the indissoluble ties that bind one to one's country. Leaders and common people alike chose to remain rooted in their ancestral soil. In 1764, General Murray estimated that "not more than 270 souls, men, women and children . . . [would] emigrate from this province in consequence of the treaty of peace." Most of these would be "officers, their wives, children and servants." Two years earlier, Gage had reported from Montreal and Burton from Three Rivers that there was no movement in favour of emigration from their districts.[25]

The English unconsciously put into practice Machiavelli's theory that you can easily govern a foreign people if you do not try to modify its ancient customs. Realists by nature, they favoured the interests of justice and of commerce, and they did not interfere with the habits and customs of the people.[26] With the peace, the country went back to work, the city folk to their business and the habitants to cultivating their land more zealously than ever. Resigned to an inexorable fate, the citizens of Montreal and Quebec had no compunction about playing an honest diplomatic card and presenting to the authorities addresses in which they recognized "the mildness, justice and moderation" of the British administration.[27] A few even temporized with truth to the extent of declaring that they were "pleased" to accept the new régime, and that they expected to

7

derive from it "advantages which they could never have enjoyed under French rule."[28]

The attitude of the clergy was frankly realistic. Beginning in 1762, prayers for the British royal family were offered in churches, and priests, following a directive from the Bishop, celebrated the proclamation of the treaty with *Te Deums*.[29] A clear-sighted hierarchy, in whom national sentiment was less imperious than care for the Catholic religion, in order to insure the preservation of religious freedom, put aside its French patriotism and declared its loyalty to the new sovereign.[30] In so doing, the clergy of Canada were anticipating the advice of Rome itself, couched in the words of Cardinal Castelli: "We must give credit to the English for their goodwill with respect to religion; and for their part, priests and bishop must, in this particular, sincerely forget that they are French."[31] The same policy inspired the request presented by the clergy for a form of oath of allegiance to the King of England to which Quebec Catholics could subscribe.[32]

In reality, however, ever since news of the Treaty of Paris had reached them, the homes of New France had been filled with sorrow and mourning. Behind the screen of official *Te Deums* and public declarations, people of all classes sought courage in their faith and consolation in their memories; but they were prostrated by the national calamity which had made their country an English province, and for them the future could not but be fraught with anxiety. Their first concern was for their religious freedom, now threatened by England's anti-Catholic laws. Laymen and church leaders, among them Charest and the Abbé de Montgolfier, who took the first steps to insure religious freedom, were supported by the Governor. Their combined efforts resulted in the consecration of a bishop, Mgr. Briand, in March, 1766, and of a coadjutor *cum successione futura*, Mgr. d'Esgly, in July, 1772.[33] A letter from Mgr. Briand expresses his satisfaction with the situation. "I can assure you," he wrote, "that things are going as well as usual, perhaps better, in the parishes and religious communities, and among the

8

people."[34] But freedom of worship for Catholics, although conceded by the authorities, was not yet sanctioned by any British law.

The administration of justice was a second cause for anxiety. When, in September, 1764, courts were created and English civil and criminal law introduced, a plea was presented for the maintenance of existing laws and for the use of French as the language of court procedure.[35] A group of citizens requested that the King maintain a court of first instance which would follow the *Coutume de Paris*, and that lawyers and parties be allowed to speak in French. "We entreat your Majesty," so ran the petition, "to permit us to transact our family affairs in our own tongue and to follow our customs in so far as they are not opposed to the general well-being of the colony."[36] Carleton affirmed that all Canadians were in agreement in their demand for the restoration of their own laws and customs.[37]

Finally, an even more urgent problem plunged "the people of all ranks into the greatest dejection." This was the fear of losing the paper money which had been left in their hands on the departure of the French authorities.[38] Paper money was the subject of their first petition to the King, in 1762,[39] and in 1764 they once more "anxiously" besought him to demand that France fulfil her financial obligations in accordance with the terms laid down in the treaty.[40] The French ministers, who were anxious to repair their country's financial condition, had begun to act even before this petition was presented. While still occupied with the prosecution of Bigot and his gang of plunderers they had attacked the problem of the Canadian debt, and on June 29, 1764, after months and months of investigation by a special commission, the terms of liquidation were fixed by royal decree. The King's debt to Canada, which amounted to 83,000,000 *livres*, was cut down to 37,606,000 by reducing certain notes to half, or even a quarter, of their face value. In payment of a debt of 15,958,729 *livres* on the books of her former subjects, France offered 6,655,000 *livres*! The royal book-keepers might well say that the operation was "advantageous for the King,"

9

a debtor whose powers were absolute. But the poor Canadian creditors had every reason to cherish bitter memories of the bankrupt's farewell with which Louis XV took leave of his colony.[41]

We have seen that the Canadians lost no time in putting their old system of petitions into practice with their new masters. They had recourse to it on other occasions when their aim was the modification of certain ordinances,[42] and their requests could not always be considered modest. In 1765, for example, in order to increase their exports of wheat, they suggested that the British government should revise its laws and bring them into accord with the new conditions arising from the conquest.[43] On the other hand, they showed, on occasion, that they were not lacking in goodwill. Thus, in 1764, they raised a contingent to fight against Pontiac.[44] Three hundred men volunteered, more or less freely, within a fortnight, and Gage congratulated their commander, de Rigauville, on this gratifying achievement.[45]

Into this French-Catholic population, conservative and resolute, the conquest immediately introduced a wave of English-Protestant immigration. The first of these new-comers were almost all provisioners and their employees, victuallers and sutlers who accompanied the English troops according to the custom of the time. The capitulation of Montreal encouraged a certain number of them to remain in the country, some to continue to supply the garrisons, others to engage in the fur trade, now opened up to them by the English occupation.[46] Before long a more important group appeared. On Amherst's invitation, merchants and commissioners came from Massachusetts and New York to Montreal and Quebec. They brought with them provisions and goods to the value of 300,000 dollars, which they sold to the military and civil population or exchanged for Canadian furs.[47]

This first core of British citizens in Canada increased with the arrival of immigrants attracted by the advantages which the country offered to merchants and tradesmen.[48] From about a hundred, their number had increased in 1764 to 200, including some Americans.[49] The latter group numbered about twenty in 1765 and more than fifty in 1774.[50] Almost all these "ancient subjects," as they were designated, were engaged in trade,[51] and for that reason they were not in favour with the military caste. Murray reported unfavourably on the British subjects in general and the colonials in particular; some of the latter were "most inveterate fanatics."[52] He was most disdainful of the merchants, "chiefly adventurers of mean education . . . [with] their fortunes to make and little solicitous about the means, provided the end is obtained."[53] The Governor added the comment that the newly-arrived British merchants were resentful because he could not appoint them magistrates nor allow them to "oppress" the new subjects. Burton accused the British immigrants of fomenting discord and lawlessness, and he too was convinced that they would stop at nothing in their determination to advance their own interests.[54]

Carleton's language was more restrained, at least at the beginning of his period in office, although he too saw the new-comers as "followers of the camp" or "adventurers in trade, or such as could not remain at home, who set out to mend their fortunes at the opening of this new channel for commerce."[55] The Canadian seigneurs were equally contemptuous of this "scheming tribe," among whom the camp followers were no worse than the agents and representatives of London merchants. All were "ill-behaved and ill-bred," and all were "contemptible in themselves."[56] Such harsh criticisms should not, however, be taken too literally. It must be remembered that they were inspired in part by the military arrogance of the age and in part by the disdain of the European for the colonial. The new-comers, unmoved, stood on their rights. They considered, with good reason, that their establishment in this conquered country would bring them greater advantages than they had hitherto known, and they did in fact very soon derive substantial profits from it. They received advances from such shrewd men of affairs as the London merchants, whose confidence they enjoyed, and one can well believe that they were not merely "a group of insignificant

11

lackeys without friends or fortune." On the other hand, their agent Fowler had later to recognize a foundation of truth in the accusation that they were "unruly and factious."[57]

If we allow for the prejudices which in Canadian society set class against class, army against civilians, officials against merchants, all prejudices which colour contemporary writings, it is quite possible to draw a portrait of those first British and American immigrants. For the most part, they were young men, active, enterprising, and aggressive, eager to realize their ambitions. They had few scruples, and they lived in an age when the unrestrained desire for wealth had its counterpart in the shameless manipulation of public finance and public works. Products of a democratic society, they hated all official hierarchies, especially the military hierarchy. Impatient of political direction, and especially of taxation by the mother country, they lost no opportunity in demanding their "British rights," specifically the right to participate in government. For these fanatics, liberty meant freedom to interpret the law to suit their own interests, while others were privileged only to obey. In an age when particularism was unknown, they could hardly fail to apply this principle in a conquered country whose people should, according to their idea, be glad to receive from them superior laws and material progress. It seemed to them quite natural that no stalwart of the papist religion, so bitterly execrated in New England, should be admitted to any public charge or even to membership in the legislative assembly; such was the law in Great Britain, and hence in the British colonies.

One is led to conclude that in the Anglo-American group, it was the American minority, "the Colonists" as Carleton calls them, who set the pace.[58] They had two reasons for taking the initiative: they were naturally more aggressive, and they had some knowledge of local conditions. Their position was clear from the outset; they expected that the military administration would be superseded by civilian government and that, as in the colonies to the south, public affairs would be directed by representative bodies. The Americans had come to seek their fortune in Canada where they meant to take full advantage of their status as British citizens. They argued that the anti-papist laws then in force in England also applied in Canada, this in spite of the fact that application of the laws would effectively deny to the whole Canadian population any possible means of political action. We have already observed that the British military officials were sharply critical of the immigrants' attitude. And a petition from the seigneurs of Quebec is charged with the bitter resentment of the Canadian people: "The former subjects, at least most of them, have, since the institution of civil government, had no other aim than to oppress and enslave us."[59] These tensions had appeared with the first contacts between the two groups. Less than three months after the proclamation of October 7, 1763, which created the province of Quebec, the London merchants, through their correspondents in the colony, refused to present New Year's greetings to the recently-appointed Governor of Montreal, General Burton.[60] Burton interpreted their gesture as one of opposition to military authority. Murray, writing in June, 1764, deplored the arrogance of the British colonists: "The Canadians have entirely overcome their national antipathy. I wish I could say as much of the British subjects. Several from New England now established here are most inveterate fanatics."[61]

Acts soon justified the Governor's judgment. Civil government was instituted by an ordinance dated September 17, 1764, and on October 16 the first jury, composed of French and English members, was convened in Quebec. Following a precedent set by the American colonies, and on the motion of a "Colonist," this jury declared itself "the only representative body of the country." The motion was recorded in the official report, but the English jurors later proved their bad faith by meeting in secret and signing supplementary articles in which they declared their opposition to the presence of Catholics on juries and to the exercise of judiciary functions by military officers.[62] It was recognized even by Fowler that such an attitude "might justly create fears and uneasiness in the minds of the

13

Canadians."[63] The French jurors, in a vigorous counter-attack,[64] charged that their British *confrères* were "opposed to the wise ordinance of the Governor and Council" and that they were trying to introduce "new constitutions" into the country.[65]

The same American spirit appears in a petition to the King in which the Governor is accused of partiality towards the Canadians. Condemning certain ordinances as "harmful to civil liberty and to the Protestant cause," the petitioners asked to be governed by a legislative assembly from which Catholics would be excluded, although they would be permitted to vote for Protestants.[66]

All the political unrest which marked this period was the result of American propaganda. On the one hand, the political agitators denounced Murray's "military despotism" and proposed that Canadians be reduced to a condition of political incapacity, while on the other, taking a lesson from Machiavelli, they tried to stir up Canadians against the government. Murray charged the "lawless traders" from New York with inciting the new subjects against the Stamp Act,[67] and Carleton was quite right when, in dispatches to London, he identified as "Colonists,"[68] that is, as American immigrants, the leaders in the movement of unrest. The Colonists, he reported, following the example of their brothers to the south, were protesting the imposition of customs duties[69] by the mother country, as well as the bankruptcy law,[70] and any other order which interfered with their business enterprises.[71]

Thus, during the first years of the English régime, political action of American origin was making itself felt in a movement directed against the military administration in the province, and even against the authority of the mother country itself. Its chief object was to obtain representative institutions modelled on those of the neighbouring colonies and legislation excluding Catholics from all public office. In 1764, with the backing of their powerful sponsors in London, the leaders of the campaign requested that Murray be recalled. They charged him with abuse of power, but the true reasons for their demand were his refusal to convoke a legislative assembly, and his determination to protect the Canadians against a minority eager to occupy and to profit from a dominating position. But, repeated statements of his dismissal notwithstanding, Murray was not dismissed. He was directed to "return to the Kingdom, in order to give His Majesty an account of the state of the colony." The report was duly presented, and Murray was completely exonerated. The wisdom of his policy was recognized and, although he did not return to Canada, he remained in office as titular Governor. In him Quebec lost a loyal friend and a champion of the political rights of her citizens.[72]

Murray's successor, Colonel Guy Carleton, who had served under Amherst at Louisbourg, arrived in Quebec during the summer of 1766. Since Murray was still in office, Carleton was commissioned as Lieutenant-Governor. He was appointed Governor in 1768. A man of lucid and dispassionate intelligence, mindful of justice and inclined towards tolerance in religious matters, the new Governor proved to be slow to act, but tenacious in the execution of his decisions. First-hand acquaintance with local conditions soon convinced him that the country was unlikely to attract British immigrants and that it would always belong to the "Canadian race."[73] Hence, he reasoned, it was essential that Great Britain should win over the Canadians by restoring French law and by making public offices accessible to them. Still basing his reasoning on this initial premise, he advised against the creation of an elective assembly which would be dominated by a minority of biased fanatics.[74] In the military sphere, he pointed out how vitally important it was that England should enlist the Canadian militia in her service, for he realized that the day might come when the American colonies, already semi-autonomous and now protesting against the levying of taxes by the mother country, would revolt. If that day did come, the colonies would find an ally in France who would surely be eager to seize such an opportunity to reconquer Canada.[75]

Meanwhile, the Anglo-American group pressed its campaign in favour of an elective assembly, in complete ignorance of the

15

Governor's ideas on the matter. In 1767, a draft petition for an assembly was submitted to Carleton by Thomas Walker, a former Bostonian now established in business in Montreal, and the following year John McCord, a Quebec tavern keeper, was busy collecting signatures for another such request.[76] Knowing that this agitation was being encouraged by the London merchants, Carleton decided, in 1770, to go to England in order to present to the government his own pro-French, pro-Catholic policy, and to urge the adoption of a Canadian constitution embodying that policy. When the "Colonists" realized that they were losing ground at Westminster, they dispatched their own delegates, Thomas Walker and Zachary Macaulay, to London, where they succeeded in enlisting the collaboration of the wily and skilful Huguenot, Francis Masères, a former attorney-general of Canada and an advocate of the gradual assimilation of the Canadians.[77] There followed a series of petitions, to the King, to Parliament, and to the ministers of the Crown.[78] The Canadians, for their part, had seized the opportunity of Carleton's presence in London to solicit the restoration of their ancient customs.[79] They also refused to associate themselves with the efforts of McCord and company to win approval for the creation of an assembly.[80] In December, 1773, a petition was drawn up in the name of Canada's French population of 100,000 inhabitants. It acknowledged with gratitude the freedom which Canadians enjoyed in the exercise of their religion, but besought the King to restore French law and to allow Canadians access to public office.[81] Such was the situation at the end of 1773.

2

THE QUEBEC ACT AND THE CONTINENTAL CONGRESS

Failure of the Colonist programme. Adoption of the Quebec Act. Terms of the Act. Gratitude of Canadians and annoyance of the pro-American party. Agitation in the British colonies. Coercive measures. The Quebec Act attacked by the Continental Congress. Address of Congress to the People of Great Britain. The true aims of the Quebec Act. Letter from Congress to the People of Quebec. Propaganda from Massachusetts.

THE FIRST phase of the American-inspired political campaign ended with the introduction of the Quebec Act in the House of Lords on May 2, 1774. The objects of the campaign were to obtain for Quebec a legislative assembly on the British-American model, and to insure that Catholics should be excluded not only from membership in the elective chamber but from all public office. As the constitution incorporating these terms would also have made the colony practically free from any intervention by the mother country, it would have placed in the hands of a few hundred British Protestants the administration of a French-Catholic country. Opposing a programme which would have made Canada another Ireland, Quebec's leaders petitioned instead for the restoration of French law, the continuance of the administrative council, with its power to appoint officials, and free access for Canadians to public office, including membership in the executive council.

Within a very short space of time, the political scene was

changed. In spite of representations from Anglo-Americans and London merchants, the "Colonist" pressure failed to prevent the adoption of the resolutions presented by Murray and Carleton. Basing their argument on the law of nations, two army officers won their case against the merchants and the plea of national privilege, and in so doing laid the foundations of a far-sighted policy of strict justice. To the honour of Parliament, the cabinet, and the ministers who held the balance, the scales tipped in favour of an alien majority and against a self-interested British minority. Neither cries of *No popery* nor last-minute petitions succeeded in preventing passage of the Quebec Act which was signed by George III on June 22, 1774, to come into effect on the first day of May of the following year.

The new law restored the province's former frontiers, from the Ohio and the Mississippi to Hudson Bay and Labrador. Still more important, it granted and legalized complete freedom to the Catholic religion, and authorized the collection of tithes. By dispensing with the oath of supremacy it opened all public offices to Catholics. It was true that in the practice of their religion Catholics remained "subject to the King's supremacy," but, as Mgr. Briand observed, this phrase was no more than a verbal form dictated by political necessity. "In the bill authorizing the Catholic religion," wrote the Bishop, "the word supremacy does appear, but we do not swear on the bill. I have raised the question with His Excellency, our Governor, and he answered: What have you to do with the bill? The King will not make use of his power in this regard; he agrees and even maintains that the Pope is your leader in the faith. But the bill would not have passed if this word had been omitted. No one has any intention of managing your religion, and our King will interfere in religious affairs less than the King of France did. You see from the oath that you are not asked to recognize his supremacy. Listen to him, and believe what you will."[1]

Finally, the Act re-established French civil law, based on the *Coutume de Paris,* and confirmed the seigniorial system of land tenure. British criminal law remained in force, and the British system of tenure "in common socage" was retained as an alternative to the seigniorial system.[2] With one blow, the new charter ruined the plans of the Anglo-American group. In an age of political antagonisms and anti-Catholic fanaticism the Act marks, in the words of the historian Lecky, "an epoch in the history of religious liberty." Carleton had devoted six years, the last four of them in London, to informing, persuading, convincing, ministers of the Crown, and when he stepped ashore in Quebec on September 18, 1774, it was with the satisfaction of knowing that he had accomplished his mission and won a victory for his policy of justice for Canadians. Addresses presented by the people of Quebec, Three Rivers, and Montreal praised his achievement and expressed the deep gratitude of Canadians of all classes.[3] The Governor could see for himself that the people of Canada, who had feared nothing so much as the "calamity" of having an elective legislature imposed upon them,[4] were completely won over to the English Crown. Now that the Crown had granted them religious freedom, French law, and access to civil and military posts, they would support it in any eventuality. A letter to Lord Dartmouth conveys Carleton's feeling of gratification at the results of his policy: "I have had the satisfaction of finding His Majesty's Canadian subjects impressed with the King's great goodness towards them in the late act of regulation for the government of this province; all ranks of people amongst them vie with each other in testifying their gratitude and respect, and the desire they have by every mark of duty and submission to prove themselves not undeserving of the treatment they have met with."[5] Addresses and letters from all parts of the province expressed "the same sentiments of gratitude and attachment of His Majesty's royal person and government as well as to the British interests."[6]

For most of the "ancient subjects," on the other hand, the Quebec Act was a bitter disappointment. Not only did it abolish English civil law, but it destroyed the hope of the American-minded minority for a representative assembly which might have been led to legislate in their favour. The British, as distinct

19

from the Colonials, although they too were disconcerted by the adoption of the new constitution even after the London city merchants[7] had petitioned against it, were uncertain as to what course they should follow. "The most respectable part of the English," those who lived in Quebec in the shadow of the Château St. Louis, disregarding advice from their compatriots in England, presented an address in which they assured the Governor of their intention to participate in the success of the new charter.[8]

Their address was, however, only the act of one group, a political gesture dictated by the circumstances of the moment. Neither in Quebec nor in Montreal did the partisans of popular government mean to abandon even a hopeless struggle, and they seized the first opportunity to reaffirm their "Colonist" principles and their opposition to any demonstration of authority on the part of the mother country. Such an occasion presented itself in June, 1774 when the port of Boston was closed by act of Parliament after a group of citizens had protested a new tax on tea by boarding ships and throwing tea cargoes into the harbour. On September 6, 1774, the Quebec merchants, incited to action by a former citizen of Massachusetts, Jonas Clark Minot, revealed their own leanings and their sympathy for a protesting colony by sending 1,000 bushels of wheat to Boston. The gift was acknowledged on October 10, with fulsome expressions of gratitude, by the Committee of Donations.[9] The merchants of Montreal collected subscriptions amounting to one hundred pounds, but for reasons of prudence the sum was not dispatched until the following February.[10]

In the course of the autumn, the so-called "laws of coercion," which abolished autonomy in the provinces, provoked a violent reaction against the mother country and the British Parliament. The Governor of Massachusetts, General Gage, who was also Commander-in-Chief of the English forces in America, and who foresaw the possibility of insurrection, wrote to ask Carleton to send him the two regiments stationed in Quebec. At the same time, he questioned him on the possibility of raising a corps of

Canadians and Indians which might, in case of open conflict, serve against the American colonies. Carleton answered that the Canadians had displayed "the strongest marks of joy and gratitude and fidelity to the King, and to his Government, for the late arrangements made at home in their favour," and that "a Canadian regiment would complete their happiness." "I am convinced," concluded the Governor, "their fidelity and zeal might be depended on." He was perhaps over-optimistic, however, when he suggested that this first regiment "might be augmented to two, three, or more battalions."[11]

In response to Gage's request, the 10th and 52nd Regiments embarked for Boston, leaving the colony almost denuded of troops. For the protection of its whole vast territory there remained only the Fusiliers in Quebec, and detachments of the 26th Regiment in Montreal, Three Rivers, and Chambly, no more than 1,000 men in all.[12] Currents of influence and reaction could already be felt on both sides of the border. The British in Canada were disturbed by the autocratic measures which Parliament was directing against their American brothers, while the colonies were alarmed to learn that Canada was dispatching troops destined to aid in the enforcement of coercive laws.

In London it was assumed that the Quebec Act had put an end to Canada's constitutional difficulties; but the struggle suddenly moved from London to Philadelphia, where the first Continental Congress of the British Colonies in North America was in session. The ferment of autonomy had been at work for years in colonies stoutly opposed to all attempts on the part of the mother country to levy taxes on them and thus force them to pay some part of the heavy debts which she had piled up during the Seven Years' War. Moreover, with the restoration of peace and in an effort to restore England's financial position, the cabinet had taken measures to suppress the enormous contraband trade which was carried on from American ports and which deprived England of a valuable source of revenue. By so doing, they had further irritated important colonial trading interests. In 1765, Parliament passed an act requiring that a stamp be affixed to every legal and official document, but the Stamp Tax aroused such vehement opposition that it was prudently withdrawn the following year. Determined, at whatever price, to force the colonies to contribute their share to the mother country's budget, Parliament passed the Townshend laws which instituted new duties on certain imports, including tea. Fully roused, the colonies, led by Massachusetts, expressed violent opposition to any tax levied by the mother country. March 6, 1770 was marked by the so-called "Boston Massacre" during which soldiers, acting in self-defence, fired into a hostile mob and killed five of the demonstrators. While the main struggle against taxation went on in an atmosphere of increasing tension, it was a minor escapade, the Boston Tea Party, which lighted the spark that fired the insurrection. On December 16, 1773, as a protest against import duties, a group of men boarded three English ships anchored in Boston harbour and threw overboard their cargo of 342 cases of tea.

Colonial leaders explicitly demanded constitutional reform based on the principle: *No taxation without representation*, but their ultimate goal was economic and fiscal autonomy. Failing that, they were prepared, as the American Cato, Samuel Adams, declared at the end of 1773, to revolt and to claim political independence. In such circumstances the tea episode created an uproar. Involving as it did flagrant infraction of English laws as well as violation of personal property, it struck horror into the hearts of the people of England. This signal act of defiance could not go unpunished. On June 1, 1774, the port of Boston was closed by act of Parliament and shortly afterwards three other punitive measures were adopted: the charter of Massachusetts was withdrawn, it was declared legal to quarter soldiers on private citizens, and anyone accused of sedition was to be transported to England for trial. These "intolerable acts" united the colonies from north to south in burning indignation against Parliament. In order to organize a common defence of their political rights, they formed an association, and on September 5, 1774 the first Continental Congress of the American Colonies opened in Philadelphia. Its business was to consider measures to be taken.

On September 17, Paul Revere, who had ridden down from Boston the day before, presented to the Congress resolutions adopted on September 9 by Suffolk County in Massachusetts. The resolutions proposed that all commercial relations with Great Britain be broken off, and that they be resumed only when the rights of Massachusetts had been restored. One resolution denounced the Quebec Act in the most forthright terms: "The late Act of Parliament for establishing the Roman Catholic religion and the French laws in that extensive country now called Canada is dangerous in an extreme degree to the Protestant religion and to the civil rights and liberties of all America; and therefore, as men and Protestant Christians, we are indispensably obliged to take all proper measures to protect our safety."[13]

It is interesting to note that it was Massachusetts, Quebec's oldest neighbour and the principal victim of Canadian forays, which sounded the alarm when the charter of 1774 reinstated French law and Catholicism in Quebec. Alerted, no doubt, by Walker and his friends, the people of Massachusetts saw in the Quebec Act the threat of papist and military invasion. But, although Congress had not initiated the anti-French, anti-Catholic resolution, it immediately approved it without reservation, and it was adopted, along with the others, without a dissenting voice. Newspapers were instructed to publish the resolutions and they were later posted on public notice boards in Boston.[14]

On October 14, Congress opened its own attack by declaring that both the laws suspending the constitution of Massachusetts and the Quebec Act were "impolitic, unjust, and cruel, as well as unconstitutional and most dangerous and destructive of American rights."[15] The declaration went on to say that the Quebec Act, by "abolishing the equitable system of English laws," was erecting a tryanny in Canada "to the great danger from so total a dissimilarity of religion, law and government,

23

of the neighbouring British colonies, by the assistance of whose blood and treasure the said country was conquered from France."[16]

Just six days later, in the deed of association which united the colonies and suspended all commercial relations with the mother country, Congress once more condemned the Canadian charter. The Act aimed at "establishing an arbitrary government . . . and discouraging the settlement of British subjects in that wide extended country: thus by the influence of civil principles and ancient prejudices . . . [it would] dispose the inhabitants to act with hostility against the free Protestant colonies whenever a wicked minister [should] choose to direct them."[17]

These last lines reveal the fundamental cause of all these vehement protestations: the colonies feared they might be invaded by Canadian troops serving under the British flag. Had not the Quebec militia under Bradstreet marched in 1764 against Canada's former allies, the western Indians? Furthermore, the American colonists had lost none of their bitter hereditary hatred for the Canadian militia. They remembered the murderous Franco-Indian incursions, those campaigns of military terrorism which had been launched by New France, in every war since Frontenac's time, against their frontier settlements. Frontier adjustments were another serious grievance against the Quebec Act, although Congress maintained a diplomatic silence on this point. The restoration of Canada's earlier frontiers would practically shut off colonial farmers from the plains of the Ohio, and colonial traders from the western fur territories.

Thus, the Quebec Act, which, for all sorts of reasons, offended the political, economic, and religious beliefs of the colonists, could be used by Congress as a powerful instrument of anti-parliamentary propaganda in the colonies. Its usefulness in this respect was not, however, limited to the colonies. In his "Address to the People of Great Britain," dated October 21, 1774, John Jay, speaking in the name of Congress, again set up the new constitution as a religious and political scarecrow. The aim of the Quebec Act, wrote Jay, whose terror tactics did not exclude prophecy, was to win over the Canadians by playing upon their religious and political prejudices, and to swell their ranks with Catholic immigrants from Europe. In that way, as their numbers increased, these auxiliaries might become "fit instruments in the hands of power to reduce the ancient free Protestant colonies to the same state of slavery with themselves." Moreover, English immigrants into Canada were already being denied the rights of trial by jury; they were no longer protected by habeas corpus, "the great rampart and palladium of English liberties." Predicting a future for Canada of bloody inquisition and persecution, the letter expressed "astonishment that a British Parliament should ever consent to establish in that country a religion that has deluged your island in blood and spread impiety, bigotry, persecution, murder, and rebellion throughout every part of the world." If, with the help of Canadian troops, the British government was victorious in America, to what lengths would it not go? And in a final flight of imagination the letter evoked the horrible vision of Canadian troops serving as an instrument of oppression in England herself: "May not a ministry with the same armies enslave you?"[18]

The letter of Congress was the basis of the charge that, in passing the Quebec Act, Parliament had been motivated by fear of insurrection in the colonies and the need to prepare for such an eventuality by winning over the Canadians. This false and fictitious affirmation, born of resentment and utilized in the interests of political propaganda, is completely disproven by the facts and documents in the case.

These are the facts. French law was abolished in Quebec by a royal proclamation of October 7, 1763.[19] On December 24, 1764, Lord Mansfield wrote to the Secretary of State, Lord Grenville: "Is it possible that we have abolished their laws and their customs and forms of judicature all at once? . . . The history of the world do'nt furnish an instance of so rash and unjust an act." And he added: "For God's sake, learn the truth of the case and think of a speedy remedy."[20] In October, 1764,

Murray had already pointed out to the minister the need for rectifying the injustices created by the political structure imposed upon the country.[21] In 1767, Carleton, in his turn, pleaded the cause of justice for the King's Canadian subjects, and Lord Shelburne answered that "as the right administration of government in Quebec is a matter of the greatest importance to that province, the improvement of its civil constitution is under the most serious and deliberate consideration of His Majesty's servants and principally of His Majesty's Privy Council."[22] But the wheels of government grind slowly. In the spring of 1766, the Governor received special instructions to study the question of French law in Quebec.[23] A year later, on August 28, 1767, these instructions were ratified by the Privy Council, and on September 15, 1769, a joint report from Carleton and Chief Justice Hey was forwarded to London. The report advised against the continuance of English law and recommended "the restoration and re-establishment of French law."[24] At the same time Carleton instructed the Abbé Jacrau of the Quebec seminary to draw up a summary of Canada's French laws.[25] In order to hasten the adoption of French law, Carleton went to London in 1770 to support the measure in Parliament.

Unfortunately the bill was delayed, both by an unstable political situation—with six changes of ministry in nine years—and by the stubborn opposition of the Anglo-Canadian minority and financial interests in London. On December 1, 1773, the Secretary of State, Lord Dartmouth, was able to announce that an act concerning Quebec would be dealt with shortly,[26] and on May 2, 1774, the Quebec Act was finally introduced in Parliament. The law had been in gestation since 1764, its basic principle had been accepted in London years before the American rebellion, and its adoption was not motivated by the outbreak of the revolution in 1775.

In Philadelphia, the Congress, after dispatching its violent protest to the people of Great Britain, launched a second attack on the Quebec Act. In a memoir addressed to the provinces, the Act was represented as an instrument of injustice towards the English in a country whose inhabitants were being called upon to contribute to the oppression of the colonies.[27] But the strangest part of this story was still to come. The document containing these fulminations against the Quebec charter, the Catholic religion, and French law was dated October 21, 1774, and the ink in which it was written was hardly dry when Congress charged three of its members, Thomas Cushing, Richard Henry Lee, and John Dickinson, with the task of preparing an appeal to the Canadian people. Lee was chiefly responsible for the text of the "Letter Addressed to the Inhabitants of the Province of Quebec."[28] Adopted by Congress on October 24, 1774, this letter marked the first attempt of the colonies to win to their cause a people for whose religion and laws they had so recently expressed supreme contempt.

The letter begins with praise for the "gallant and glorious resistance" of the people of Canada during the last war. It then proceeds, somewhat tactlessly, to invite them to rejoice at the happy outcome of their defeat and to thank the Divine Being who "would bestow upon [them] the dispensations of his over-ruling providence by securing for [them] and [their] latest posterity the inestimable advantages of a free English constitution of government." The letter then goes on to discuss political issues. The "first grand right" and base of the prosperity of the English colonies is that "of the people having a share in their own government by their representatives chosen by themselves, and, in consequence, of being ruled by laws which they themselves approve, not by edicts of men over whom they have no control." For, if they participate in the political direction of the country, the representatives of the people can, by refusing to grant the subsidies required for its administration, force the reigning power to remedy any abuse. The letter further specifies the "inestimable rights" which stem from representative government: trial by jury, habeas corpus, freedom from the corvée, freedom of the press, all rights conferred on man by natural law.

In comparison with the representative system of government,

the letter continues, what does the Quebec Act offer you? Freedom of conscience? But "God gave it to you, and the temporal powers with which you have been and are connected firmly stipulated for your enjoyment of it." As for the restoration of French laws, How can you be sure that these laws will really be restored, since the Governor and council can change the law "arbitrarily" in virtue of their power to appoint "such criminal, civil and ecclesiastical jurisdiction as shall be thought proper." But the most dangerous clause in this new constitution is the one which establishes an excise tax, "the most odious of taxes." The oracle, Montesquieu, has spoken: legislative authority resides in the people or its representatives, and there is no liberty where the legislative, executive, and judicial powers are not separated. Since by the Quebec Act all powers are united in the hands of the ministry, Canadians have no protection against *despotism, taxes,* and *arbitrary rule.*

After defining the constitutional rights of Canadians and predicting the evils which will result from the Quebec Act, the letter reveals its essential purpose, which is to win the support of the Canadian people. The argument may be summed up in the following terms. What must be your conduct when your neighbours are engaged in a struggle for liberty? Do not your interest and your happiness alike urge you to become the friends of the rest of North America? You have everything to gain from such a course. Do not allow difference of religion to be a cause of division, and do not allow self-interested sycophants to "sacrifice the liberty and happiness of the whole Canadian people." We do not ask you to take the offensive, but simply to join us. Elect delegates to form a provincial congress which will in turn elect delegates to represent you at the next Continental Congress, which will assemble in Philadelphia in May, 1775. The violation of your rights is a violation of ours, and we have demanded redress. May Heaven guide you to join the united forces of America for the triumph of our cause![29]

This letter gave Canadians their first lesson in constitutional law. Considering the state of mind of the two groups concerned, it is, on the whole, as skilful and diplomatic as circumstances permitted. In an argument which was coherent, solid and lucid,[30] it presented the best case possible in the circumstances, considering that it was directed to a people without the least experience in constitutional questions.[31] It praised the Canadians for their valour, defined their rights as British citizens, warned them against the danger of taxes, and invited them to associate themselves with those colonies which were defending the rights of all.

The task of having the letter translated, printed, and distributed in Canada was entrusted to the delegation from Pennsylvania. It was also recommended that the provinces of New Hampshire, Massachusetts, and New York should collaborate in its distribution.[32] The translation was completed with great dispatch by a Frenchman, Eugène du Simitière, and a French printer, Fleury Mesplet, ran off 2,000 copies of which 300 were sent to Boston.[33]

Meanwhile, this time in Boston, another effort to win Canada was being organized. On October 21, 1774, the Massachusetts Congress adopted a proposal to send an agent to Canada with a commission to establish relations and initiate communication with the Canadian people.[34] The question was discussed during the sittings of October 22 and November 26, and finally, on December 6, the delegates appointed a committee of "correspondence" which included the three leaders in the anti-British movement, Samuel Adams, Joseph Warren, and John Hancock.[35] No further action was taken, however, before the end of the year, although the Massachusetts Congress forwarded copies of the letter from the Continental Congress, and paid the cost of their distribution in Canada.[36]

3

THE CAMPAIGN AGAINST THE QUEBEC ACT

British pro-rebel committees in Montreal and Quebec. Propaganda against the Act directed towards Canadians. Loyalist counter-offensive of Canadian leaders. Attitude of the different social classes. American agents in Canada. Brown's mission. Anglo-Canadian policy. Enforcement of the Quebec Act.

TWO OR three weeks after the adoption by the Continental Congress of the Suffolk County resolutions, with their condemnation of the Quebec Act, news of the adoption reached Montreal, where it created a sensation in the British colony, and especially among the American group. Carleton, who was immediately informed of the excitement, was not quite sure whether the Montrealers had "caught the fire from some Colonists settled among them," or whether "in reality letters were received from the General Congress, as reported." In any case, Britishers flocked to the Coffee House to hear the latest news. There, encouraged by the American protests, they discussed their own grievances and considered means of redress. A time was set for a later meeting but, in order that their activities might be less apparent to the government, it was agreed that subsequent gatherings should be held "at the house of a person then absent" rather than at the Coffee House. Further meetings were held and a committee of action was set up. Three members of this committee, Thomas Walker, James Price, and John Blake were "old subjects" from the British colonies; the fourth was Isaac Todd. Walker assumed a position of leadership and

30

undertook to draw up a plan of reform and to raise subscriptions.[1]

Once the movement had been set on foot in Montreal, the committee moved to Quebec, where it summoned British citizens to meet at the tavern of Miles Prentice. A committee of seven was chosen and instructed to consult with the delegates from Montreal. Several American-style town meetings were held, open to all comers, as well as joint meetings of the committees. The committees decided to thank the mayor and the city of London for their help in the campaign to prevent passage of the Quebec Act. They also thanked the Colonists' adviser in London, Masères, and rewarded his services with a handsome honorarium. Finally a motion was adopted to address petitions to the King, the House of Lords, and the House of Commons.[2]

The petitions, dated November 12, 1774, were signed by 185 citizens. They protested against the substitution of French for British law, a substitution entailing the loss of habeas corpus and trial by jury. They pointed out that Canada's French population was no more than 75,000 and that the number of British settlers, which had now reached 3,000, was constantly increasing. They claimed that the petition presented in January, 1774 in the name of the Canadian people had been "in a secret manner carried about and signed by a few of the seigneurs, chevaliers, advocates, and others in their confidence, at the suggestion and under the influence of their priests," and that it had not been "imparted to the inhabitants in general" who would have been "alarmed" at such a step.[3] The British petitioners could hardly have claimed accuracy for their figures since Masères himself had stated, some years earlier, that an elected assembly "would be a representative only of the 600 new English settlers and an instrument in their hands of domineering over 90,000 French citizens."[4] The three petitions for repeal of the Quebec Act were forwarded to Masères who delivered them in January, 1775.[5]

Opponents of the Act did not include all Britishers in Canada. A certain number of "discreet persons" declined to enlist in the campaign. The Canadians, for their part, were unanimous in their refusal to co-operate with the committee. Not only had they already expressed "gratitude and attachment" to England, but they were now worried at the efforts of "meetings and nocturnal cabals to disturb the minds of people by false and seditious reports." For the adversaries of the Act, urged on by Walker, had been actively engaged in soliciting signatures among the different social groups which they represented. The aim of the petitions, as declared by these spokesmen, was to protect Canadian lives and property, and to take from the Governor the power to call Canadian citizens to military service, to send them and their families "up the country among the savages," or, if he so chose, to dispatch them to wage war against the New Englanders. In short, the one aim of the petitions was to save Canadians from the bondage into which they were being led by laws made by the British Parliament.[6]

This propaganda, whose object was to create an atmosphere of suspicion and alarm, derived a certain force from the fact that it was disseminated by presumably faithful and loyal British subjects. It was all the more dangerous since, until the appearance of a translation on December 8, four months after the publication of the English text, most Canadians had no first-hand knowledge of the Quebec Act. Leading Canadian citizens expressed "indignation and impatience at being solicited to join in such proceedings." They were also anxious lest "some of their countrymen, under the awe of menacing creditors," might have been induced to sign.[7] While the Governor assured Canadians that opposition and intrigue would not then or later bring about any modification of their new privileges, he was also convinced that the government could not guard "too much or too soon against the consequences of an infection, imported daily, warmly recommended, and spread abroad by the Colonists here and indeed by some from Europe, not less violent than the Americans."[8]

Events were following an inevitable course, since political agitation was the only weapon with which the Colonists, whether north or south of the border, could fight the Quebec Act. For the Americans, haunted by memories of devastating French raids,[9] and convinced that the purpose of the new constitution was to mobilize the people of Canada against the rebellious colonies, the chief objective was to dissuade their neighbours to the north from taking up arms against them.[10] At the same time the protests of Congress and its "Letter to the Inhabitants of the Province of Quebec" gave fresh impetus to the movement in favour of a representative assembly in Canada. Specifically, the letter suggested a tactical line to be followed in dealing with the French population, the line of skilful diplomacy. Following this line, the Colonists would present themselves as good neighbours, desirous only of freeing their fellow subjects from the alleged "oppression and enslavement" which the laws of Parliament sought to impose upon them.[11] During the last weeks of 1774 and the first months of 1775, the pro-rebel forces maintained their unceasing efforts to kindle in the common people of Canada a spark of the spirit that prevailed in the province of Massachusetts.[12] By the middle of November, the letter from Congress had been distributed from one end of the province to the other. English merchants ranged over the countryside and, on the pretext of buying wheat from farmers, read them the letter and incited them to rebellion, while in the towns Britishers of every stripe harped on the same theme.[13] Thus town and country alike were subjected to constant political indoctrination and to an unremitting campaign of anti-English propaganda.[14]

Taking up the ideas of the congressional address, agents spread through the country elementary notions of political theory, and explained the advantages of a form of representative government in which the members, elected by the people, discuss and fix taxes. In short, the campaign constituted a complete social doctrine, illustrated by concrete examples drawn from the local and contemporary scene. To Canadians without experience in public affairs it revealed a whole world of new ideas tending to engender opposition to the Quebec Act and to any attempt to enrol them in the service of England against her rebellious colonies. The Anglo-American propagandists, playing on the theme of fear already introduced in the letter from Congress, repeated insistently that the new Act concentrated all power in the hands of the Governor, who could confiscate land, exile families, or, "at his own pleasure," send militiamen to war.[15] They even maintained that, under French law, Canadians would be led like slaves and that *"lettres de cachet* were to be brought into use again."[16]

They also had recourse to the tax argument, always effective with farmers, and especially with Canadians who, throughout the period of French rule, had remained stubbornly averse to paying taxes of any sort. When the Quebec Act came into force, it was averred, the authorities would impose heavy taxes[17] in order to meet the expenses of the province and to pay the salaries of the Governor, judges, members of the new council, and other officials;[18] and of course they could not fail to increase the duties on wines and spirits.[19] As a last resort the "Congressists," as they were called, even attempted, by appealing to the pecuniary interests of the rural population, to foment opposition to the clergy and the seigneurs. Since the conquest, parishioners had frequently protested the rates at which tithes were fixed, and seigneurs had been unsuccessful in their schemes to increase rents. Now, however, the new constitution would sanction higher rates for both rents and tithes. Thus the Quebec Act would subject Canadians once more to "the despotism of their ancient masters."[20]

This active and persistent propaganda made "a deep impression on the minds of the country people."[21] One contemporary reported that wicked Englishmen and Americans in the colony had poisoned the countryside and parts of the towns with their talk of some imaginary liberty.[22] For the first time Canadians could be heard discussing constitutional and political questions and talking of liberty and the rights of the people. Disturbed by the campaign of "false and seditious reports" and the confusion it was creating in the minds of an ill-informed population, the country's leaders came to the defence of the charter and seized every opportunity to point out those articles in the Act which gave complete satisfaction to the aspirations of the Canadian people.[23] Their task was considerably facilitated by the publication of the Act, in French, in the *Quebec Gazette* of December 8.[24]

Shortly after the publication of the translation, a circular letter, signed *Le Canadien Patriote*, appeared in the same paper, and copies, transcribed by students at the Quebec seminary, were distributed throughout the province.[25] Refuting the allegations of the Colonists, the author pointed out that French law brought greater benefits to the Canadian people than did English law, and that it had nothing to do with *lettres de cachet*, prisons, war, taxes, or absolute power for the Governor. Furthermore, these benefits were guaranteed by the Quebec Act. One of the clauses of the Act, explained the *Patriote*, "not only allows you the free exercise of the Roman Catholic religion but . . . lays open to you all the employments and places of trust in the province. This is the thing that shocks these Englishmen and makes them declare in the public newspapers that the said act of Parliament is a detestable and abominable act authorizing a bloody religion, which spreads around it, wherever it is propagated, impiety, murder and rebellion. These violent expressions reveal the true character of their authors and show us how deeply they have been mortified at not having been able to obtain an assembly from which they had proposed to exclude you. . . . Should we not make ourselves perfectly ridiculous if we were now to express dislike of an act which grants us everything we had desired, the free exercise of our religion, the use of our ancient laws and the extension of the boundaries of our province? . . . To be sure, these laws do impose certain taxes on liquors. But were there not taxes of the same kind in the time of the French government? And are not the taxes laid upon such articles as are least necessary to our subsistence? As to the proposal of a Canadian regiment, would it not be to the advantage of the Canadians themselves to raise such a regiment?"[26]

The next move on the part of the defenders of the Act was

to compare the fine words of the "Letter to the Inhabitants of the Province of Quebec" with the fanatical and violent language of the "Address to the Inhabitants of Great Britain," in which the Congress had expressed supreme contempt for the Catholic religion. The Address was translated, and the translation was circulated privately, or read, when occasion offered, to gatherings of people. Readers and audiences to whom this evidence of flagrant double-dealing was presented were filled with indignation at the perfidy of the two-faced Congress. At the same time they called down blessings on their gracious sovereign and swore to obey the ruler whose humanity was constant and extended to all religions. But, while the duplicity of the Congress angered audiences to whom the English letter was read, these audiences made up only a very modest aggregate. For in French Canada there was neither a committee nor any special group with an immediate interest in exposing the deception and trickery which formed the basis of the American offensive.[27] Consequently, little use was made of a weapon which could have been very effective, especially in the country districts. And how could a few scattered rebuttals hope to counter an incessantly active Anglo-American campaign for political rights and social and economic progress?

Carleton was the first to perceive clearly the effect on the whole country of all this American-inspired agitation. In a letter of February, 1775, he observed that, although the Quebec Act had given great satisfaction, the gentry did not "relish commanding a bare militia," for "they were never used to that service under the French government." As for the habitants, who had "in a manner emancipated themselves," it could hardly be expected, considering all the new ideas they had acquired in the last ten years, that they would be "pleased at being suddenly and without preparation embodied into a militia, and marched from their families, lands, and habitations to remote provinces, and all the horrors of war." Furthermore, any suggestion of enrolment for military service would confirm in their minds the claim of the "sons of sedition" that the aim of the new constitution was to serve the interests of the government by restoring the despotism of their former masters.

Carleton saw quite clearly that the weakness of the government in the war of propaganda arose from the fact that the new constitution was not to come into effect until May 1 of the following year. "Had the present settlement taken place when first recommended," he wrote, "it would not have aroused the jealousy of the other colonies, and it would have had the appearance of more disinterested favour to the Canadians."[28] At the same time, the Governor pointed out the great mistake of the British Cabinet. As a result of the interminable delays which had retarded by ten years the solution of the Canadian problem, the Quebec Act, when it was finally passed in 1774, had the appearance of something which it was not, a military threat against the insurgent colonies and a political manoeuvre to woo the Canadian people.

In spite of the categorical statements of the man who was chiefly responsible for the decision made in London, it is sometimes still argued that the Quebec Act was not a disinterested measure of justice towards the people of Canada. According to this thesis, Parliament, driven to action by the threat of revolution in America, adopted the Quebec Act solely in order to win over England's new subjects to her cause. It has already been shown, however, that this contention is disproved by the evidence.

The Massachusetts Congress had reached the conclusion that a rupture between the mother country and the colonies was inevitable and imminent. It was also convinced of the intention of the British government to solicit and win over the people of Canada and the most distant Indian tribes, with the design of harassing and devastating the colonies. Spurred on by these and other considerations, of which one was the colony's hereditary fear of Franco-Indian raids, the Congress decided to act, and on February 15, 1775, asked Boston's correspondence committee to establish relations with the province of Quebec.[29] A member of the committee, John Brown, volunteered for the mission and was accepted.[30] He left Boston with twenty pounds in his pocket and a letter from the provincial Congress soliciting support from Canadians and inviting Canada to send delegates to the next Continental Congress. The letter, dated February 21, was addressed to Thomas Walker, Isaac Todd, John Blake, James Price, the brothers Heywood and other citizens of Montreal, and to Zachary Macaulay, John Aikin, John Patterson, John Lee, John Wells, and Ronald Monteith, of Quebec.[31]

Brown delivered his letter in Montreal in March. He was well received by Walker and Blake, who informed him that Carleton, "a man of sour and morose character," had established a censorship and refused to allow the "Letter to the Inhabitants of Quebec" to be printed. They assured him, however, that, thanks to the activities of friends of the American cause and their warning threats to Canadians, the government was incapable at that moment of raising ten men in the province.[32] On Saturday, April 1, Brown held a secret meeting at Lachine with the British merchants,[33] and on April 4, American sympathizers gathered at the Montreal Coffee House to hear the American spokesman and to choose two delegates for the Continental Congress which was to convene in Philadelphia on May 10.[34] An attempt was made to entice some Canadians to the meeting, but "there was not a single one," and the British merchants admitted that "the Canadians did not want to join the proposed union."[35] After reading the letter from Boston, Brown spoke in support of it, and Walker too made a long speech. Both recommended that a committee be set up to hold a watching brief and maintain relations with Massachusetts, and that two delegates to the next Continental Congress be appointed. But the meeting refused to adopt these recommendations,[36] for although they were in sympathy with the spirit of the resolutions, these men, both British and Colonists, were first and foremost merchants, and they were afraid that participation in the revolt might provoke restrictive measures limiting their freedom of action.

The answer to Massachusetts' invitation to unite in a common struggle for liberty was written by Walker and Price, and dated April 28. It expressed regret that, although their sympathies were with the American cause, members of the British group were restrained from taking action by "their own interests" and the "unlimited powers of the Governor." They explained the position in which they were placed. They could not join the next Congress, for the Canadians would unite with the government to overrule them. The authorities and the upper classes did not share their views, but "the mass of the people," both English and Canadian, favoured the colonies and would refuse to serve against them although the gentry would be quite willing to do so. Would the Congress accept these restrictions and the further provision that Quebec should be excluded from any agreement to cut off all import and export trade with England, and, given these conditions, would Congress agree to admit their delegates? A postscript recommended that the letter be kept secret for fear of consequences.[37] In short, the Anglo-Americans of Montreal would support the rebel cause on condition that they should not have to do anything which involved either their persons or their own little business interests.[38] Specifically, they were afraid that they might lose the fur trade to Canadians.[39]

Meanwhile emissaries from the colonies continued to range through the country districts. In February, a certain Mr. Woolsey distributed copies of the letter from Congress at Saint-Charles, Lachenaie, Terrebonne, and various other points. Posing as horse dealers, other agents went from parish to parish, denouncing the Quebec Act and pleading the cause of the rebels to the south. In Montreal, Walker and George Measam spoke in the market places or wherever opportunity offered, repeating the same criticisms of the Act and making the same appeal in the name of liberty.[40] On April 4, Walker declared bluntly to the Abbé Brassier of the Seminary of Saint-Sulpice, that the only means of preventing the ministry from despoiling the people of Canada of their rights and their property was to send delegates to the next Continental Congress.[41] In La Prairie

Brown distributed letters to the curés of four neighbouring parishes.[42] In the course of conversation with Canadians he told them that it would be folly for them to join the handful of British troops in the province, since such action would result in confiscation of their property by the rebel forces. He assured them that the agents of Congress came not as enemies but as friends, that they too were British, well-disposed towards the King and the constitution, and that they were sent by the partisans of liberty to prevent Canadians from being reduced to slavery by the King's ministers, a group of wicked men seeking to undermine the constitution. They never wearied of repeating their refrain, that, with the help and under the protection of the American Colonies, Canadians would be freed from taxes, tithes, rents, and corvées, and that the humblest habitant would have a voice in public affairs.[43]

In this offensive, open threats of invasion and devastation were mingled with warm protestations of friendship. Brown asserted that if a single Canadian had the audacity to march against the New Englanders, 30,000 men would immediately invade Canada and ravage the country.[44] Other champions of "liberty" spoke in the same vein,[45] and other emissaries followed Brown, among them a certain Jabez White, who appeared in Quebec and Three Rivers. Under the guidance of Canadian sympathizers, they moved about freely preaching the gospel of American "liberty."[46]

It was in this atmosphere of intrigue, unrest, and anxiety that on May 1, 1775 the Quebec Act came into force. On that date the former administrative council ceased to exist and the commissions of judges and civil servants were revoked. On April 26, in order to prevent a condition of chaos in the judicial sphere, the Governor had proclaimed the appointment of six "conservators of the peace." These officials were to perform the functions of judges, although the establishment of permanent courts was deferred to a later date.[47]

Montreal, the most convenient point of arrival for information and propaganda from Boston and New York, was naturally the most important centre of political and pro-American activity. It was also the scene of the only incidents which marred the inauguration of the new constitution. On May 1, early morning visitors to the Place d'Armes saw the bust of George III with its face blackened. Suspended about the King's neck was a rosary of potatoes with a wooden cross and the inscription: *Behold the Pope of Canada or the English fool.*[48] This insult to the sacrosanct majesty of kings, obviously an expression of violent opposition to the Act, was attributed to Walker.[49] It aroused a storm of indignation, and the officers of the 26th Regiment offered a reward of fifty pounds for the capture of the culprit. The next day, when M. de Bellestre remarked to a group of bystanders that hanging was the proper punishment for the criminal guilty of such an insult to royalty, a certain Mr. Franks attacked him with his fists. In the course of another incident, a Jew called Salomon asserted that the outrage must have been committed by a Canadian, and when M. Le Pailleur retorted that it was more probably a Jew, Salomon struck him in the face. Both men were later haled into court.[50]

Reports of these incidents, exaggerated and spread abroad, did little to calm the minds of citizens, especially since a new source of dissatisfaction had further troubled the Canadian political scene. A proclamation had announced the names of members of the new Council for the Affairs of the Province of Quebec, created by the Act. Of the seventeen councillors, nominated by the Governor and appointed by royal order, seven were Catholic Canadians, all chosen from the minor nobility and the seigniorial class.[51] The selection, which completely ignored leaders in the professional and business groups, dissatisfied both the townspeople and the tenant farmers.[52] For this reservation to the seigniorial clan of membership in the legislative body of the province naturally inspired the just fear that it would be followed by a rise in farm rents.

Such fears were not without foundation. For, since the adoption of the Act, some seigneurs had become more aggressive in their attitude towards their inferiors,[53] and a small group had tried to take advantage of the change of régime in order to add new rates to those already paid by their tenants. All these facts, taken together, gave weight to the arguments advanced by opponents of the Act, with the result that it became the victim of circumstances. In spite of the sympathetic spirit in which it was conceived and framed, the Quebec Act was opposed by the majority of Britishers and received with suspicion by the rural population.

4

CANADA'S POLITICAL AND MILITARY SITUATION

Outbreak of war at Lexington. Invasion of Canada under Arnold and Ethan Allen. Appeal to the militia and call for volunteers at Saint-Jean. Propaganda from the Continental Congress, Massachusetts, and New York. Loyalism of Canada's élite. Neutralist tendencies of the rural population. The country's military situation. Support of Mgr. Briand for the Governor's efforts. Martial law. Creation of a militia. Declaration of the Six Nations. Carleton's temporizing tactics. Appointment of a legislative council.

BY CLOSING the port of Boston and abolishing the colony's constitution, the British Parliament had chosen to make Massachusetts the scene of the inevitable explosion. The shots between Colonists and English soldiers which lit the spark of revolution were fired at Lexington on April 18, 1775. Now that war had become a reality, the rebel provinces turned their eyes towards the north, as a possible scene of military action. For British invading forces could come down from Canada to attack the colonies in the rear; Lake Champlain provided a highway and Fort Ticonderoga a suitable starting point for an invasion. Moreover, Ticonderoga was well stocked with the cannon and munitions which were so badly needed by the colonies, and its garrison, under Captain Delaplace, counted only forty-seven soldiers, while Crown Point, fifteen miles down the lake, had a mere token guard of ten men.

Expeditions against these posts were immediately organized, one under Benedict Arnold, a horse dealer from Connecticut, and the other under the bold and dashing adventurer, Ethan Allen. The volunteer contingents were established independently, but they united in a plan to capture the isolated forts before the news of war should reach them. The plan was completely successful; Ticonderoga was taken by surprise on May 10, and Crown Point on the following day.[1] With the forts, the rebels captured 500 cannon and six mortars. A few days later, Arnold set out again, with about thirty men, in a schooner which had been seized at Skenesborough. They sailed down the Richelieu to Saint-Jean, and on May 17, seized the fort with its ten men, and the King's sloop which lay at anchor. Prisoners and equipment from the fort were put on board the sloop, and the expedition set out on its return journey. The invading party had reached Saint-Jean early in the morning, and the whole operation was completed before ten o'clock. A retired officer, Moses Hazen, rode posthaste to carry the news to Montreal, whence Colonel Templer immediately dispatched a force of 140 men under Major Preston.[2]

As Arnold and his detachment were making their way up the Richelieu, they passed Ethan Allen with a contingent of eighty men in four boats. Allen's party was on its way to launch its own attack on Saint-Jean, and they hoped also to capture Fort Chambly, a few miles down the river. At Saint-Jean they made contact with a rebel sympathizer, an English merchant from Montreal called Bindon, who, on the pretext of attending to some private business, had obtained permission to cross the St. Lawrence with Preston's soldiers. From Longueuil, Bindon had galloped ahead to Saint-Jean and informed Allen that a relief force was on its way to the fort. The next day, May 18, when Preston's soldiers reached Saint-Jean after having met Bindon on his way back to Longueuil, they found Allen's men already re-embarking for Ticonderoga. They fired a few ineffectual shots at the retreating rebels, and their fury at Bindon's betrayal knew no bounds. When they reached Montreal two days later, a group of soldiers seized the traitor and were preparing to hang him when officers of the troop intervened to save him.

On May 19, Colonel Templer issued a proclamation calling a general meeting of the citizens. At the meeting, which took place in the Récollet church, English and Canadian citizens agreed unanimously to make preparations for the defence of the town. A second meeting, held the following day, decided to organize militia companies which would appoint their own officers. Eight citizens, seigneurs and *bourgeois,* were chosen by "the people" to draw up lists of men to be called up. Tenant farmers who would constitute a corps of defence against invasion were to be enrolled by their seigneurs. At the same time a message was sent to the Indians of the region, ordering them to be ready to take up arms. However, although the seigneurs displayed great zeal in the execution of their duty, neither argument nor example succeeded in persuading the militiamen to enlist for service. Only fifty Canadian volunteers from the seigniorial and *bourgeois* groups came forward to form the detachment which, under Lieutenant Samuel McKay occupied Fort Saint-Jean until the arrival of regular troops. As for the Indians, they refused to make any move.[3]

Before leaving Saint-Jean, Allen had written a letter to the merchants of Montreal and asked Bindon to deliver it to James Morrison. He informed the merchants that the Lake Champlain forts were in the hands of the Colonials, and he asked them to send him provisions, ammunition, and spirits, to the value of 500 pounds. These were to meet the needs of his detachment, the advance guard of the Colonial army, and would be duly paid for. He urged them to believe, and to assure the people of the province, that his directions from the Colonies were "not to contend with or any way injure or molest the Canadians or Indians but on the other hand treat them with the greatest friendship and kindness."[4]

Arnold too had been active and had already established communication with Walker. After a first short prudent message, he wrote from Crown Point on May 24 to ask for information on the number and movements of British troops.[5] The letter also contained a warning to Canadians. If any of them joined the troops, reprisals would follow: the Colonials would send an army into the heart of Canada.[6]

Connecticut was proud of the part played by her sons, Arnold and his men, in the capture of the Lake Champlain forts. To follow up this exploit, the colony's General Assembly appointed a committee to meet James Price, the rich merchant from Montreal. On May 22, Price reported to the committee that, while Canadian officers were in Carleton's pay and were trying to rouse the Indians to action, to the Canadian people—as distinct from the gentry—the idea of marching against the Colonies was extremely repugnant.[7] This report was forwarded to the New York Provincial Congress, which decided, at the meeting of May 26, to send a message to the colony's northern neighbours.[8] The letter, written in highly rhetorical style, first declared that the question at issue between England and her colonies was whether citizens of the latter should be subjects or slaves. It then expounded the American political doctrine as it applied to Canada and to Canadian-American relations. No power had the right to dispose of the property of Canadians or to deprive them of religious freedom. The capture of the Lake Champlain forts had been a necessary act of self-defence on the part of the Colonials. Canadians must not allow themselves to be deceived on this point and plunged into the horrors of war. They must refuse to be slaves, and they must enjoy the liberty which was their birthright.[9] The assembly ordered 1,550 copies of the letter, 1,500 in French and fifty in English, to be dispatched to Montreal.

Philadelphia, delighted and reassured by the capture of Ticonderoga, was in festive mood on May 18, when John Brown, newly arrived from Canada, appeared before Congress.[10] He came as the bearer of good news, gleaned from letters which had been intercepted on their way from Malcolm Fraser to Carleton. The Canadians were offering stubborn resistance to the proposal that they raise a regiment, while the British in Canada were giving free expression to their dissatisfaction at seeing the political capacity of the new subjects increased at their expense.[11] After hearing this report, Congress concluded that England was preparing to send an invasion force into the colonies from Canada, and that it was therefore essential to garrison the Lake Champlain forts.[12] A week later, on May 26, it appointed John Jay, Samuel Adams, and Samuel Deane as a committee to compose a second letter to the Canadian people. The next day James Price, representing rebel sympathizers in Montreal, presented his picture of the situation in Canada, and on May 29, Congress approved the letter which had been composed by Jay and presented in the name of the committee. It was agreed that the letter be translated and printed, and that 1,000 copies be sent to Canada for distribution.[13]

In its effort to provoke anxiety and suspicion in the French-Catholic population of Canada, this second letter sought to prove, in language more vehement than accurate, that the Quebec Act was nothing but "a form of tyranny," which reduced Canadians to the status of slaves at the mercy of the Governor and his council. Their American fellow subjects urged them to consider their sad plight: "You are liable to be transported into foreign countries to fight battles in which you have no interest. . . . Nay, the enjoyment of your very religion, on the present system, depends on a legislature in which you have no share, and over which you have no control. Your priests are exposed to expulsion, banishment, and ruin. You have already been called upon to waste your lives in a contest with us." After appealing to the Canadians as Catholics, the letter then plucked the cord of French patriotism with a prophetic warning: "Should war break out with France, your wealth and your sons may be sent to perish in expeditions against her islands in the West Indies." The message ended with the familiar refrain on the theme of brotherly affection between colonials: "We are your friends, not your enemies. . . . These Colonies will pursue no measures whatever, but such as friendship and a regard for our mutual safety and interest may suggest."[14]

As if the colonies had already become conscious of the American genius for publicity, they all entered whole-heartedly

47

into the propaganda campaign. The tireless Ethan Allen was the author of the next letter to the inhabitants of Quebec whom he addressed as: "Friends and fellow countrymen." He declared that the Colonials desired neither to harm nor to molest their fellow subjects, the Canadians, nor to deprive them of their liberty or their possessions. He could not doubt that the Canadians for their part were disposed to be sympathetic towards the rebels or at least to remain neutral spectators of the struggle between the British colonies and the mother country. "To fight the King's troops." continued Allen, "has become a necessary and incumbent duty. The colonies cannot avoid it. But pray is it necessary that the Canadians and the inhabitants of the English colonies should butcher one another? God forbid, there are no controversies subsisting between you and them." For Canadians, then, the part of wisdom would be to stand aside and turn a deaf ear to the interested exhortations of their leaders.[15]

As they became more and more preoccupied with the Canadian question, the northern colonies maintained a steady flow of propaganda across the border. On June 3, the New Hampshire Congress addressed a message to its companion assembly in Massachusetts. In view of England's design to arm the Canadians, it was a matter of the utmost importance to inform the latter that the Colonies had no intention of attacking them but were acting solely to protect themselves.[16] One June 12, the Massachusetts Congress considered this communication and forwarded to Philadelphia a resolution proposing that the Continental Congress should once more solemnly declare the Colonies' intention and desire that their "brothers in Canada" achieve full and free enjoyment of their civil and religious rights.[17] On the same day, the New York Congress after having conferred with James Price, composed a letter. This time the message was addressed to the English merchants in Montreal. It made the point that while the Colonies were offering armed resistance to ministerial injustice, they did not aim at independence. Price was sent back to Montreal with two copies of this message and 800 copies of the letter from the Continental Congress to the inhabitants of Quebec.[18]

At the same time, a system of observation was organized along the Quebec frontier, with scouts and agents penetrating deep into the country. The province was patrolled by two companies of fifty Americans, one operating in the neighbour-hood of Montreal, and the other in the Lake Champlain country.[19] Massachusetts charged Andrew Gilman with the mis-sion of sounding out the temper of the Indians of Saint-François and the people of Quebec.[20] In July, James Dean returned from his missionary post among the Indians and reported both to the Congress of New York and to the Continental Congress.[21]

Meanwhile, the political climate of the province of Quebec was becoming more clouded every day. Incessant, insidious, and skilful Colonial and pro-rebel propaganda had succeeded in dividing the country. The clergy, the seigneurs, and the leading citizens, the competent and well-informed element in the coun-try, had adopted a realistic and far-sighted policy of support for the British ministry and for the authorities in Canada. On the other hand, incessant American warnings had achieved their object of confusing a majority of the common people, who were now worried about the possible consequences of the Quebec Act and were reluctant to be drawn into a quarrel which did not concern them. In a letter to the Lord Chancellor, Chief Justice Hey refers to the influences which had created this state of mind: "I am sometimes willing to think that fear, joined with extreme ignorance and a credulity hardly to be supposed of a people, have been over-matched by the subtlety and assiduity of some colony agents who were very busy here last winter. They are not at bottom an ungenerous or disobedient people."[22] As for the subjects of British origin, most of them were stub-bornly opposed to the new constitution, while an extremely active and energetic minority worked openly in favour of the rebellious colonies.

On May 19, a dispatch from General Gage had informed General Carleton of the outbreak of hostilities on Lexington

Green. The following day Captain Hazen had brought the news that the Americans, after taking Ticonderoga and Crown Point, had also captured the King's sloop and the little garrison manning the fort at Saint-Jean. The evening of the same day it was learned that Ethan Allen, who had led a second attack on Saint-Jean, had escaped with his men before the arrival of Preston's troops. The people of Canada were shaken by the news of these engagements, and Carleton reported that "the consternation in the towns and country was great and universal." Although the Governor knew that the country was "in no danger of internal commotions," he also knew just how inadequate were its defences. The regular force could not muster "six hundred rank and file fit for duty," and, since the peace, the militia had fallen into a state of complete disorganization.[23]

Although faced with a problem apparently impossible of solution, the Governor sent two boatloads of troops from Quebec, with artillery and ammunition, to re-fortify Saint-Jean. He also sent detachments to Sartigan at the head of the Chaudière and to Saint-François-de-Beauce to guard these two possible points of entry into Canada. A third detachment was dispatched to Fort la Galette (Ogdensburg) on the St. Lawrence. Finally, the garrisons of Montreal and Three Rivers were placed under the orders of General Preston and sent to Saint-Jean.[24]

At the same time, acting on his conviction that when the Church spoke Canadians were the most submissive and obedient of sons, Carleton persuaded Mgr. Briand to issue a directive dealing with the American raids. The Bishop, who had felt, after the Treaty of Paris, that religion in Quebec might actually benefit by the change of rule,[25] had already (1768) circulated a message warning Canadians against "false reports" based on "vain hopes" that Canada would be reconquered by France.[26] When the Quebec Act had become law, he had seen the path of duty clearly marked before him. It was equally clear in this moment when the country was threatened with invasion. The Church prescribed the duty of obedience to the established sovereign, in this case the King of Great Britain, the representa-

Mgr Jean Olivier Briand

Sir Guy Carleton

Sir Frederick Haldimand

tive on earth of divine authority. In its exposition of the duties of the subject, eighteenth-century civil and common law was quite as absolute and quite as categorical as canon law. Moreover, Mgr. Briand could not but be conscious of special factors in the local situation. England had recognized almost complete religious freedom for Canadian Catholics, as the Bishop himself had recently reported to the nuncio in Paris. "I am not impeded in the exercise of my charge"; he wrote, "the Governor likes and esteems me, and the English do me honour."[27] When the Jesuits' case was presented to Carleton, that "kindest of men"[28] had agreed to leave them in possession of their property, and this at a time when the Society had been expelled from both France and England and suppressed by the Pope.[29]

In such circumstances, the Bishop could hardly refuse the Governor's request that he substitute an episcopal mandate for the letter of advice which he had intended to circulate in the diocese. Besides, he was embarrassed by the attitude of his flock. He found an excuse for their error in the false arguments which the British Colonists had been spreading abroad for two years, and he was anxious to undo some of the harm already done. Accordingly, he hastened the promulgation of a mandate which he composed and had transcribed between eleven o'clock and two.[30]

The mandate of May 22, 1775 was brief, but it was composed with great skill. The Bishop first observed that the invaders were "subjects in revolt against their lawful sovereign who is also ours." The aim of the rebels was to involve the Canadians in their revolt or at least to obtain from them a promise not to oppose "their pernicious designs." He then abjured his charges, when they were subjected to these self-interested appeals, to remember the "singular kindness and mildness" of their present government, and especially "the recent favours" which it had heaped upon the Canadian people by restoring French law, permitting them to practise their religion freely, and ensuring their enjoyment of all the privileges of British subjects. Finally he reminded them of an essential precept of

Catholic teaching: "Your oath and your religion impose upon you the solemn obligation to defend your King and country to the utmost limit of your power." The subject of military service was introduced discreetly at the end of the document. "There is no question of carrying war into the farther provinces; all that is asked of you is that you lend your aid to repulse the enemy and to withstand the invasion which threatens this province."[31]

Although it set out the doctrine of the citizen's duty to protect his country, and appealed to the people's sense of gratitude for favours received, the mandate was no more than an exhortation to duty. Mgr. Briand directed it to the vicariates of Montreal and Three Rivers, the centres of pro-American activity. But, acting with the approval of Lieutenant-Governor Cramahé he withheld it from the peaceful Quebec area. Naturally, the citizens of Quebec soon heard about the order, and the Bishop was grieved to learn that they were sharply critical of it. "The mandate has been the object," he wrote, "of mean and pitiable comment, quite contrary to the spirit of religion."[32]

In the ardour of his conviction, Mgr. Briand had urged the curés to do their utmost to make his pastoral order an occasion for stimulating the zeal of their parishioners.[33] To further the realization of this desire, the Vicar-General of the Montreal region, who was also the superior of the seminary of Saint-Sulpice, prepared an outline for a sermon which could be used by the curés under his jurisdiction. The plan is interesting as evidence of the arguments used by the clergy in favour of the government and against the American cause. M. de Montgolfier presents his doctrine under four headings: 1. As a patriot, the Canadian owes it to himself to defend his country against invasion, for to remain neutral is to declare oneself for the enemy. 2. As a subject who has sworn allegiance, the citizen who refuses to obey orders is thereby a traitor to justice and to the fidelity he owes his King, in this case the guarantor of the property rights of Canadians and of freedom of religion in Canada. 3. As Catholics, Canadians must show that their religion, which teach-

es them to revere God, also teaches obedience to their sovereign.
4. By obeying, they repay the debt of gratitude which they owe
the King, for his generous treatment of them; and the Governor,
for his zeal in defending their cause. M. de Montgolfier then dis-
cusses possible objections to his precepts. Why, it might be
asked, should we meddle in a quarrel which does not concern
us? A victory for the mother country would be of no advantage
to us, and if we were to take part in a conflict from which the
colonies emerged victorious, they would take vengeance on us.
But, countered the Vicar-General, would not a victorious mother
country find, in your refusal to obey, justification for withdrawal of all her favours? Remember the example of the
Acadians. Prudence, honesty, gratitude, and your religion all
dictate to you the duty of fidelity to the King.[34]

While the clergy strove to rally the people to support the
government, Carleton went up to Montreal, where he arrived
on May 26. There, in the strategic heart of the country, the
population welcomed the Governor with every sign of satisfaction, and the citizens presented themselves to him in a body.
But Carleton "received them coolly" although "most of them
had shown themselves to be good and faithful subjects." The
eight deputies, who had been chosen to draw up a census and
a military roster reported on the results of their labours. "They
had found the people ill-disposed"; some deputies had even been
victims of "disagreeable incidents, notably the two who had
been sent to the suburb of Saint-Laurent, where the women
tried to throw stones at them." M. Sanguinet, a highly-esteemed
and influential citizen, suggested the organization of militia
companies as they had existed under the French régime, and
the Governor agreed to adopt this practical and diplomatic
measure.[35]

Although he had always been favourably inclined and sympathetic towards the Canadians, the Governor now found himself
struggling in a complex and difficult situation. He could see
quite well that the one defect of the Quebec Act, unfortunately
a fatal one, was that it had been passed four years too late and

at an inopportune moment. In a letter to Gage, written in February, 1775, he had expressed his regret that the Act had not been adopted immediately after his arrival in London in 1770. "Many advantages might have resulted therefrom at this juncture, which must now be deferred to a more distant occasion."[36] For time would have made it possible for Canadians to appreciate the generosity of the privileges accorded by the Act and forestalled any possible imputation that it had been conceived as an interested measure designed to enlist the Canadian people in the struggle against the colonies in revolt.

It was also true that Carleton had seriously overestimated the influence of the seigneurs and the clergy. He was equally deluded when he supposed that recently-conquered habitants would leave their farms and hasten to the defence of their conquerors. He had forgotten too that the victors had on several occasions burned and ravaged villages and farmsteads for no better reason than that militiamen had dared to defend their farms and their country. Misled by unfounded assumptions, the Governor had acted rashly when, acceding to General Gage's request for reinforcements, he had denuded the country almost completely of its troops. Furthermore, out of respect for British rights, he had refrained from any attempt to prevent English and American propagandists from urging Canadians to neutralism, disaffection, and overt defiance of authority.[37] The result was complete confusion in a country divided against itself, with no regular defence force and no effective militia. Demoralized by Anglo-American propaganda, the common people wavered in their loyalty and militiamen refused to march in Beauce as well as in Montreal.[38] The gentry and the clergy were eager to prove their loyalty, but both had "lost much of their influence over the people." Carleton was convinced that the source of the evil was to be found in the treasonable theories of British Americans. "To defame their King . . . to speak with the utmost contempt of his government, to forward sedition and applaud rebellion seem to be what too many of his British American subjects in those parts think their undoubted right."[39]

Angry at the people's lack of zeal and mortified by his own lack of insight, Carleton began to doubt the possibility of reviving the militia.[40] But he had no more than 800 regular soldiers to defend the country from Beauce to Lake Champlain,[41] and after the raids of Arnold and Allen, he realized that there was no alternative. A proclamation of June 9 established martial law and called up the militia to defend the province against the American rebels threatening invasion on the pretext of protecting the people of Canada from "taxes and oppression by the government." At the same time all militia officers who had been commissioned since the capitulation of Montreal were ordered to report for duty in the service of the King.[42] Two weeks later, the Governor ordered certain officers to visit the parishes, review the militia, confirm commissions, and instruct officers to hold ten men from each company ready to march at the first order.[43]

Profoundly troubled by the success of the congressists and the refractory attitude of the rural population, Carleton once more turned to Mgr. Briand for help. To meet this new crisis the Bishop chose to issue a simple circular letter rather than a formal mandate. He expressed approval of the decision to revive the militia companies, and emphasized the advantages which the parishes would derive from them. The militia would help to maintain order and commissions would be coveted honours. Moreover, the Governor's intention was to commission as officers only candidates who were "acceptable to the public." Obviously the prelate was well aware of the need to recognize a new spirit abroad in the country.[44]

Whereas the earlier mandate had been an exposition of Catholic doctrine in its application to a local situation, the letter gave episcopal support to a specific government order. The result was a storm of protests. The Bishop was accused of setting himself up as "the country's general," and was informed without ceremony that "his job was to give [his people] priests," not to issue military instructions.[45] This hostile spirit was expressed in a letter from Quebec, and, to the great sorrow of the Bishop, it also manifested itself in a number of other parishes.

In sharp contrast to the humbler classes, Canada's *élite*,—professional men, seigneurs, and leading business men—took every opportunity to refute the claims of pro-American agitators and to exalt the merits of the new constitution.[46] The country now had one newspaper, the *Quebec Gazette*, which was printed on Canada's one printing press. Short anonymous articles in the *Gazette* of July 6 and July 13 denounced the two-faced American policy. On the one hand the representative body of the Colonies declared that they were not hostile to the Canadians' religion, while on the other its letter to the people of Great Britain represented Catholicism as a superstition which had caused rivers of blood to flow, and spread murder and rebellion throughout the world. "There we have one proof," wrote the journalist, "of their friendly feelings towards the religion of this province." Doubtless the invasion was another "inevitable consequence of their friendship."[47]

These first articles were followed by others. On July 20, "a patriotic Canadian" protested against the ridiculous idea entertained by some persons that they could remain neutral "between their sovereign and his enemies." As members of the state, they must be with the Sovereign and support him. Moreover, Canadians owed a special debt of gratitude to the King who had restored their full property rights and their ancient laws. Self-interest pointed the same lesson; as faithful British subjects, they did not run the risk of being paid in worthless paper money or of seeing their commerce cut off by a British naval blockade. Where religion was concerned, "New England fanaticism was notorious." Would these men, who had neither spared nor accepted their brothers, the Quakers, be kinder to adherents of a religion which they accused of having spread murder throughout the world?[48] In another article (August 10) a reader confessed that he had allowed himself to be perverted by "an enthusiast for liberty." Now, however, that he recognized in George III his father and his Sovereign, he realized that it would be treason for him to refuse to defend his country and to protect his own property and that of his compatriots.[49]

In Montreal, the Governor, taking some hope from the authority of the clergy and the influence of the seigneurs, undertook to organize the militia in his district. He chose as officers for the French division Colonel Dufy-Desaulniers, Lieutenant-Colonel Neveu-Sevestre, and Major Saint-Gorges-Dupré, but from the outset these officers antagonized their recruits by favouring members of their own families. Still more serious, "the common people refused to be enrolled . . . and claimed that Colonel Templer had promised that they would be grouped in companies of thirty men which would choose their own officers."[50] The English merchants refused to sign up under any conditions. Carleton threatened to vent his anger by burning Montreal and withdrawing to Quebec;[51] but, when the case was put to them by Chief Justice Hey, most of the recalcitrant British agreed to serve under Major Robertson, Captain Gray, and Lieutenant Todd. After this first double reaction of opposition, the Montreal militia came into being and was reviewed on the Champ-de-Mars by Carleton, on July 9. The Canadians especially seemed "well disposed to carry out their duty and to repulse the *Bostonnais*,"[52] and the Governor notes "with pleasure" their zeal and enthusiasm.[53]

In the rural districts, however, the effort to revive the militia companies met with stubborn resistance, and argument was useless. The habitants "could not be convinced of the error into which they had been led by the specious reasoning of a few ill-disposed old subjects who kept repeating that the Americans desired only to relieve them of the taxes about to be imposed on the province."[54] However, on July 9, when Carleton reviewed companies at Longue-Pointe and Pointe-aux-Trembles, as well as at Montreal, he was well satisfied with their attitude.[55]

Some of Carleton's difficulties were the inevitable result of his lack of familiarity with places and persons. In a number of cases the seigneurs and former army officers[56] whom he commissioned were "youths more heedless than wise." One of these, the Sieur La Corne, committeed a whole series of blunders at Terrebonne, from threatening to put recruits "in prison and in irons," to striking two or three of them, and announcing that he was going to call in the regulars to enforce his orders. In the face of this last threat, the men of Terrebonne, Lachenaie, Mascouche, and Repentigny assembled to offer resistance to the troops, but at that point Carleton intervened to reprimand La Corne. He also sent an officer to reassure the protesting habitants, who dispersed and returned home.[57]

Finally, thanks to his conciliatory attitude and to active support from seigneurs and clergy,[58] Carleton succeeded, though with some difficulty, in forming militia units in almost all the parishes of the Montreal district. He was unsuccessful only in a few "where the people were most corrupted, some by a more immediate intercourse with the rebels upon their borders, and others by the friends of rebellion residing amongst us."[59] In the district of Three Rivers, the proclamation instituting the militia was read in the parishes on June 13, and the companies were organized promptly and without incident.[60]

Quebec, the oldest of the administrative districts, was also the one where subversive propaganda had been least effective. There the government appointees, Captains Nairn and Lécuyer and the Fraser brothers, reorganized the militia during the months of June and July. Most of the parishes accepted the revival of the companies without too much demur,[61] although some declared their intention to remain strictly neutral.[62] There were also a few parishes whose members were critical of the order or openly defiant. In May, the seigneur had succeeded in re-forming the militia at Sainte-Marie-de-Beauce under the command of Captain Etienne Parent, but his activities were carried on in the face of the violent protests and "improper objections" from Louis Marcoux and Pierre Camiray. The parishioners of the neighbouring village of Saint-Joseph met and decided "unanimously" neither to submit to the Governor's order nor to obey the exhortations of their curé, the Abbé Verreau, and the meeting dispersed without even allowing the seigneur to speak. The parishioners of Saint-François refused to allow the formation of a militia company.[63] When Mgr. Briand was informed of this movement of opinion, he sent his mandate to the Abbé Verreau with a message directed to the people of the parish: "Make this point quite clear to them; not only are they committing a sin by being false to their oath, they are also liable to severe punishment." On the other hand, the Bishop suggested that, while no order to this effect had been given, it was probable that if they mended their ways their misconduct would not be reported.[64]

In the city of Quebec, both Canadians and English had offered their services and declared their willingness to be enrolled.[65] To complete his military preparations, Carleton had also been in communication with the Indians in the villages along the St. Lawrence and the chiefs of the Six Nations. They had all promised to support the English cause, and in fact a certain number had been serving at Saint-Jean since June 18.[66] On August 3, some five or six hundred Indians from the mission villages and the Six Nations met in council and decided that their warriors would dig up the hatchet to defend Canada, but that they would resort to arms only if they were attacked.[67]

After sending reinforcements to protect the frontier forts, and re-creating at least the framework of a militia, the Governor next turned his attention to recruiting a battalion for active service. But he hesitated in the fear of possible failure.[68] For he was well aware that inscription of a name on a roster did not necessarily mean that a man was ready to take up arms and fight. At the same time his natural tendency was to play for time and to pin his hopes too exclusively on reason and conciliation. Reluctant to use force, he failed to take any of the measures which the circumstances demanded,[69] and, as Chief Justice Hey observed, by some "strange negligence or timidity or ignorance of local government," he did not make use of his authority either to combat subversive propaganda or to impose censorship. Instead of forcing enemy agents and apostles of disobedience to respect the law, or even subjecting them to regular surveillance, he left them free to execute their nefarious designs.[70]

Carleton himself recognized that the most dangerous agents for the Colonials were to be found in Canada where British American subjects were known "to forward sedition and applaud rebellion."[71] And yet it was his failure to act and his tolerance of their activities that made it possible for these agitators to preach their doctrine of sedition. Either with the object of gathering information or in the hope of reawakening loyalty in a disloyal subject, Carleton went so far as to talk to James Price, on the latter's return to Montreal from Philadelphia. He even allowed that arch-spy in the colonial service to go to Quebec, gather information on the state of Canadian opinion, and carry his report back to the Continental Congress.[72] To the dismay of loyalists and Canadian leaders, Carleton took no measures to suppress the propaganda of his audacious visitor nor that of his confederate Walker, even though correspondence had been intercepted between the latter and the enemy.[73] It is very difficult to explain the Governor's failure to act at a time when small parties of armed men were appearing on the south shore of the St. Lawrence, and when four dispatch bearers had actually been captured.[74] Agents and publicity men circulated the most fantastic stories: that the Americans had invaded the country in order to prevent the imposition of the Stamp Act; that vessels were anchored in Quebec harbour, waiting to transport habitants to Boston; that the Governor had sold them to the Spaniards and had already been paid for them.[75]

It was in this clouded and anxious atmosphere, in the midst of an unstable military and political situation, that the Governor arrived in Quebec and, on August 17, convened the first meeting of the legislative council established by the new constitution.[76] Apparently unaware of the critical turn which events were taking, the twenty-two members of the council, of whom seven were Catholic Canadians, confined their deliberations to the discussion of two bills dealing respectively with the creation of courts of justice and with trading regulations.[77] These questions were still undecided when an army of American rebels crossed Canada's southern frontier. The fate of the country was at stake and was to remain so for many long months.

5

CANADA INVADED BY THE COLONIALS

March of Montgomery on Saint-Jean. Inactivity of the militia. Neutralism in parishes on the Richelieu. Livingston's activities. Attack by Canadians on a presbytery. American camps at Saint-Mathias and Longueuil. Neutral sentiment at Lanoraie and Lavaltrie. Lack of response to militia duty, especially in the Quebec region. Slight influence of clergy and gentry on the people. Neutrality a result of American propaganda and failure to take counter measures.

SOUTH of the frontier, two irreconcilable concepts—supremacy of the mother country and complete autonomy for the colonies —were leading the country steadily in the direction of an armed struggle. The Continental Congress, ever mindful of the danger of invasion from the north, did not slacken its vigilant watch over Canadian opinion, nor its efforts to woo Canadian sympathy. On June 1, 1775, Congress adopted a resolution to refrain from undertaking any expedition into Canada. As the resolution was framed to reassure not only Carleton but the Canadians, it was translated, and copies of the translation were sent to Canada for distribution.[1] Congress exchanged letters with Walker using as messengers Indians from the village of Sault-Saint-Louis (Caughnawaga),[2] and it received news of Canadian affairs by various other avenues. A Quebec sympathizer reported to Congress in July.[3] In August, John Duguid brought confirmation of the rumour that the Canadians south of Quebec and along the Richelieu wanted to remain neutral, and that they refused to recognize the militia officers appointed by Carleton.[4] There were repeated reports that the country people were protecting the Colonies' emissaries, and that, although the threat of punishment made it impossible for them to take up arms, they were hoping to see the American army. They even promised to provision it as it passed through.[5]

Armed with this information, and the knowledge that Carleton's opposing forces consisted of 800 regulars divided among a number of different posts, the members of Congress concluded, in the course of the session of July 27, that the moment had arrived to seize the initiative and invade Quebec. They immediately instructed General Philip Schuyler, a retired officer who had served in Canada during the war, to visit Ticonderoga and Crown Point and to gather information as to the attitude of the Canadian population. If the general considered that the enterprise could be carried out without alienating the Canadians, he was to proceed at once to seize Saint-Jean, Montreal, and any other fortified places in the country, and to take any other measures tending to ensure the peace and safety of the Colonies.[6] Schuyler set to work at once, concentrating troops at Ticonderoga and Crown Point, and, with the help of American agents or pro-rebel sympathizers, spreading the news of his invasion plans in Canada.[7] At the same time the province was flooded with copies of the second letter of Congress to the Canadians, and of the letter from the New York Congress. In the vicinity of Montreal, the following enigmatic announcement was posted on house doors:[8]

> *Onis soit qui mal y pence.*
> *A celui qui ne suivra le bon chemin.*
> Baston.

James Livingston, a former American lawyer and now a grain merchant on the Richelieu, was actively engaged in conditioning the minds of his neighbours. At the same time he distributed circular letters to militia captains announcing the arrival of American troops.[9]

On September 4, 1775, an army of 2,000 came down from

Lake Champlain[10] and took possession of Ile-aux-Noix. The force was commanded by Richard Montgomery, a former British army officer who had served under Amherst. On September 7, an advance party was ordered to penetrate farther into Canadian territory, but it was driven back by a group of Indians patrolling the region.[11] From their camp on the island, the invaders continued to send out small detachments of armed men and emissaries "to debauch the minds of the Canadians and Indians, in which they proved too successful."[12] On September 5, at the first report of invasion, Prescott, who was in command in Montreal, had sent "orders to the country districts calling up fifteen men in each militia company, but the habitants, who were ill-disposed," had disregarded the orders and had taken no action whatsoever.[13]

The following day, Carleton sent out his instructions from Quebec: each parish between Châteauguay and Sorel[14] was to call up one militiaman for ten enrolled. Pierre Guy distributed similar orders from Lachine to Les Cèdres, but although the officers reported in Montreal, their militiamen did not follow them.[15] On the other hand, "the gentry, the clergy, and most of the *bourgeois* . . . [showed] the greatest zeal and fidelity to the King's service, and exerted their best endeavours to reclaim their infatuated countrymen."[16] Under their influence a detachment of 120 Canadian volunteers was raised in Montreal, and on September 7, this detachment, under the command of M. de Longueuil, was sent to reinforce the garrison at Saint-Jean.[17] "The English merchants flatly refused to join up. The Canadian militia mounted guard in Montreal, and the *bourgeois*, who did not belong to the militia, formed a company of volunteers. The Sieur Perthuis was killed in a skirmish at Saint-Jean between the Americans and thirty of these volunteers led by M. de Longueuil."[18] Even when faced with the reality of invasion, the country was divided; some Canadians persisted in maintaining a specious neutrality, while others were resolved to fight the invader.

Meanwhile the war of propaganda went on. A letter of

September 5, written by General Schuyler at the American Camp on Ile-aux-Noix, informed the Canadian people that Congress had ordered the invasion in the certainty that American invaders would encounter no opposition. The object of the intervention was to free Canadians from bondage and "to restore to them the rights which can be claimed by any subject of the British Empire, from the highest to the lowest, whatever his religious opinions may be." Schuyler explained further that the orders which he had received, and which would be carried out by the soldiers under his command, were to protect the liberty and property of Canadians. Finally, he added that he had already concluded a treaty with the Indians in the Colonies, and was counting upon the friendship of the Indians in Canada.[19]

Schuyler selected Ethan Allen to carry his message through the countryside. Armed with copies of the letter, and accompanied by Brown and interpreters, the adventurous courier set out on September 8. He was well received at Chambly, where the Canadians even provided him with a guard. Several militia captains and leading citizens called on him and received copies of Schuyler's letter. Allen also talked to the Indians at Caughnawaga, who assured him that they would remain neutral. As a matter of fact, after the first skirmish at Saint-Jean, where they had observed that the Canadians were not taking up arms, the Indians had gone back to their village. The people in the Richelieu valley were not completely won over by the American envoys; for, as Allan observed, they did not think the American troops were strong enough to protect them if the invasion proved unsuccessful. However, they agreed to maintain their attitude of neutrality and to ignore the appeals of Carleton and the Catholic hierarchy.[20]

Livingston had also been active in Allen's service. With James Duggan, a wig-maker turned grain merchant, and a blacksmith called Loiseau, he had established a guard on the Chambly river. He claimed to have assembled 300 Canadians at Pointe-Olivier (Saint-Mathias), but a contemporary, Sanguinet, estimates the total at not more than forty or fifty.[21] The men had been lured by a bonus and a distribution of provisions, and Allen confessed that their fidelity cost him dear. It required all his eloquence too, for the seigneurs were bending their efforts towards rallying their tenants to repulse the invaders. Allen had to keep pleading for funds to pay these unreliable supporters at least a part of what he had promised them. If he could pay half of what he owed, he assured Schuyler, they would wait for the rest.[22] Livingston and Duggan sent a circular letter to militia captains between Pointe-Olivier and Quebec asking them to provide supplies of flour, and to form a corps of volunteers to join their compatriots from the Richelieu country.[23] In another letter Livingston exhorted the people to ally themselves with the Americans whose only desire was to make them masters of their property by abolishing the taxes that the authorities were trying to impose upon them.[24]

With inadequate military forces—less than 1,000 men for the defence of the whole country—with no reserve troops, and with the Canadians contributing only the hundred volunteers at Saint-Jean, Carleton was powerless to act. He had to remain on the defensive and wait for the enemy to make the first move. Fully aware of the critical weakness of the government, Livingston, with valuable help from Loiseau, succeeded in obtaining promises of collaboration from most of the people in six parishes on the Richelieu.[25] Militia officers and prudent members of these communities condemned the attitude of their fellow parishioners, and in at least one case led them to acknowledge their error. On September 5, the people of Saint-Denis begged Carleton to grant them an amnesty.

In answer to the plea Carleton sent the Sieurs Orillat and Léveillé to Saint-Denis with a proclamation of amnesty. At five o'clock in the morning of September 17, as the Governor's messengers were asleep in the presbytery where they had been lodged, the house was surrounded by a detachment of twenty Americans led by rebel sympathizers from Saint-Mathias, Saint-Charles, and even Saint-Denis. When the curé presented himself "he was treated with little respect (it was even said that he was seized by the scruff of the neck and that his cassock was torn). He was told to hand over the two men in his house, and that, if he refused, the house would be set on fire. As the curé went back into the house to relay the order to his guests, a servant who showed her head at the window was shot and killed. The two men were seized by the rebels and taken to the camp on Ile-aux-Noix."[26] For the first time in their history Canadians had gone beyond disregard of ecclesiastical directives. Not only had they threatened a priest with violence, they had actually placed violent hands upon him.

This exploit, against which no reprisals were taken, encouraged the movement of resistance. Other habitants joined the group at Pointe-Olivier, whose numbers were further swelled by the arrival of Ethan Allen with twenty New Englanders. Parties from the camp infested the neighbouring countryside, cutting off communication between Sorel and Chambly, and pillaging seigniories. Meanwhile Canadians on the north shore declared themselves ready to march with the Montrealers against the rebels, "on condition that a large enough troop of British soldiers could be assembled to support them if they were repulsed. If no regular troops could be supplied, they preferred to remain neutral."[27]

Since the Americans had already made their peace with the Indians of Sault-Saint-Louis, a neutral militia made it possible for them to establish camps at Longueuil and La Prairie, across the river from Montreal, and to watch Carleton's movements from there. Practically "all the countryside south of the river was at the service of the *Bostonnais* who got [the militiamen] to mount guard for them, . . . and who were supplied with fresh food and carts by the farmers."[28] The Canadians of Pointe-Olivier had become such passionate partisans of the American cause that M. de Montgolfier, the Vicar-General of the region, considered it quite useless to send them a missionary. He reported to Mgr. Briand that a missionary "would not even be safe" among men who committed such acts "of revolt and

67

treason" as stopping convoys and firing on British troops. These were the acts which caused the Governor to class them as "rebels."[29]

The members of two parishes on the north shore of the St. Lawrence, Lavaltrie and Lanoraie, where it was suspected that "very few are royalists," soon exhibited their sentiments quite unequivocally by talking "insolently and seditiously" and by refusing to support the royal cause in any way. On September 16, the whole militia company of Lanoraie refused to obey the orders of the officers appointed by the Governor. Their neutrality reflected pro-American propaganda, and some of the arguments with which they met ecclesiastical admonitions and governmental orders were curiously revealing. The object of the revolt was "foreign to religion," and consequently "foreign to the Christian ministry and preaching." It was a national dispute in which each party claimed rights about which Canadians knew very little, since these matters of right and fact had yet to be put to the test of proof. Moreover, neutrality was not only allowable, it was a duty. "Since in one kingdom the subjects form one family," Canadians could not raise their hands against their brothers who were perhaps the victims of unjust treatment. Furthermore, by disarming the Canadians, the British authorities had released them from any obligation to serve. Their final argument was based on the premise that distance inevitably weakens the link binding colonies to a central authority. "The mother country is losing some of her power, and our province, abandoned by her, will be exposed to the fury of the Colonies which are so close to us and so much stronger than we." For all these reasons, Canada must think of her own safety and remain entirely free.[30]

These arguments, which anticipate theories of Quebec autonomy, were reported to Mgr. Briand by the curé of Lanoraie, the Abbé Saint-Germain. In his answering letter, the Bishop pointed out that none of these "false reasons" could possibly justify an act of disobedience "contrary to natural law, to Christian law, and to the obligations of the oath of allegiance."

He therefore ordered the curé to refuse the sacraments to anyone who professed such ideas. The Bishop added that he was astounded to see his poor people, intelligent, but ignorant and unenlightened on the subject of their own religion, setting themselves up as casuists. If they could reason more clearly, they would be "convinced and persuaded" that their best friends were "their curés and those better able [than they] to advise them and to make safe decisions for their temporal and spiritual good. . . . How little faith there is in Canada, though the shell of religion still remains!"[31] The prelate, who had fought so hard for the principle of religious liberty, and for its guarantee in the Quebec Act could not but be bitterly disappointed to see some members of his flock repudiate his spiritual direction.

After the appearance of the Americans at Saint-Jean, instructions were issued in the town of Three Rivers and the *côtes*, or parishes, of the district to call up the militia. But when the word went out from the pro-rebel Richelieu parishes to resist the order, since the mission of the invaders was to save Canada from "oppression," most of the parishes believed the story and their men refused the call to arms. There were a few volunteers in Rivière-du-Loup, Machiche, and Maskinongé, but not a single one from the parishes of Nicolet, Bécancour, Gentilly, and Saint-Pierre-les-Becquets. The little town of Three Rivers followed the example set by Quebec and Montreal, and, with the neighbouring village of Pointe-du-Lac, gave proof of loyalty by sending twelve men, under Tonnancourt and Bellefeuille, to swell the numbers of the garrison at Saint-Jean.[32] Militiamen also mounted guard in the town of Three Rivers itself. In October, when the Vicar-General of Three Rivers led a novena for the success of the royal arms, large numbers of the townspeople participated, although some of them declared that they were praying for victory for the *Bostonnais*.[33]

When Montgomery's army entered Canada, the Governor delegated men of influence to call up a certain number of men from each militia company in the Quebec district, but almost all the parishes refused to obey the summons. Recruits from Saint-

Joachim, who tried to offer their services, were stopped on their way to Quebec by the men from Saint-Féréol led by Chrétien Giguère.[34] The men from Pointe-Lévis, who took the lead in the movement of resistance, sent an invitation "to the neighbouring parishes to join them in resisting the action of the government." They also set up a guard "to await the arrival of the rebels." The result was a league of parishes which established an armed camp and made ready to resist government troops if the need for such action should arise. Included in the league were the parishes of Beaumont, Saint-Charles, Saint-Michel, Saint-Vallier, Berthier, Saint-François-du-Sud, Saint-Jean Deschaillons, and Saint-Henri-de-Beauce.[35] The villagers of Saint-Thomas-du-Sud were on their way to join the camp when they learned that it had been dispersed.[36] Five other parishes: Cap Saint-Ignace, les Islets, Saint-Roch, Sainte-Anne, and Rivière-Ouelle, set up guards to prevent execution of military orders.[37]

The movement of defection spread rapidly. A certain number of parishes, la Vieille-Lorette, la Jeune-Lorette, Charlesbourg, Berthier, and Cap Saint-Ignace, flatly refused to recognize the militia officers designated by the Governor.[38] In a number of parishes—Sainte-Anne-de-Beaupré, Saint-Féréol, Gentilly, Saint-Pierre-les-Becquets, Lotbinière, Saint-François-du-Sud,[39] Sainte-Foy, and Saint-Augustin[40]—officers refused to accept the King's commission. When the Governor's delegates on the Ile d'Orléans tried to raise fifteen men in the parish of Sainte-Famille, and threatened to set fire to the village if they were opposed, a young man called Drouin, who had refused to accept a commission immediately retorted: "We are ready for you." Then, setting out with the rebels from Saint-Famille, he gathered recruits from Saint-Pierre and Saint-François and set up a camp at the end of the island where about twenty men from Saint-Jean joined the group.[41] In the village of Saint-Pierre, when Mabane, Grant, and Boisseau proclaimed the King's orders, François Chabot and Pierre Choret expressed opposition to the summons. They agreed, however, to the appointment of officers who went into the presbytery of Mgr. d'Esgly, the Bishop's coadjutor, to confer with the government delegates. Thereupon, two brothers, Joseph and Gabriel Langlois, started the cry: "Follow me, let's kidnap the officers," and with a dozen followers tried to force their way into the house. Most of the group held back, however, and Mgr. d'Esgly's resolute attitude stopped the leaders at the threshold. While Saint-Pierre and Saint-François sent squads to the camp at the end of the island, Saint-Laurent and Saint-Pierre-les-Becquets limited their activities to mounting guard before the church.[42]

In spite of this wave of resistance in the Quebec region, resistance born of the determination of one part of the population not to fight in a quarrel which did not concern them, even the dissident parishes had their royalist sympathizers. Although in most cases the loyalists had to accept passively orders dictated by the opposition, a few groups gave proof of firmness and showed a good deal of spirit. Captain Louis Gouin and twenty-two volunteers from Sainte-Anne-de-la-Pérade marched to Montreal to join the forces, and six men from Saint-Roch with their captain, François Pelletier, passed through several neutral parishes on their way to offer their services to Lieutenant-Governor Cramahé in Quebec. Captain Alexandre Dionne led a group of ten men all the way from Kamouraska to Pointe-Lévis, but they did not succeed in finding boats to take them to Quebec.[43]

In that autumn of 1775, while the country people displayed their determination to remain strictly neutral at whatever cost, the clergy, the seigniorial class, the *bourgeoisie*, and almost all city dwellers gave strong support to the government.[44] They constituted a minority of the population, but they were the *élite*; those with the best knowledge of the situation and of the privileges accorded to Canadians by the Quebec Act. Conscious of the inestimable value of the rights guaranteed by the Act—rights, it must be observed, from which their groups would draw the greatest benefits—they freely accepted the corresponding obligations. They did not, however, succeed in converting to their point of view the village artisan or the farmer.

Apart from this select minority, there were, according to one observer, no more than a hundred Canadians willing to fight for the government.[45] Virtually all potential members of the militia refused to perform the military service required by the Governor's decrees. And they persisted in their refusal in spite of episcopal mandates and pastoral exhortations. Far from being received with approval and in a spirit of submission, the Bishop's word met with bitter criticism and violent opposition. The country's rulers, including Carleton and Mgr. Briand, had counted too much on the implicit obedience of the Canadian to the voice of the Church. They forgot the individualistic and disputatious character of the average Canadian Catholic, whose spirit of independence had been fostered in the climate of the New World, and who, under English rule, had lost some of his earlier inhibitions. Even before the invasion, Mgr. Briand had admitted that his charges had become "less docile and less submissive in their attitude towards their pastors," and that they had created "very grave difficulties" for him.[46]

Men who refused to submit to their Bishop were naturally even less willing to accept advice or censure from their seigneurs. For, apart from the conditions of his tenure, the tenant farmer was in fact, and on occasion showed that he was, completely independent of the lord of the manor. He deferred neither on the point of social authority nor in matters of opinion. Under the old régime he had served as a militiaman, not under his seigneur, but under officers chosen from his own community.[47] It was also true that the old régime had produced, along with understanding and competent seigneurs, others who had sought to exploit their farmers.[48] After the conquest, when the intendant was no longer there to protect the tenant, some seigneurs tried to take advantage of the situation by raising their rents. Others affected an air of superiority befitting the importance which the snobbish attitude of British officers and officials imputed to them. The appointment of seven of their number to the legislative council had further increased their pretentiousness,[49] and the arrogant attitude of a few when the attempt was being made to raise a militia had exasperated the habitants. The net result of all this was that the seigneurs ceased to exert any influence and that they "could not raise a single man."[50] The *bourgeois* class, composed of professional and business men, was not, at that time, strong enough either in numbers or in prestige to lead the people in the loyalist path, or to persuade them to take up arms in defence of the government.

So it came about that in the country districts neutrality and inaction were followed by resistance to orders, and even by active aid to the invaders. And yet, following a policy unknown in an age when the state or empire was conceived as a single monolithic unit, the Quebec Act had accorded generous advantages to a small population different in race, religion, and language from the ruling country. To be sure, it had come too late[51] to allow Canadians to appreciate the profound spirit of justice which had inspired it; but, even considering the delay, how can we explain the fact that a charter which gave the Canadian people everything they had demanded[52]—religious freedom, French law, admission to public office—evoked, in rural Canada, neither enthusiasm nor gratitude nor satisfaction? For, as Chief Justice Hey had observed, the Canadians were "not at bottom an ungenerous or disobedient people."[53]

The first explanation is to be found in the "subtlety and assiduity" of the campaign carried on by the Continental Congress and its British partisans in Canada, who took infinite pains to set the average Canadian against the new constitution.[54] They represented it as an arbitrary measure empowering the Governor to seize their possessions and to send them to war.[55] They perhaps played their strongest card in presenting the régime instituted by the Quebec Act as one which would make it possible to levy taxes,[56] for taxes were the special phobia of a people which had obstinately refused to be taxed right up to the very end of the old régime.[57] At the same time the adversaries of the Act represented it as what it was, a victory for the Church and the seigniorial class. The Church had won on the question of tithes and the seigneurs on that of land

73

tenure. So the pro-rebel agents promised Canadians that exemption from seigniorial rents and abolition of tithes would follow as natural consequences of a Colonial victory.[58]

It must also be remembered that, precious as it was in law, in fact the Quebec Act did not change the lives of the country people, who had never ceased to practise their religion nor to follow the *Coutume de Paris*. Moreover fifteen years of peace and stability had procured for them a life of ease and comfort, even of luxury.[59] And now, frightened, misled, and completely demoralized by American propaganda, they could see nothing in the new constitution except that which might interfere with their domestic economy; always a sensitive area in the reasoning of any peasant. Far from deriving any satisfaction from the Act, the habitant regarded it with anxiety and suspicion; so that a law which was passed for the explicit purpose of pleasing Canadians and satisfying their demands became for them an object of dissatisfaction and aversion.[60]

A second and no less powerful motive restraining the Canadians from taking up arms was the weakness of the government's military forces.[61] At the time of the Seven Years' War, the regular forces in Canada—marines and land troops—counted about 5,000 men. These formed the main battle line while the militia, as a rule, served as auxiliaries. But now, when the Americans had 2,000 soldiers at Saint-Jean and the whole country was threatened with invasion, the strength of the regular army was reported as 750[62] in the official record, and as 500 by Chief Justice Hey.[63]

The Governor had given the order to raise ten militiamen for each company, a total of 1,500 or 2,000 for the province. That meant that the militia would bear the main weight of defence, a situation which seemed completely unjustifiable to the militiamen concerned; it was incumbent on the King of England to defend the colony, as the King of France had done. Moreover, Canadians had not forgotten the bitterness of defeat, nor the ravages committed by the English troops, and it seemed completely unreasonable to expect that defeated men would be

74

transformed overnight into defenders of their present masters, or that they would support the latter in a family quarrel in which they (the Canadians) had nothing to gain and everything to lose. Why should they risk their skins when the British in Canada refused to fight, and even joined forces with the Americans?[64] So the Canadians refused to take part in a war of political principle, of no interest to them, between two groups of their former enemies, a war in which Great Britain was apparently powerless to protect them.

As contemporary observers realized, the root of Canadian neutralism was to be found in the military weakness of Great Britain. Carleton reported to Lord Dartmouth that "every individual seemed to feel our present impotent situation,"[65] and Daniel Claus attributed the defection of Canadians directly to the defenceless situation of the country.[66] Gage wrote that "a good force alone is wanted in Canada to set them all in motion,"[67] while Cramahé considered that "some troops and a ship of war or two would in all likelihood have prevented this general defection."[68] In the last analysis then, American propaganda and British military weakness together created a spirit of neutralism in Canada and provoked the refusal on the part of Canadians to serve as a buckler for the British and a target for the Americans.

6

ENGLISH INDECISION. AMERICAN PROGRESS

Carleton's play for time. La Corne's plot. Defeat of Allen at Longue-Pointe. Volunteering of militiamen. Arrest of Walker. Declaration by Montreal of its loyalty and by Three Rivers of its decision to remain neutral. Pro-rebel incidents at Lavaltrie, Lanoraie, Berthier, and Verchères. Condemnation of neutralism by the Bishop. Opposition to the clergy. Abundance of militiamen in Montreal. Failure of Carleton to take action at Longueuil. Capture of Chambly by the Americans. Failure of MacLean's expedition. Capture of Saint-Jean. Canadian help for the invaders.

CAUGHT between the American invasion and the defection of the militia, Carleton was incapable of making a decision. Chief Justice Hey deplored his friend's timid hesitancy, and his misjudgment of human nature. He considered that the incursions of Arnold and Allen should have prompted an immediate enrolment of the militia, by force if necessary, and that the Governor's hesitancy and his fear of irritating the Canadians had caused the situation to deteriorate seriously.[1] Hey was at once right and wrong; he was wrong in supposing that with an army of 500 men, stationed at the frontier posts, the Governor could force the hand of 1,500 militiamen, but he was right in condemning the Governor's failure to act. Carleton's error, then and later, was his unwillingness to hasten events or to hustle people, his confidence that time, which arranges everything, would lead Canadians back to the tradition of obedience and Americans to their British loyalty.

76

This disposition doubtless explains the Governor's conduct in such cases as his meeting with James Price, a liaison agent between Philadelphia and Montreal, and his failure to arrest Walker, whose correspondence with the enemy had been intercepted. He displayed the same leniency towards the American Livingston, who had a son in the army of invasion, was in constant communication, through the Indians, with the enemy, and held meetings of pro-rebel British subjects in his house. In Montreal, Carleton took no action with respect to foreign visitors, while in Quebec, Cramahé merely issued a proclamation (September 16, 1775) that they were to appear before a judge and declare the object of their journey.[2] Espionage and pro-rebel propaganda were left free to flourish. Public confidence was at such a low ebb that towards the end of September a group of influential Montrealers, under the leadership of a former officer, the wily and cunning Saint-Luc de La Corne, established communication with Montgomery, whose army was camped outside Saint-Jean. Their object was to prepare the way for surrender on terms which would ensure the protection of their property. In reply, Montgomery stated his conditions. He would require hostages and a loan, and the Canadian people must promise not to oppose the establishment of a free government. They must also send delegates to the Continental Congress as soon as such action became possible.[3]

Suddenly, on September 24, it was rumoured that the enemy was about to attack Montreal. The people on the outskirts were ordered to bring their ladders inside the walls, but they refused to carry out the order and threatened with violence anyone who might attempt to force them to obey.[4] The rumour was well-founded; Carleton's inaction and the sympathatic neutrality of the Canadians had encouraged Ethan Allen and Major Brown to make a bold bid for fortune's favour. Brown was to cross the river from La Prairie with 200 men, while Allen's force would embark farther down the river at Longueuil. They would then attack the city simultaneously from two directions.[5] On September 24, Allen took up his position at Longueuil according to plan with thirty Americans and eighty Canadians from the camp at Saint-Mathias. At ten o'clock in the evening he crossed the river with Duggan, Loiseau, and a few companions, and called on several citizens in the Quebec *faubourg* at the eastern gate of Montreal. Meanwhile, his detachment crossed at Longue-Pointe, where he joined it on the morning of the twenty-fifth. Carleton was still ignorant of the fact that the enemy was only a few miles away, and it was a man called Desautels who, startled to see Americans in several houses in the village, ran through the fields to alert Montreal.

The city gates were immediately shut and a general alarm was sounded. Without waiting for orders, citizens flocked to the Champ-de-Mars and thence to the barracks where they were supplied with powder and shot. A force of 300 Canadians and thirty British merchants, led by thirty regular soldiers, marched out of Montreal. The other British merchants had refused to volunteer. "That," observes Sanguinet's eye-witness, "was where the traitors could be recognized most clearly."[6] Allen's force was made up of thirty-seven American soldiers and about sixty Canadians whom he had engaged at thirty *sous* a day and with whom he had promised to share equally the booty to be captured from the city. At the approach of the Montrealers under Captain Crawford, a large number of Allen's Canadians disappeared. They had not expected a battle; they had come not to fight but to pillage, and they had expected to be joined by the people of the *faubourgs* and the neighbouring parishes.[7] At the Ruisseau-des-Soeurs the two forces clashed, and after losing six men Allen surrendered. His force had dwindled to twenty Americans and eleven Canadians.

Allen and his soldiers were sent as prisoners to England; but Carleton, still conciliatory, chose not to inflict the same punishment on the Canadians, who were imprisoned in Canada.[8] For Carleton, who knew that the city merchants had led the habitants astray, pitied the culprits more than he blamed them.[9]

If it had not been for that sortie of volunteers, five-sixths of them Canadians, Montreal would have fallen into the hands of the Yankees.[10] On their return, the leaders of the expedition proposed to Carleton that they should seize the enemies' boats and surround the *Bostonnais* who were attempting to escape to them. It would have been easy to overtake the fugitives, and their capture would have doubled the importance of the victory, but Carleton refused to agree to the plan.[11] One immediate result of Allen's defeat was that La Corne placed Montgomery's letter in the hands of the Governor, who ordered it to be burned in public.[12] "The affair of September 25" made a deep impression on the country people. "Since then," observed M. de Montgolfier, the habitants of all the parishes on this island have come to offer their services to the general."[13] It was true that this small royalist triumph had awakened the Canadians and given them the confidence they needed if they were to take up arms. Beginning the very next day, September 26, volunteers arrived in the city every day. On September 30, Captain McLeod led twelve soldiers and thirty militiamen "in red tuques and blanket coats" in a successful attack on the American camp at Longueuil. The Americans were put to flight and their store of provisions was seized.[14] Loyalist militiamen at Saint-Denis succeeded in capturing two pro-American agitators, Orillat and Léveillée, although the men put up a stiff resistance.[15]

Unfortunately, this favourable change of opinion did not move Carleton to decisive action. He still hestitated to renew his order to raise fifteen men for each militia company, although he allowed Colonel Dufy-Desaulniers of Montreal to do so in his name. Within the next few days, men converged on the city in ever-increasing numbers. Twenty-two came from as far away as Sainte-Anne-de-la-Pérade on the north shore of the St. Lawrence, and even the presence of the Americans did not slow down the movement on the south shore. Three hundred men came in from the single parish of Varennes as well as a number from Saint-Ours who had ignored the colonials' threat to burn their barns and granaries. Militiamen from several parishes on the island volunteered to march against the enemy, and one day a hundred Indians came in from the Lac-des-Deux-Montagnes and Saint-Régis.[16]

While recruits kept pouring into Montreal, loyalist Canadians in Quebec launched a counter-attack against neutralist propaganda. *Civis Canadensis,* whose ecclesiastical style revealed his calling if not his name, published an article in the *Gazette* of October 5. Recalcitrant Canadians, explained the author, had been misled by the rebels and were guilty of resisting God from whom comes all power. For to disobey a King who recognized their religion and to whom they had sworn an oath of fidelity was to resist God. Deceived by the enemies of that same religion Canadians were bringing disrepute upon themselves. The enemy would take all their possessions and pay for them with paper money. In conclusion, the article declared that true liberty consists in obedience to one's king.[17]

The following week there appeared an *Adresse aux Canadiens* of which 400 copies had been printed for distribution by the government. The King, said the government's spokesman, would be justified in saying to Canadians that while he had protected their property, their religion, and their laws, they had taken up arms against him. God could not leave unpunished such a crime of human and divine lese-majesty. The Governor, too, had spent his efforts in their service; could he expect such conduct in return? Under English rule, they had enjoyed prosperity and had "paid no taxes"; in short, Canadians could consider themselves the happiest of peoples. And the author terminated his address with the wish that they repair their fault.[18]

From his residence in L'Assomption, Walker had been corresponding with the enemy, receiving enemy agents, and preaching neutralism and open sedition to the habitants. When, on October 5, Carleton finally ordered his arrest, and he was put in irons in Montreal,[19] this decisive action was immediately followed by a new influx of volunteers. They came "in large numbers" from all the parishes in the island,[20] and the movement continued throughout the month of October. From L'Assomption itself, the parish of Walker and the "mutineers," came a group of "160 warriors" who were granted pardon for their previous disloyalty. However, although the region was as a whole disposed to be loyal, there still remained a few intractable parishes even in the immediate vicinity of Montreal. Sault-au-Récollet and Longue-Pointe, Sainte-Geneviève and Pointe-Claire maintained such a rebellious attitude that Carleton threatened to quarter soldiers in private houses. The Vicar-General, M. de Montgolfier, for his part, decided to deprive the rebellious parishes of their curés. Threats proved more effective than the "ingratiating kindness" which the Governor had previously shown. They worked "marvels" and for the time being suppressed the movement of revolt.[21] Thus, after Allen's defeat and Carleton's decisive measures, the Montreal region as a whole gave evidence of a will to defend the country.

In the district of Three Rivers, on the other hand, the temper of the people remained stubbornly neutral. This spirit showed itself quite openly on October 8, when, in answer to the Governor's order to call up fifteen men for every hundred enrolled in the militia companies, almost all the parishes refused to obey. Godefroi de Tonnancourt and the notary Badeaux went to Nicolet, whose citizens had set the example of resistance, and explained to the habitants that their religion required them to be faithful to the King, as they had sworn to do, and that the penalty for disobedience was hanging. After a long discussion, ten men joined up, received the curé's benediction, and marched off to Three Rivers, reciting litanies and singing as they went.[22] On October 10, a detachment of sixty-seven men under Lanaudière and Tonnacourt set out from the rallying point of Three Rivers for Montreal. However, they were stopped between Berthier and Saint-Cuthbert-du-Chicot by a group of habitants under the leadership of Captain Merlet. The two commanders were taken prisoner, and Father Pouget had to intervene in order to obtain their release.[23]

The parish of Lanoraie was equally stubborn in its refusal to comply with the Governor's order, and the Vicar-General decided to take strong measures. The curés of Berthier and

Saint-Cuthbert, Fathers Papin and Dubois, were withdrawn from their parishes, and the Abbé Saint-Germain was ordered not to officiate at Lanoraie, although he continued to serve the village of Lavaltrie, whose attitude had been more satisfactory. Alarmed by the action of M. de Montgolfier, the parishoners of Berthier and Saint-Cuthbert dispatched a deputation to Montreal to declare their submission, to ask pardon for their offence, and to beseech the Vicar-General to restore their curés to them. Carleton agreed to pardon them,[24] but M. de Montgolfier refused to send the priests back to their presbyteries. Thereupon, a "large number of mutineers" displayed their contempt for the punishment meted out to them. "To show that they could do without a curé," they rang the church bells and took it upon themselves to authorize "assemblies and public prayers in the church." The boldness of the act, which came very close to schism, struck horror to the heart of M. de Montgolfier. "In order to prevent things from going any further" he sent Fathers Papin and Dubois back to their parishes "to sustain the faithful and to restrain the impious."[25]

In spite of such incidents, the situation was improving and opinion was veering towards some measure of support for the government. Berthier was now the only parish on the north shore which still refused all military service, and its refusal had been provoked by an unwarranted assumption of authority on the part of the seigneur Cuthbert. Cuthbert had summoned his farmers to the manor house, but they had answered that if he wished to speak to them he could meet them at the shrine by the crossroads. The seigneur went to the appointed meeting place, but insisted that his tenants were bound to serve by the terms of their tenure. They answered that they would provide the required quota, fifteen men for each company, but Cuthbert insisted that the full strength of the company must be enrolled, to which they answered that military service was not the seigneur's business, and that not one man would follow him. Then, after agreeing among themselves not to take up arms against

General Richard Montgomery

General Benedict Arnold

Benjamin Franklin   Marquis de La Fayette

the Americans, the farmers dispersed and went back to their farms.[26]

Cuthbert's excessive display of zeal was followed by a second unfortunate incident. On October 15, a party of militiamen under Rigauville was sent out from Montreal with orders to speed up recruiting on the south shore. As their boats were leaving Montreal the Americans opened fire on them from their post at Longueuil, but the detachment proceeded on its way to Longue-Pointe, and thence across the river to Verchères, where it arrived on October 17. The men of Verchères explained that the reason for their failure to report for military service was the fear of having their houses pillaged by the pro-rebels, but that now fifty of them were ready to march. However, when Rigauville ordered the arrest of the wife and children of a defecting militiaman, the volunteers refused to follow him. They even threatened to call in the Americans from Longueuil, and announced that fifty men from Contrecoeur were armed and ready to resist any order from Rigauville. As the recruits were dispersing for the night, Rigauville sat down to table without placing any sentries, and got royally drunk. Between four and five o'clock in the morning the village was invaded by some sixty Americans who had been informed of the situation by the malcontents. The militiamen immediately faded away, Rigauville, still drunk and dressed only in his shirt, was taken prisoner, and his detachment went back to Montreal with nothing to show for its pains.[27] However, these two incidents, both provoked by the display of excessive zeal and authority, had little effect on opinion. The country people kept coming to Montreal in a steady stream, a good number of them from parishes which until then had been refractory.

In the Quebec region, Allen's defeat produced very little reaction in favour of the government. Mgr. Briand observed that the attitude of the people, usually calm and sensible, was now definitely unsatisfactory,[28] and that the tendency to remain neutral seemed to be increasing. Since by persisting in their inactivity, the country people were actually favouring the cause of the invaders, the prelate saw only one remedy for the situation. "We should have troops"; he wrote, "they would be more convincing than the word of God which we proclaim."[29] And it was not long before the neutralist members of his flock justified the opinion of their Bishop.

On September 29, at Saint-Michel-de-Bellechasse, as Father Lefranc was expounding the doctrine of obedience to the temporal power, a habitant shouted from the back of the church that "he had been preaching too long for the English." When he was informed of the fact, Mgr. Briand wrote to the curé of the parish, M. Lagroix, and pronounced judgment on a miscreant who had not only failed in his duty "to the King, his oath, and the virtue of obedience," but who had also been guilty of disrespect for "the temple of the Lord." The Bishop asked to be informed of the name of the offender. "For," he continued, "we are resolved to maintain the right even at the risk of our lives, [since] . . . people glory in opposing it and regard us as persons who have sold ourselves to injustice. . . . They say that the clergy is preaching war; no, I preach not war but obedience and respect for authority, and the fidelity they have promised to their oath and their King." The bitterness of his indignation can be gauged by the decision at which he had arrived: "If you cannot find the guilty man we are resolved to pronounce an interdict on yours and the neighbouring parishes[30] until this affair is settled."[31]

Saint-Thomas-de-Montmagny was the scene of another incident involving disrespect for the clergy and insubordination. Even though the order to furnish fifteen men from each company was supported by exhortations from the curé, M. Maisonbasse, only about fifteen militiamen in all volunteered. The women professed the same sentiments as the men, and the parishioners answered their curé with one voice: "You are an Englishman, and you want to force us to submit and to become English too."[32]

Faced with insults to its doctrine and its priests, the Church adopted a firm and uncompromising attitude. "As soon as any instance of excessive insolence is reported," declared Mgr. Briand, "I write to the parish and I punish."[33] M. de Montgolfier, the Vicar-General of Montreal, expounded with great clarity the doctrine of the Church in the matter of civil obedience. "All those who violate their oath of allegiance and take up arms against the King, (and this includes those who have not formally sworn the oath) are excluded from the way of salvation, unworthy to receive any sacrament, and unworthy of Christian burial if they die bearing arms. Only excepting burial, the same is to be said of all those who knowingly fan and incite rebellion, and even those who give any aid or encouragement to rebels, unless they are actually forced to do so. Those who are known to have been guilty of these excesses, even though they may be repentant, may not be admitted to the sacraments, even *in articulo mortis*, until they give outward and public expression to their repentance."[34]

A letter from Mgr. Briand to M. Maisonbasse of Saint-Thomas expresses the Bishop's horror and dismay at the gravity of the movement of rebellion: "My authority is no more respected than yours; they say of me as they say of you that I am English. . . . It is true, I am English; as you should be, and as they should be, since that is what they have sworn to be." The Bishop then showed the curé quite clearly where his own duty lay: "Since they repudiate the teaching of the Church and the Bishop, they are schismatics, and you cannot administer the sacraments to them without committing mortal sin." The letter ends with a stirring call for devotion to Christ and to his Church: "We must be ready to maintain the religion of Jesus Christ and the essential discipline of his holy bride, the Church, even at the cost of our lives." Measures of discipline to be applied to delinquents were strictly defined by the Bishop: no marriage would be performed and no banns published until the offender had given a sworn promise of submission, no sacrament would be administered "even in the hour of death," unless the offender retracted in public and made reparation for his offence, no offender could serve as a godfather or witness. In his determination to root out the evil of civil and religious rebellion, the Bishop seemed ready to go to the most extreme lengths. "I ought," he wrote, "to place all the churches and most of the parishes under an interdict."[35] The country had never known such a revolt against the Church; schism was knocking at the doors of the cathedral itself.

The Montreal region presented a curious contrast. There, although the whole district had been subjected to intensive indoctrination by rebel sympathizers, the situation continued to evolve in the government's favour. During the month of October, "more than twelve hundred habitants" from the country parishes came to join some 600 militiamen from the town, and their numbers continued to increase daily. About 500 more loyalists were in camp at Sorel and a considerable number of habitants from the north shore were ready to march with the troops. Rifles were distributed, and everyone expected the Governor to give the order for an attack on the American post at Longueuil. The Americans, who were aware of the existence and the strength of the loyalist army, "had loaded their boats and were ready to abandon their post the moment they heard that the little army was on the march."[36]

All opinions were agreed that offensive action was an imperative necessity. Montgomery's army, reinforced and now 1,000 strong, had left its camp on Ile-aux-Noix, and, on September 18, had laid siege to Saint-Jean which still barred the way to an American advance on Montreal. Montgomery was trying to reduce the town by famine, but he had no artillery, and the capture of the post at Longueuil, which the Americans themselves had given up for lost, would have forced him to abandon the siege.[37]

But, still temporizing, Carleton took no offensive action. A proclamation of October 14 ordered militia officers to require that habitants who had remained on their farms should harvest the crops of those who had been called to service in the militia. He also gave permission for militia detachments to reconnoitre the south shore from Longueuil to Boucherville, but they were "expressly forbidden to fire on the *Bostonnais.*" The people were completely bewildered by the Governor's policy of inaction. "Everyone muttered and complained, and people were persuaded that the General had orders from the English court to avoid shedding the blood of English subjects in the hope that the American colonists would return to the path of duty."[38] Carleton had received no such orders, but that in effect was his policy: to avoid fratricide and thus preserve the possibility of reconciliation between the rebels and the mother country.

Meanwhile, after weeks of inaction, the rural communities were becoming restive, "weary of delays, and anxious about their farm work,"[39] for it was now time to begin the ploughing. People kept asking one another why they were not taking the offensive, when the siege of Saint-Jean could have been raised in a week. As Carleton appeared stubbornly determined not to act, the people became more and more dissatisfied,[40] while militiamen "complained out loud." Some of them asked for and obtained permission to go and see their families, and the number of departures increased every day.[41] Meanwhile, "the town was full of spies, both foreign and resident." The citizens mounted guard regularly, but the farmers on the outskirts, indoctrinated by James Price during a recent visit, refused to do so. Price had invented a new and specious argument which was sedulously repeated by the pro-Americans: Canadians had no right to enlist since after the conquest they had sworn not to take up arms against the English. They must therefore remain strictly neutral.[42]

Considering the anxious and difficult situation in which the Governor was placed, it was hardly surprising that he should adopt a policy of delay and conciliation. How could he take the offensive with only a few hundred soldiers of whom some had to be left to garrison strategic frontier posts? Could he count on the fighting spirit of militiamen except in a strong framework of regular troops? In view of their recent attitude, could he even be sure that they would give solid support to the regulars? After the devotion and the unwearying effort with

87

which he had struggled to obtain legal recognition of their rights, he might well be chagrined at the conduct of this unhappy people, unable to see the path of honour or of duty, or even of its own interest. Embittered by what he called the "stupid baseness of the Canadian peasantry,"[43] he dared not place much confidence in them. They shared with the Indians the defects of being "easily dejected" and likely to "choose to be of the strongest side, so that when they are most wanted, they vanish."[44] As M. de Montgolfier observed in a letter to the Bishop, Carleton, who was not at all sure of his army of habitants, realized also "that the slightest reverse might be of the greatest consequence." In these circumstances, asked the Vicar-General. could the Governor run the risk of a defeat which would be disastrous for the country? After weighing all these considerations, he concluded that a policy of temporization was probably "the best and safest."[45]

However, towards the middle of October, Carleton appeared to be about to act. Three hundred men, under his personal command, cruised along the Longueuil shore in front of the American post. They then returned to Montreal without having effected a landing. This timid reconnaissance apparently gave some satisfaction to the Governor, but the townspeople were dismayed and frustrated, and the most clear-sighted among them began to feel that they were facing certain defeat. Finally, on Monday, October 30, Carleton announced that a real expedition was to be sent against Longueuil. About 800 Canadians, 130 troopers, and 80 Indians embarked in a fleet of forty *bateaux* and smaller boats. As they approached the shore, three-quarters of a league above the enemy's position, they perceived a guard of ten men; but just as the troops were about to begin their landing, the order was given to the *bateaux* which were in the lead to "draw away from the shore." The flotilla then cruised in front of Longueuil, "out of range of rifle fire." Leaving thirty soldiers in their fort, 130 Americans hastened to join the guard; whereupon the Governor retreated with his army which disembarked on the Ile-Sainte-Hélène, while a small band of Canadians and

Indians who had come within range of Longueuil exchanged rifle fire with the enemy. Three Indians were killed, and two were taken prisoner. The Sieur Lemoine and the wigmaker Lacoste were also captured. Finally, about five o'clock, Carleton led his army back to Montreal.[46]

What possible end could be served by such a sortie, when the general who ordered it and who commanded about a thousand men refused to attack a post defended by force of 170? A letter from the Vicar-General offers a curious comment on the Governor's plan for his expedition: "It appears that the original intention of His Excellency . . . was not to disembark at all."[47] This futile parade of force thus became an admission of weakness, not only in the eyes of the Americans, but even more, in the eyes of the Canadians, at the very moment when the services of the militia were most needed and when it was essential to inspire them with confidence.

Meanwhile, with the help of hard cash, Montgomery was increasing his pressure on Saint-Jean. He bought the neutrality of the Indians from Caughnawaga and the other villages for four hundred pounds,[48] and enticed the habitants, with the promise of good wages, to dig trenches and build breastworks.[49] The Canadians were willing to work for the rebels in this auxiliary capacity, but they had no illusions as to the strength of the American troops. Ever shrewd and practical, they refused to declare themselves and were careful to refrain from any overt act of hostility.[50] Most of the workers were adventurers or idlers, who had been attracted from the nearby parishes[51] by promises of pay and loot. For the Americans' chief recruiting agent, the barber Duggan, had followed Allen's example and promised that they would be allowed to pillage the forts.[52]

But the besieging army had no artillery and it was short of ammunition, while Saint-Jean was well defended and well supplied with provisions; so the siege dragged on. It was in these circumstances that Montgomery's Canadians suggested an attack on Fort Chambly, which was well stocked with arms and provisions, and the defences of which were much weaker than those

89

of Saint-Jean. A detachment of 150 Americans and 300 [53] Canadians was organized under the orders of Majors Brown and Livingston. Brown had persuaded the Canadians to join the expedition by promising that they would have an equal share of the stores from the fort, with the exception of its arms.[54] On October 17, after a siege which had lasted only two days, Major Stopford surrendered ignominiously with his garrison of eighty officers and soldiers.[55] By some strange aberration, he failed even to prevent his stores from falling into the enemy's hands, and, instead of throwing them into the river which flowed right outside the walls of the fort, he handed over 227 barrels of provisions and a still more valuable prize of arms, cannon, and 127 barrels of powder.[56]

Colonel MacLean, who was stationed in Quebec, had been instructed by Carleton to form a detachment which could be sent to relieve Saint-Jean. On October 14, he arrived in Three Rivers with a group made up of Scottish volunteers from Quebec and militiamen who had been recruited along the way. After gathering in a few more recruits at Three Rivers, the little band crossed the St. Lawrence. MacLean had hoped to enlist a few men at Nicolet, but after discovering that the entire population of the village had fled to an island in the Nicolet River, he pressed on to Sorel. There a number of pro-rebel Canadians from the parishes on the Richelieu joined his company, but they remained only long enough to be provided with rifles and to demoralize their fellow Canadians with Colonial propaganda, after which they returned to the American camp. MacLean continued his advance up the Richelieu, but his militiamen were beginning to desert, and when he learned that the bridge at Saint-Denis had been destroyed he returned to Sorel, where he received the news of the fall of Saint-Jean. Since relief of the fort was no longer a practical possibility, he embarked with his force, and, after stopping at Three Rivers to take on provisions and military stores, the expedition returned to Quebec.[57] The arms and ammunition captured at Chambly had made it possible for Montgomery to take offensive action. On November

1, forty cannon balls and 120 bombs fell on the fort of Saint-Jean. The defenders' stock of ammunition was exhausted, and their stores had been reduced to three days' rations. With the news of Carleton's fruitless excursion to Longueuil all hope of relief vanished, and on November 2, Major Preston agreed to surrender the fort with its garrison of 536 officers and soldiers, seventy-nine Canadians, and eight English volunteers.[58]

The surrender of Saint-Jean, coming so soon after that of Chambly, was a military and political disaster, the effects of which could be seen in the reactions of the people. The Richelieu habitants, who had already been won over to neutralism and in some cases to peaceful co-operation with the invaders, now came out openly in their favour. Henceforth the Americans could count on support from the parishes on the south shore, where the farmers made them welcome and supplied them with food. Moreover, some five hundred Canadians volunteered to accompany the Colonial army,[59] doubtless in the hope of participating in the sack of Montreal. The American victory at Saint-Jean marks a decisive moment in the invasion. It paralyzed the recruitment of militia and spread neutralism throughout the province. Still more important, it opened wide the road to Montreal. Canada's prosperous metropolis, waiting behind its wall, would be the next target of the half-disciplined rebel troops.

7

CANADA DURING THE AMERICAN INVASION

March of Montgomery on Montreal. Retreat of Carleton to Quebec. Surrender of Montreal. Pro-American feeling in the suburbs. Surrender of Three Rivers. Arnold's invasion by the Chaudière. Invaders welcomed. Washington's letter. Formation of militia companies in Quebec. Siege of Quebec by Montgomery and Arnold. Appointment of a committee by Congress to study and advise on the Canadian situation. Lack of response to American appeals for Canadian volunteers. Defeat of the Americans at Quebec. Death of Montgomery.

WITH the capture of Saint-Jean and with increasing evidence of neutralism among the Canadian people, Montgomery's hopes soared, and on November 9 he sent a message to the citizens of Montreal. Pierre Du Calvet, to whom the letter was addressed, was a wily, untrustworthy Huguenot. He combined the functions of justice of the peace and seigneur with his activities as a merchant, and he meant to play both the British and American sides of the board for his own profit. Unfortunately for Du Calvet, the letter, which summoned the town to surrender and thus avoid bloodshed, was intercepted by the British authorities, who took careful note of the name of Montgomery's intermediary.[1] Montgomery was also worried because his soldiers, who had signed a limited engagement, were beginning to ask for their release. However, on the promise that they would be free to go home immediately after the capture of Montreal, they agreed to remain in the army, thus making it possible for the

92

General to carry out the next steps of his plan of campaign.[2] Advance guards were sent to capture Sorel and Three Rivers, strategic points on the way to Quebec, while the main force pressed on towards Montreal. At La Prairie boats were collected, and on November 11, the army crossed to the Ile des Soeurs, one league above the town.

When Carleton learned that the Americans were in La Prairie, he issued orders preparatory to abandoning Montreal: volunteers were to be sent back to their farms, guns were to be spiked, boats which were not in use were to be destroyed, baggage, ammunition, and supplies were to be loaded on ships in the harbour. Then, about five o'clock in the afternoon of November 11, the very day on which Montgomery occupied the Ile des Soeurs, a fleet of eleven vessels bearing the Governor and a force of ninety soldiers sailed out of the harbour of Montreal. When they reached Sorel, after having been delayed for two days by contrary winds, American batteries already commanded the narrow channel. The fleet could not hope to pass, but a small craft might do so, and Carleton decided to make the attempt. Dressed in the homespun suit of a habitant, he boarded a whaler whose skipper, Bouchette, had volunteered to take him to Quebec. As they slipped down the river they could hear the cries of the American sentries on the shore, but by taking infinite precautions, at one point even paddling with their hands, the Canadian sailors succeeded in guiding their boat past the danger point. They reached Three Rivers just as the first American troops arrived there, but thanks to his disguise, the Governor had made good his escape. At Three Rivers he boarded a waiting brigantine, and on November 19 he landed safely in Quebec.

The members of the legislative council and leading citizens immediately assembled at the Château Saint-Louis where the Governor thanked Captain Bouchette in the warmest terms.[3] Meanwhile the flotilla, under Prescott's orders, had surrendered. The pilots had refused to expose the vessels to fire from the American batteries.[4] Fortunately Captain Bellet, a Canadian officer in charge of the powder supplies, showed greater presence of mind than Stopford had done at Chambly, and threw the powder overboard.[5]

After the Governor's departure, Montreal was left to its own devices. The pro-Americans among the British at once laid down their arms. They had been "grimacing long enough," they said. The city gates were closed and the loyalists remained under arms, but the Canadians on the outskirts refused to take shelter within the walls. Heywood, the associate of James Price, and the traitor Bindon slipped out through a gate where the latter was standing guard, and hurried to the Ile des Soeurs to inform the enemy of the state of Montreal's defence. The next day, Sunday, November 12, at nine o'clock in the morning, the American troops landed at Pointe-Saint-Charles. By four o'clock in the afternoon, fifty men were in possession of the Récollet suburb to the west of the town, while pro-rebel sympathizers from the *faubourgs* came to join the American camp.

Soon after the Americans landed, some of the leading citizens came as delegates to Montgomery who gave them four hours to prepare terms of capitulation. The terms, drawn up by six Canadian and six English citizens, included protection of property, free exercise of the Catholic religion, freedom of trade, and exemption from any obligation to serve against England. They also requested the return of prisoners, the institution of judges "elected by the people," a promise that troops should not be quartered on the inhabitants, and the exclusion of Indians and rural inhabitants from the city until the American forces should have taken formal possession.[6] At seven o'clock, three delegates, one of whom was James Price, were sent to discuss these conditions with the citizens' committee, but while the discussion was still in progress, the deputies from the town met Montgomery in the Récollet suburb, where he signed the treaty and gave his answer to the proposed terms.

Montreal, he declared, was not organized for defence and could not claim the right to formal capitulation. Nevertheless, he would grant its citizens free possession of their property as well as religious freedom. The merchants would be given passports allowing them to engage in the fur trade. The General hoped soon to see the creation of a "virtuous" provincial convention which would protect the political rights of the people. His reply ended with the assurance that citizens would not be forced to serve against the mother country, that the occupying power would establish courts of justice, and that troops would be quartered on the inhabitants only in cases of necessity.[7]

The American army took possession of the city on November 13, and on November 14, Montgomery received a letter from the people of the suburbs "who had shown themselves to be not very good subjects." The letter, which bore forty signatures, had been composed by Valentin Jautard, a Frenchman with some of the attributes of the soldier of fortune. In grandiloquent phrases it saluted the General who brought liberty to Canada and it condemned those citizens of Montreal who refused, in their pride and contempt, to participate in any "fraternal union." For their part, they, the signatories of the letter, welcomed the union. They had accepted it tacitly ever since 1774, when they had read the letter addressed by the Continental Congress to the people of Quebec. Only fear of persecution had prevented them from declaring themselves openly. The General could well imagine how much they had suffered. Montgomery could now inform Congress that they accepted the association offered to them by their brothers in the British colonies with "the same laws, the same prerogatives, proportionate taxes, sincere union, and permanent peace."[8]

The little town of Three Rivers — 800 citizens defended by a simple log palisade — had decided to capitulate even before the enemy had appeared on the horizon. Accordingly, the citizens prepared an address to Montgomery in which they sought protection for their persons and property. Messieurs Badeaux and Morris set out with the letter on November 9, but they did not deliver it to Montgomery in Montreal until eleven days later, on November 18. On November 20, envoys received a written answer from the General. It assured the people of Three Rivers that they would be well treated, and it expressed the hope that their province would "soon possess a free government."[9] At the end of November, Captain Loiseau of Saint-Mathias with about sixty pro-rebel Canadians carried out a search of loyalist houses in Three Rivers and confiscated all weapons.[10]

Once in possession of Montreal, Montgomery turned his attention to the tasks of reorganizing his army, providing winter clothing for his troops, and trying to increase the strength of his army. In order to achieve this last object, he decided to proceed without delay to recruit a Canadian regiment. The men would serve for one year and the regiment would be commanded by James Livingston, now promoted to the rank of colonel. Fully aware of the political implications of the invasion, the General also informed the people of the colonies' intentions. On his return from Quebec, which would, of course, be captured, he would call a meeting of the people in order that they might choose delegates to the Continental Congress. Montgomery also made an agreement with Father Floquet, a Jesuit, whom he found "very reasonable." For he realized that in dealing with a Catholic population he would need support from the clergy. He promised Father Floquet that the Jesuits' house would not be used to lodge prisoners of war, and he also assured him that, in the event of union between Canada and the American colonies, the Jesuits would be left in undisturbed possession of their property. Although he knew that the clergy were creating every possible difficulty for him, and that they were even refusing absolution to those who served with the Colonials, Montgomery continued to ignore their opposition and to show them every mark of respect, for he did not wish to lay himself open to criticism or calumny on that score.[11]

Unlike its religious leaders, the population on both shores of the St. Lawrence gave the Americans a sympathic welcome,[12] and Montgomery reported to Schuyler that he could get as many Canadian volunteers as he could afford to pay. At least, that was his first impression; but he soon perceived that the

Canadians' zeal was in direct proportion to the superiority of the American forces.[13]

Although Montgomery chafed at the delay, the business of re-forming and equipping the army required time, and it was not until November 28 that the contingent left Montreal to pursue the main objective of the campaign, the capture of Quebec. An American army was already encamped before the provincial capital, for in September, acting on a suggestion from Benedict Arnold, Washington had decided to send a second expedition into Canada by way of the Kennebec and Chaudière rivers. Since Arnold himself combined the necessary qualities of courage, audacity, and energy, he was placed in command of the force of 1,100 men which set out from Newburyport on September 18, 1775.[14] The enterprise proved to be a particularly difficult and hazardous one. Not only did the invaders have to contend with frequent rapids in their journey up the Kennebec and down the Chaudière, but the rivers flowed through 320 miles of virgin forest, which offered no possibility of renewing their supplies. After seven days of such travelling, Colonel Enos and three companies of soldiers, worn out with fatigue, abandoned the expedition and returned to civilization.

Undeterred by this massive desertion, the army pressed on. Sparing no effort of endurance, surmounting indescribable difficulties, and suffering the most extreme privations, they finally approached the end of their long journey. On October 30, after forty-two days of extenuating exertion, Arnold knocked at the doors of the first Canadian houses. He had gone ahead with a small escort, and, when the farmers proved to be friendly, he immediately sent provisions to his troops who had been reduced to living on roots. On November 3, the main force of starving, ragged, exhausted soldiers arrived at the farmsteads. They were welcomed with the greatest show of sympathy by the Canadians, who cared for the sick and supplied the provisions which were so sorely needed.[15] With the exception of a few, more wary than the others, the people continued to be very hospitable, although there were some who took advantage of the situation to sell their produce at exorbitant prices.[16]

Arnold made haste to establish contact with the villages in the region and to distribute copies of a letter from Washington to the Canadians.[17] In the letter, which began with a greeting to his "friends and brethren," Washington declared that the quarrel between the Colonies and the mother country could only be settled by arms, and that the Americans were stronger than their adversaries. Furthermore, the English, in their ignorance, imagined that Canadians were incapable of distinguishing between freedom and slavery; they thought that by gratifying the vanity of a little circle of nobility they could blind the people of Canada. On the contrary, the Canadians had shown that they were enlightened, generous, and virtuous, and the Americans invited them to become partners with them in an indissoluble union. This had been the aim of Congress when it had sent an army into their country, not to despoil them, but to protect them. A second army was about to set forth under General Arnold, and any help given to it would be paid for liberally. Washington therefore urged Canadians, as friends and brothers, to supply the army with the provisions it needed, for the cause of liberty was the cause of every good citizen, whatever his ancestry or his religion.[18]

Adding his own word to Washington's exhortations, Arnold seized every occasion to proclaim that the Americans would respect the persons, property, and religion of Canadians.[19] For it was true that Washington had enjoined him to maintain the strictest discipline, not to countenance any looting, and to pay the full price for all supplies and services.[20]

Thanks to one Jacques Parent, Washington's manifesto was read to the assembled parish of Sainte-Marie-de-Beauce as early as November 2. Parent had gone to meet the invading army with a message from the habitants of Pointe-Lévis. The latter urged the Americans "to come promptly, because the King wanted them to take up arms and had already taken away all the boats" from the neighbouring villages.[21] On November 5, Arnold reached Sainte-Marie and installed himself in the manor house. Taschereau, the seigneur, had made himself still more unpopular by arresting a militiaman who refused to serve against the Americans, but the farmers had protested so vehemently that he had had to release the prisoner.[22] Three days later, Arnold reached Pointe-Lévis and established his headquarters in Major Caldwell's mill. The seigneur's agent, John Halstead, handed over to him the entire stock of wheat and flour, and the troops were billeted with the farmers, who seemed well-disposed towards both officers and men, and ready to do what they could to insure their comfort.[23] On November 8, answering a letter of October 29, Arnold congratulated Montgomery on his success and informed him of his own plan to cross the river with 700 men and attack Quebec.[24]

Some six months before these events, the capital had begun to prepare its defence. On June 28, after the first raids on Saint-Jean, the citizens of Quebec, English and Canadian, presented an address to Carleton, who was then in Montreal, and offered to serve as volunteers.[25] But on July 19, when they tried to organize the English militia, only seventy men presented themselves. The large number of abstentions among British merchants, business men, and other inhabitants, was a clear indication of their leanings.[26]

Acting with his customary deliberation, Carleton waited until the beginning of September to appoint Noël Voyer colonel, Jean-Baptiste Dumont lieutenant-colonel, and Jean Baptiste Lecompte-Dupré major, of Quebec's Canadian militia.[27] On September 9 and 10, Lieutenant-Governor Cramahé reviewed first the British militia under Major Caldwell, and then the Canadian company.[28] Cramahé worked so energetically at the organization of the militia that, on September 17, eleven Canadian and six English companies paraded before him at full strength.[29] Acting as Commander-in-Chief in the absence of Carleton, he also gave orders for strengthening the fortifications and for arming a certain number of ships.[30]

After Allen's unsuccessful landing at Longue-Pointe on September 25, the pro-Americans in Quebec called a number of public meetings. In the course of informal discussions, the "congressists" who, until then, had acted with great discretion, betrayed their true sentiments by spreading the news of Montgomery's successes, and by using every possible means to influence both old and new subjects. Since the enemy was superior in numbers, they argued, the prudent course for the people of Quebec was to remain neutral and thus obtain better conditions when the enemy captured the town, as it could not fail to do. Quebec could not possibly be defended, and if a defence were attempted, it would result in the ruin of every citizen. The best course, in their opinion, was then to surrender without offering any resistance. When news of Arnold's expedition reached Quebec, the rebel sympathizers even went so far as to draw up terms of capitulation.[31] But the net result of all this activity was that American partisans in Quebec now stood revealed in their true colours.

Quebec's fortifications were strengthened, and beginning on September 17, a regular guard was maintained by the citizen volunteers. The Canadian companies, which counted 974 officers and men,[32] were distinguished by their excellent discipline. The creation of such a spirit appears still more remarkable when we remember that it was sixteen years since Canadian volunteers had last borne arms. An article in the *Quebec Gazette* marks the lines of opinion which separated Canadians: "Alas!" writes the journalist, "if the country people, instead of allowing themselves to be shamefully corrupted by dangerous rebel spirits, had chosen to follow the example set by their seigneurs and by educated Canadians both in the towns and in the country, the rebels would never have dared to disturb our peace by invading this province. There is, however, every reason to hope, that the little band of loyal Canadian subjects, who are preparing themselves to follow the orders of their brave and generous Governor, will suffice to drive out the invaders."[33] A helpful, though somewhat vague indication of the general feeling may be found in the fact that of twenty-eight masters of posting stations between Montreal and Quebec, twenty-five volunteered for the defence of Quebec.[34]

Towards the end of October, a letter from Arnold to an English merchant, John D. Mercer, was intercepted, and Cramahé learned of the existence of the Kennebec army and its march towards Quebec.[35] He immediately ordered that all boats at Pointe-Lévis should be destroyed so that the enemy would have no means of crossing the river. On November 2, a dispatch from Admiral Howe of the Atlantic fleet informed the Lieutenant-Governor that so late in the season the navy could do nothing to help Quebec.[36] Cramahé then called a council of war which, after examining reports on the state of the city's forces and supplies, resolved to defend it to the utmost extremity.[37] The gravest danger, however, lay in the attitude of the rural population. "The rebels," wrote Cramahé, "being in force, have upon their side the Canadian peasants, whom neither the zealous exertions of the gentry, clergy, or *bourgeoisie* could prevail upon to do their duty, and for want of a force, we could neither awe or compel them to it; two battalions in the spring might have saved the province. I doubt whether twenty would regain it."[38]

In spite of the order to destroy all boats, Arnold had succeeded in gathering together enough small craft to transport his men, and on the morning of November 14 his little army paraded on the Plains, 800 feet from the ramparts. The Americans gave three hurrahs, and the garrison answered with three cheers for the King. Quebec's batteries then opened fire and the Americans were forced to retreat. Since, without artillery, Arnold could not lay siege to the town, he established a camp at Pointe-aux-Trembles, where the habitants provided him with supplies, without, however, compromising themselves too seriously. Arnold was shrewd enough to pay in cash, for he realized that experience under Bigot and Vaudreuil had left Canadians with very bitter memories of paper money.[39] On November 28, he wrote to urge the people of Pointe-Lévis to send no supplies to Quebec, for the British authorities were trying to deny the rights and liberties of humanity in general, "and of this colony in particular."[40] Meanwhile, on November 19, Cramahé had sent a dispatch to inform the Secretary of State of the colony's vital need for reinforcements, and to urge that these be sent to reach Quebec as soon as the river was open in May.[41] On the same day, Carleton reached Quebec and at once turned his attention to the task of hastening the work of defence in preparation for the siege which appeared imminent.

On December 3, after a week's march, the American force from Montreal joined the Kennebec contingent at Pointe-aux-Trembles, and two days later an army of about a thousand American soldiers laid siege to the capital city and the one fort in Canada over which the British flag still flew. Protected by its ramparts, defended by 1,800 men, soldiers, sailors, and militia, provisioned for eight months, Quebec with its population of 8,000 could withstand a long siege.[42]

Montgomery quickly recognized the weakness of his forces and the difficulties of his situation. At first he placed his hopes in the help he would get from the regiment of Canadians to be raised by Livingston. But, faced with the disappointing results of his recruiting effort, he was forced to admit that the Canadians could not be counted upon. They would be friends of the Americans as long as the latter could maintain their own position,[43] but the province of Quebec would wait to join the union until the Americans were masters of the whole country.[44] It was easy to apply the conclusion to the case in point. True Normans, shrewd and argumentative, the habitants meant to remain neutral in the struggle and masters in their own province. They had no intention of going off to be killed either for the English or the American cause.

In Quebec, Carleton was quickly informed of pro-American sympathies and intrigues, and on November 22, he declared by proclamation that any citizen refusing to join the militia must leave the city and the district within a week, taking his family with him. After December 1, those who refused to "serve in arms" would be treated as "rebels and spies."[45] As a result of this order a "large number" of English notables left the city with their families.[46] The English militia lost about 170 men, while the Canadian companies gained fifty-three recruits.[47] Montgomery wrote to Schuyler that many of their "friends" had had to leave the city,[48] among them Bondfield, Antill, Wells, Zachary Macaulay, Murdoch Stewart, John McCord, and four or five militia officers. But the pro-rebel Allsopp managed to remain and to retain his post as commissioner.[49] Among Quebec's other American sympathizers were Hector McNeil, Udney Hay, John White Swift, J. D. Mercer, John Halstead, James Jeffrys, Freeman, and Holton.[50]

During all this time Congress had been mindful of Canada and of the vitally important drama being played out there. It kept up its supplies of cash, munitions, and clothing for the invading army,[51] and on November 4, it ordered the secretary to publish both Montgomery's letter announcing the surrender of Chambly and the terms of capitulation.[52] Two days earlier it had appointed a committee of three, John Langdon, Robert Treat Paine, and R. R. Livingston, to undertake an important mission, and on November 8, a long and detailed memorandum of instructions was presented to the committee. It was to proceed to Ticonderoga to consult with General Schuyler on the Canadian military and political situation, and it was to exert its "utmost endeavours to induce the Canadians to accede to a union" with the other colonies. As a first step towards such a union, the people of Canada would be asked to "form from their several parishes a provincial convention and send delegates" to the Continental Congress. The instructions also insisted on the importance of raising a Canadian regiment whose officers would hold American commissions.[53]

On November 15, dispatches announcing the capture of Saint-Jean reached Philadelphia. They were followed, on November 29, by others bringing news of the fall of Montreal. Congress was fired with enthusiasm, and on December 9, Montgomery was promoted to the rank of Major-General.[54] Two weeks later, on its return from Ticonderoga, the committee of three presented a report on its conference with Schuyler. After describing Montgomery's difficulties in prolonging the period of service of his volunteers, the committee reported that, although the general had begun to raise a Canadian regiment, he was very doubtful of the possibility of bringing it to full strength. As conditions were unfavourable for travelling, the delegates had decided not to undertake the journey to Canada. Instead, they had written to instruct Montgomery "to inform the Canadians of the sentiments of Congress when he should find a proper opportunity to communicate them, and to pave the way for the reception of any committee which the Congress might think proper to send when the ice should render the journey more practicable."[55]

In Montreal, after Montgomery's departure, General Wooster had 300 copies of Washington's letter printed and distributed, but the results were disappointing. For the people of the Montreal region were beginning to suffer from the annoyances of a military occupation and the excesses of undisciplined troopers. The presence of the soldiers was becoming irksome, although there were some people who seemed attached to the *Bostonnais,* especially those whose business was going badly and who hoped that a change of rule would free them from their debts. Meanwhile, declared partisans of the Colonists continued to work actively for their cause. Their leader, Walker, who had been freed when the boat on which he was a prisoner was captured, went to L'Assomption to persuade his followers to join the American army besieging Quebec, but with one voice they refused to volunteer. He came back a second time with James Price, meaning to disarm them, but the wily villagers had hidden their weapons. On the other hand, the people of Pointe-Claire, Sainte-Geneviève, Sault-au-Récollet, and a few other parishes, succeeded in getting Wooster to discharge the militia captains whom they did not like.[56]

Wooster, who had engaged a French secretary, Valentin Jautard, thought that he could recruit soldiers for Montgomery. With this end in view, he sent an order requiring the captain

104

of each militia company to provide fifteen men as reinforcements for the American army which had come to Quebec to establish English liberty and to oppose the re-establishment of French law.[57] But Wooster's plea brought practically no results. Canadians who had refused to take up arms for the King, were equally reluctant to fight for the Colonies. In short, as long as the fate of the country was uncertain, they would maintain an attitude of friendly but passive sympathy towards the army of occupation.

Meanwhile, Montgomery had succeeded in surrounding Quebec, but his artillery was quite inadequate for an attack. At the same time, his amateur soldiers were beginning to show signs of impatience. On December 6, therefore, he dispatched a message to the city. The letter, addressed to the Governor, was couched in the haughtiest and most uncompromising terms. It announced the imminent capture of Quebec and warned Carleton that if the stores were destroyed he would have to answer for the consequences. A second letter, of which copies in French and English were distributed to a number of citizens, urged the people to surrender in order to save themselves from useless fighting and their town from destruction by fire.[58] The tone of these letters, designed to intimidate the townspeople and the garrison, betrayed Montgomery's own fears and anxieties. His half-trained soldiers lacked the discipline of a regular army. Three companies, due to be released from their engagement, refused to face the risks of an assault, and in an effort to put more spirit into his troops, the General promised them a share of the loot from the captured city.[59] He had recruited only 160 Canadians,[60] and he was threatened with the loss of some of his men when their engagement expired at the end of the year. Since, in circumstances such as these, there was little to be gained by waiting, he decided to risk an attack. He was even reported to have made the rash prophecy that he would eat his Christmas dinner "in Quebec or in Hell."

The prophecy was not realized, but Montgomery gathered all possible information on the capital's vulnerable points and when, on the night of December 30-31, a wild winter storm created the conditions for which he had been waiting, he ordered his troops into action. While a detachment of Canadians and Americans under Livingston and Brown feigned an attack on the Saint-Jean gate,[61] two bodies of troops, under Montgomery and Arnold, advanced to attack simultaneously from both ends of the Lower Town. Their plan was first to capture the Lower Town and then to unite their forces before scaling the heights to the Upper Town. Arnold's men wore papers in their caps with the inscription *Liberty or Death*. They advanced, 550 strong, towards the western end of the Sault-au-Matelot, the northern bastion of the Lower Town. But deserters had given warning of the attack, and the garrison, alerted by the enemy's signal flares, was ready for it. From their positions along the ramparts, defending sailors poured down rifle fire on the Americans advancing to the attack. Shortly after the firing began Arnold was wounded in the knee and was forced to withdraw, but his men pushed on under the command of Captain Morgan. After offering suspiciously feeble resistance, Captain McLeod's troopers allowed the enemy to capture the first and second barriers, but they were stopped at the third, where Major Nairn led a vigorous defence. Two Canadians, Lieutenant Dambourgès and a militiaman, Charland, knocked down the scaling ladders and all further attacks were repulsed. When Carleton ordered Captain Law to lead a detachment out through the Palace Gate, the enemy was caught between two fires and Arnold's force, now reduced to 426 officers and men, surrendered. The troops engaged in this encounter — Canadian militia, the regiment of Fusiliers, and the Royal Emigrants — had all displayed great coolness and courage.

Meanwhile, Montgomery's force of 350 men had set out on its mission to attack the Lower Town's right flank. Marching in close formation, the contingent followed the narrow road at the base of Cape Diamond, and reached the post of Près-de-Ville, closing the entrance to the first street into the Lower Town. The post, commanded by Captain Chabot, was defended by thirty Canadian militiamen and a battery manned by fifteen English sailors under Captain Barnsfair. Chabot allowed the assailants to advance to within forty paces, then opened fire with his nine guns. The snow was red with blood as Montgomery, the officers leading the attack, and a number of his men, fell under the deadly fire. The main body of troops, surprised by a spirited defence and demoralized by the loss of its officers, turned and fled back to the American camp. In spite of the tactical skill of their leader and the courage of the American soldiers, the attack was a complete failure. The defenders' casualities were limited to seven dead and eleven wounded, while the enemy's losses amounted to thirty dead and 450 prisoners.[62]

8

WEAKNESS OF THE AMERICAN OCCUPATION

Refusal of Carleton to counter-attack. Failure of the besiegers' plan. Refusal of the militia to fight for the Americans. Intervention by Congress. Appointment of a pro-rebel chaplain. American commissions for militia officers. Enlistment by few Canadians. Self-interested collaboration of country people. Rebel sympathizers among the professional classes and the women. Loyalist attitude of many parishes. Clergy almost entirely loyalist. Capture of priests by pro-rebels. Pro-rebel priests.

IMMEDIATELY after the failure of their bold attempt to capture Quebec, the Americans tried to conceal their defeat and their heavy losses. They announced that the royalists had lost 600 men against a mere fifteen on their side, that the Americans were in possession of the Lower Town, and that Montgomery had gone off across country to get reinforcements. But the very next day, January 1, 1776, a horde of vagabonds appeared in the Saint-Roch suburb, hoping to take advantage of Montgomery's promise of loot.[1] When the hope proved vain, the would-be pillagers quickly spread the news of the American defeat throughout the province.

The loyalists in Quebec supposed that Montgomery's death would be followed by an order for the sortie which would have sealed the victory. For the Governor could be sure that the rebel army was too weak to sustain an attack and would have to abandon the siege.[2] Arnold, who was now in command, was fully aware of the danger. He realized, as he said himself, that a counter-attack would "completely ruin" the whole American

108

plan. However, since the garrison appeared to be making no move, he maintained the siege with his reduced force of 700 men.[3] Carleton had under his orders 2,000 well-armed, disciplined men; he was opposed by an army one-third the size of his own and made up of ill-disciplined volunteers demoralized by defeat and ready to run at the first sight of red coats. But even under these advantageous conditions, the inveterate temporizer remained on the defensive.

Carleton's hesitations did not, however, alter the fact that the Americans were in a very perilous position, still exposed to the risk of a sudden sortie by the garrison. To add to the danger, "Colonist" propaganda had been no more successful than Colonial arms. Montgomery had consulted an influential French citizen, Christophe Pélissier, director of the Saint-Maurice forges, on the possibility of forming a Canadian assembly; but after making inquiries in various quarters, they had concluded that it would be useless to try to convene a provincial congress while Quebec was in loyalist hands. At the same time, the loyalists, who were still active in Montreal and Three Rivers, kept insisting that the small American army faced inevitable defeat, especially since a powerful English force would arrive with the first days of spring. Canadians guilty of collaboration were warned that they had no alternative; they must renounce their error, and support the government cause if they would save their homes from fire and pillage, and themselves from death in battle.

Pélissier, although he was a zealous partisan, had admitted that the "friends of America" were few in number,[4] and had recognized the necessity for strong measures if the rebels hoped to influence the mass of the people. He recommended the immediate capture of members of the armed forces, civil servants, and the principal loyalists. However, notwithstanding the zeal of the clergy for the royalist cause, he advised that full freedom of religion should be maintained. He further warned the would-be conquerors that they should not attempt to levy taxes. For, if they did so, the Canadian people, who had never paid direct taxes, would think the royalists were right when they claimed that the object of the American conquerors was to make Canadians pay all the expenses of the war.[5]

Pélissier's programme had been partly elaborated in Montreal, and it was in Montreal that the intrepid Wooster tried to implement it. Early in January, after drawing up a list of sixty-four loyalists, he had twelve of them, almost all Canadians, arrested. He intended to deport his prisoners to the Colonies, but, when the citizens of Montreal protested that he was violating the terms of capitulation, he set them free. Then, on January 6, he ordered captains and officers of militia to publish the following notice: "Any citizen or other inhabitant of Canada convicted of . . . prejudicing the interest of Congress or the progress of our arms, whether by injurious speech, seduction of loyal subjects, or protection of deserters, as well as any person suspected of furnishing food and maintaining or promoting communication with the city of Quebec, likewise any person guilty of disobeying officers created by us, will be declared by us enemies of liberty and traitors to their country, and as such will be severely punished, imprisoned and even transported from the province if such action be necessary."[6]

This order was posted on the doors of the parish churches, among them the church at Three Rivers, where three Récollet brothers, recently arrived from Quebec, violated it by reporting that the capital was well supplied with wood and provisions. The priests were arrested and taken to Montreal.[7] On January 16, when three Montreal suburbs expressed repentance for "the steps they had taken and the letter they had written," Wooster ordered that they be disarmed, and also that they hand over William Gray and René Ovide Hertel de Rouville as hostages.[8] This latter request was refused. Wooster's order and the refusal to comply are significant symptoms of a change of opinion among the common people. The rural population had another reason for dissatisfaction: the price of wheat had fallen considerably, while merchandise had increased in price. An invasion which no longer offered immediate advantages had now brought about a situation with little promise for the future.

The American commanders were harassed by still graver anxieties. For the army camped before Quebec reinforcements were an immediate and absolute necessity, and these reinforcements could only be supplied by Canadian collaboration. But even the promise of good pay did not draw volunteers. As a last resort the invaders used fear in their effort to win recruits. Canadians who had betrayed their neutralist leanings were reminded that they had made themselves liable to punishment at the hands of the English. If they did not join the rebels and help them to capture Quebec, they would all be ruined, for the royal forces would be sure to burn their houses in reprisal for their failure to support them. But this argument too was received with silence. The rebels' great banker, James Price, tried vainly to recruit reinforcements for the American army from among the "country people" between Montreal and Quebec.[9] At the same time the pro-rebel militia captain, Maurice Desdevens of Pointe-aux-Trembles, distributed an appeal from Arnold among the other militia captains of the Quebec region urging them to enlist all the volunteers they could find for Duggan's troop. The men were to engage themselves until the end of May or the taking of Quebec, and they were to receive forty livres a month and rations.[10] The appeal met with little or no success. Captain Etienne Pagé did not enlist a single recruit in any of the parishes of Cap-Santé,[11] Campanais, or Sainte-Anne-de-la-Pérade,[12] and the same lack of success was reported in Saint-Roch and Saint-Charles.[13]

Meanwhile, in the Colonies, Congress was disturbed at the slow progress being made by the American expedition in Canada. On January 8, 1776, it ordered Schuyler to dispatch more troops and to take measures to combat any attempt on the part of the British to send a fleet up the St. Lawrence.[14] On January 17, the assembly was thrown into a state of consternation by the news of Montgomery's defeat and death. On January

111

19, its dismay was translated into various emergency measures. Every possible source of troops was to be explored, recruiting was to be stimulated with promises of gratuities, and companies already in existence were to be sent immediately to reinforce the army of invasion. Although it would not be "expedient" to send a congressional committee to Canada, orders were passed for the dispatch of specie, and Washington was asked to appoint a general officer to replace Montgomery. At the same time a second Canadian regiment of 1,000 was authorized. An enlistment bonus of six dollars would be offered, and the men would serve for a year or the duration of the war.[15] On January 22, Moses Hazen was appointed colonel, and Edward Anctill lieutenant-colonel, of the projected regiment, and they were directed to choose Canadian officers in consultation with James Price.[16] Finally, William Livingston, Thomas Lynch, and James Wilson were instructed to compose a new message to the Canadian people, and on January 24 this message was submitted to Congress and adopted.

In their first address, said the letter, the Colonies had set forth their rights and their grievances. Now Canadians must realize that their own liberty and happiness were at stake in the quarrel in which the Colonies were engaged, and that, although they had given evidence of their sympathy and rendered valuable service to the common cause, reverses were still possible. But no obstacle could halt the progress of the friends of liberty; Congress would not abandon the people of Canada to the "unrelenting fury" of the enemy. Two regiments were about to set out for Quebec and they would be followed by six others, which would arrive before the British reinforcements. Congress had undertaken to raise two regiments in Canada, and hoped that Canadians would be quick to seize this opportunity to participate in the Colonies' success. The essential thing was to unite against the common enemy. To this end, concluded the message, it was important for Canadians to establish associations in the parishes, elect deputies to a provincial assembly, and instruct the assembly to choose delegates to the Continental Congress.

Signatures were appended to the document, and orders were given for its translation and its distribution in Canada.[17]

Arnold's situation before Quebec was becoming more critical every day. Not only was he ill-provided with troops and guns, but he was threatened with the loss of all the men whose engagement was about to expire. Already the latter were deserting in such numbers that General Wooster had to place a guard at Saint-Jean to stop and arrest them.[18] Arnold also had to try to restore the morale of his Canadians partisans, dismayed by Montgomery's defeat. To their first announcement that they had captured the Lower Town, the Americans added reports of the capture of the Bishop's palace and the powder magazines.[19] Then they circulated a rumour that in Quebec sixty Canadians had been hanged by the garrison without trial.[20] Finally, changing their line of approach, they repeated insistently that "large numbers of *Bostonnais* from the *Continents*" were on their way to Quebec.[21] There was even talk of an army of 20,000.[22] But during the month of January, only eighty-four soldiers arrived to swell the ranks of the army of invasion.[23]

For the moment, Canadian enlistments presented the only possible source of reinforcements. Arnold's first move, a very skilful one, was to seek out a chaplain who would give absolution and communion to Canadians serving in the rebel forces. For priests, obviously acting on instruction from the Bishop and the Vicars-General, "refused to confess" these Canadians "in spite of the persecution" which they suffered as a result of their refusal.[24] In January, Arnold found the man he needed in the person of the Abbé Louis de Lotbinière, the n'er-do-well son of a noble family. This former Récollet and Franciscan had been interdicted by Mgr. de Pontbriand. He had declared himself an apostate and had tried to discredit Mgr. Briand, then Vicar-General, with the British authorities. Moved by compassion for the enemy who had slandered him, the new Bishop had re-admitted him to the secular clergy, and this was the man who, on January 26, 1776, received Arnold's commission as chaplain to Livingston's regiment with a salary of sixty dollars a month[25]

113

and the promise of a bishop's mitre after the conquest of the country.[26]

In Montreal, General Wooster adopted other means of strengthening the authority of the rebels and encouraging enlistments. Early in February, he ordered captains of militia to surrender their commissions. He also ordered that parish meetings be held to elect new officers who would receive their commissions from Congress.[27] Most of the Montreal officers, both English and French, complied with the order, but a few refused. Dufy-Desaulniers, Neveu-Sevestre, Saint-Georges-Dupré, and Edward William Gray were among a group of refractory officers arrested on February 7, 1776, and sent as prisoners to Chambly.[28] In the district of Three Rivers, where Captain Goforth had the order posted in each parish, commissions were surrendered without protest and nominations for new officers were made.

The elections, the first of their kind, aroused lively interest and keen rivalry. Competing candidates plotted, intrigued, and even offered bribes. In some cases the military authorities had to intervene in order to insure that all candidates had fair treatment.[29] In the Quebec region, where the Americans adopted the same procedure, the new commissions, issued in the name of the Congress, were much sought after and hotly disputed,[30] and in the course of the winter, elections were held throughout the province.[31]

About the same time, probably at Wooster's instigation, a surreptitious attempt was made to appoint delegates to the Continental Congress. On February 5, some of the Montreal merchants called a meeting in the Récollet church. Although the ostensible reason for the meeting was to solicit fur-trading permits for the spring, the real intention of those who had convened it was to choose twelve deputies, half of them English and half Canadian, who would represent Canada at the Congress in Philadelphia. But the Canadians present were resolutely opposed to the appointment of delegates.[32] At this juncture, probably on February 8, Hazen and Anctill returned from the

American colonies. They brought copies of the last message from Congress, which were distributed by the Frenchman, François Cazeau.[33] But the letter made little impression on the Canadians, who "did not want to call an assembly, and who wanted still less to send deputies to the Congress."[34]

The two Canadian regiments which the Americans hoped to raise were to be known as "Congress' Own." Duggan continued to seek out men for Livingston's regiment, while Hazen immediately began recruiting for his own unit. On February 10, the public crier in Montreal read Hazen's proclamation inviting Canadians to enlist for one year or the duration of the war. Volunteers would receive a bonus of forty *livres* or eight dollars, and be paid forty *livres* a month. Clothing and equipment were to be provided or paid for by the men themselves.[35] Recruits came in very slowly:[36] at the end of February there were only 150[37] on the roster and a month later about 250,[38] most of them very unpromising material.[39] "The greater number were French soldiers who had remained in Canada after the conquest, . . . real blackguards," according to the loyalists.[40]

Colonel Hazen had dealt with the religious difficulty by enlisting Father Floquet, who had already been won over by Montgomery's promises, to serve as chaplain and "give absolution to his soldiers." But in spite of efforts to encourage recruiting, desertions continued to reduce the strength of the regiment. In the Brindamour company alone, nine recruits out of twenty-two deserted. It should be added, however, that they had not been paid regularly. The only volunteer of mark in Hazen's regiment seems to have been a Frenchman, Pierre du Calvet,[41] a judge and seigneur already in the American service. His name on the payroll provided useful publicity, but it does not necessarily indicate that he was on active service. Finally, with "the handful of men" that he called "a regiment" Hazen joined the army camped before Quebec.[42]

Anctill was busy recruiting in the Quebec region, where five men enlisted on February 16.[43] Meanwhile, Duggan's agents, especially the zealous and indefatigable Clément Gosselin and

115

his father-in-law, Germain Dionne, both from Sainte-Anne-de-la-Pocatière, and Pierre Hayot from Kamouraska,[44] succeeded in adding a certain number of volunteers to Hazen's unit. Duggan himself had suddenly "disappeared."[45] The recruiting campaign continued through the month of March, but with very meagre results. By the middle of the month, there were about a hundred Canadians with the American army before Quebec,[46] and at the end of the month the number had not changed.[47] Between Three Rivers and Rimouski, the rebels enrolled only 112 Canadians,[48] of whom a number had enlisted for short periods of two or four months.[49] The men who did volunteer were by no means those whom the recruiting agents would have chosen from their communities. Neither Colonial nor Canadian observers had a good word to say for them. Ainslie considered them "wretched idle profligates";[50] for Father Porlier they were "vagabonds" or "paupers,"[51] and Mgr. Briand pronounced them "miserable beggars and drunkards."[52]

In 1775 and 1776, the population of Canada was 90,000; at that time, according to the table drawn up by an American officer, 500 Canadians were enrolled in the rebel army.[53] This figure is confirmed by Hazen's statement, in April, 1776, that there were 200 men in Livingston's regiment, and about 250 in his own. He added that "not one more" name would be added to the roster.[54] A loyalist estimate, that of Mgr. Briand, also fixed at 500 the number of habitants who had joined the invading army.[55] The almost complete failure of a recruiting campaign carried on with great fanfare and supported by promises of bonuses and army pay becomes still more significant when it is compared with Carleton's achievement. Without offering any reward, the Governor had raised 2,000 volunteers. The failure of the Americans in this regard reveals the fixed determination of virtually the whole population to remain neutral.[56]

The Canadian was a good Norman, however, quite capable of distinguishing who was master at the moment; and of serving him for his own profit.[57] Just as, at the beginning of the invasion, he had allowed Carleton to govern the country with an army

116

of 800 soldiers, so now, he allowed Montgomery, Arnold, and Wooster successively, with 1,000 men, to rule the province as they chose. In most parishes the people obediently followed the orders of the rebels. But they refused to risk their skin for them as they had refused to risk their skin for the Governor. The Americans' hold on the country was the result of a combination of factors: the blockade of the British forces in Quebec, neutralism in the rural areas, the activity of pro-rebel militia officers, the co-operation of British sympathizers.[58] Favoured by these circumstances, the Americans assumed direction everywhere. All the resources of the province were available to them. The Anglo-Americans of Montreal provided financial facilities, merchandise, rum, and ammunition.[59] Having grown rich on the profits of fruitful exchange with the great business houses of Albany,[60] the pro-rebel element in Montreal's population now devoted its efforts to converting the people of the province to the American cause.[61] As for the Canadians, the country people, who hated military service and "adored money," were at the beginning, only too pleased to sell their products to the Americans. They were also willing to supply labour which was paid for in cash.[62]

Collaboration between the country people and the invaders was particularly active in the vicinity of the besieging army before Quebec. In February, 1776, most of the parishes from Bécancour to Kamouraska, and from Cap-de-la-Madeleine to Saint-Féréol had complied with Wooster's order and elected militia officers to hold commissions from Congress. Almost all these parishes had agreed to provide labour or supply wood, or make ladders and fascines. "As long as they were paid," a certain number of parishes procured provisions for the rebels. In several places, militiamen even mounted guard in order to intercept loyalist communications and to protect the American camps at Quebec and Pointe-Lévis. The parishes between Saint-Michel and Kamouraska later organized a chain of signal fires to give warning of the approach of English ships.[63]

In several places, the *Congréganistes* as they were called,

117

scoffed at, threatened, disarmed, or captured royalists.[64] A few, moved by hostility or cupidity, seized property belonging to their victims. At Sainte-Marie-de-Beauce the Taschereau manor house was sacked. Captain Gouin was robbed of arms, effects, and money at Saint-Pierre-les-Becquets. Wine was stolen from Father Maisonbasse, the curé of Saint-Thomas, wheat from the seigneur of Cap Saint-Ignace, and farm produce from the Quebec seminary at Saint-Joachim.[65] Certain parishes were especially zealous in the rebel cause, among them Saint-Henri, Saint-Joseph, Saint-François-de-Beauce, Pointe-Lévis, Beaumont, Saint-Michel, Berthier, and Cap Saint-Ignace.[66]

Lists of pro-Americans indicate that almost all these partisans were modest farmers, and that very few were drawn from the professional class. At Saint-Thomas a notary, Lévesque, collected signatures for a letter inviting rebels to come to the parish, and served as the rebels' informer.[67] In the neighbouring parish of Cap Saint-Ignace the Sieur Lebrun, a former lawyer, played a double role "now as a zealous subject and now as a thorough-going rebel." He joined Beaujeu's royalist troop, but only to advise the Americans of its movements. In his heart, he was a *Bostonnais*.[68] Finally a second notary, Joseph Dionne from Sainte-Anne-de-la-Pocatière, convened "an assembly to exhort the people of this parish to come out on the side of Congress."[69] These three appear to be the only members of Canada's professional *élite* who took a stand against the government, and they did not play an important role.

Curiously enough, several women were active in the pro-American movement. At Saint-Pierre-d'Orléans the wife of Augustin Chabot, known as *la reine de Hongrie*, "went from house to house, perverting almost all the habitants with her seditious talk."[70] At Pointe-aux-Trembles, the wives of Jean and Joseph Goulet went from door to door repeating that the loyalists wanted to "lead the militia to slaughter."[71] The wife of Captain Pierre Parent of Sainte-Marie-de-Beauce converted her husband to the American cause, indulged in seditious talk, and "on many occasions spoke most impertinently of curés."[72]

Another *reine de Hongrie,* the widow Gabourie, held assemblies in her house at Saint-Vallier, "where she presided" and where she gave free rein to her inclination "to rouse people against the government and . . . in favour of the rebels. In order to further her nefarious aims, she gave them strong liquors to drink."[73]

The Americans could also count upon the aid and services of a number of active and zealous sympathizers who maintained a steady stream of propaganda in Montreal and Three Rivers. The most notable of these partisans were recent arrivals from France: Pierre du Calvert; Valentin Jautard, an adventurous lawyer and scribbler and a somewhat dubious character; François Cazeau, a prosperous merchant with a considerable fortune; and Christophe Pélissier of the Saint-Maurice forges, a man of some influence in the district of Three Rivers.

There were also a few active and influential workers in the country districts. The most remarkable of these, Clément Gosselin, was constantly on the move, generally between Three Rivers and Kamouraska. He was a real "roving congressional officer," and "in that capacity he recruited and sometimes commissioned officers." Gosselin had an enthusiastic second in Germain Dionne, a rich bailiff whose natural gift of persuasion gave him a great influence over the people's minds. These "two notorious rebels . . . helped and assisted the enemies of the government to the full extent of their power."[74] Another "famous rebel," Pierre Hayot of Kamouraska, also "stirred up people's minds and engaged them on the side of Congress."[75]

Such a display of activity in favour of the invaders might lead one to believe that, as Mgr. Briand said later, "almost the whole colony wanted Quebec to be taken." But here again, as on an earlier occasion when his ire was aroused and he threatened to place "almost the whole diocese under an interdict," the Bishop was guilty of gross exaggeration. He had assured the Governor that his flock was obedient to the Church and loyal to the State, and he was at once sad and angry at this evidence of insubordination.[76]

119

In reality, although in the face of pro-rebel threats they could not or dared not declare themselves, there was throughout the province a considerable body of loyalists whose opinions were in complete agreement with the directives of the Church. In the Montreal region 1,200 volunteers answered Carleton's order to report for service.[77] Arnold's estimate of Montrealers in general was that they were "virulent enemies" of the Americans.[78] Although the Quebec region was contaminated by a pro-rebel coterie, several parishes, among them l'Ange-Gardien, Beauport, and Saint-Joachim, were bold enough to adopt a hostile attitude in the presence of the invaders.[79] Even on the partisan Ile d'Orléans, militiamen at Sainte-Famille, Saint-Jean, and Saint-Pierre resisted the orders of captains holding congressional commissions.[80] Loyalists at Pointe-aux-Trembles, les Ecureuils, Cap-Santé, Saint-Nicolas, and Saint-Vallier were disarmed, seized, insulted, or beaten by the "congressists,"[81] while in other cases parishes refused to co-operate in any way with the invaders.[82] Nine parishes on the south shore, from Saint-François to Kamouraska,[83] furnished volunteers to march against the American post as Pointe-Lévis, thus indicating their desire to cleanse their communities from "the stain of rebellion."[84]

Apart from the seigneurs and the town notables, who consistently supported the government, the clergy exerted the most resolute and undeviating loyalist influence. Professing the doctrine expounded by their Bishop, they preached obedience to the established authority and opposition to the American cause. They were inflexible in their refusal to administer the sacraments to rebel supporters. Naturally this conduct exposed them to criticism, insult, and even persecution and imprisonment. The province witnessed scenes unheard-of before that time: priests betrayed, denounced, arrested, and dragged off to American camps by their own parishoners. During the winter of 1776, the habitants even began to lodge complaints with General Wooster. They alleged that their curés "refused them absolution because some of them had chosen to take up arms for the *Bostonnais*." As a result of these denunciations and others of the same sort made to Colonial officers, guards were ordered to arrest certain curés, and "several country priests were ignominiously charged and haled before courts set up in the American camps." They were even threatened with being sent as prisoners to the Colonies. The famous James Price went with two Canadians to the Seminary of Saint-Sulpice intending to force the superior, who was also Vicar-General of Montreal, to promulgate new instructions. When the Vicar-General refused, General Wooster anounced his decision to send him to the Colonies with a number of other members of the clergy; but, on the intervention of Mrs. Price, M. de Montgolfier and his junior priests were spared this indignity.[85] In April, members of the parishes of Repentigny and Saint-Sulpice seized their own curés, the Abbés Saint-Germain and Robert, and took them as prisoners to the American camp at Three Rivers, where the Abbé La Valinière, a friend of the rebels, obtained their liberation.[86]

Similar incidents occurred in the regions of Quebec and Three Rivers. A parishioner of Charlesbourg lodged a complaint with the rebels against his curé, M. Borel,[87] and a man called Lespérance, from Saint-Joachim, sent the Abbés Corbin and Gravé, as prisoners to a rebel camp. However, at the request of twenty of their parishioners, these priests were promptly released.[88] Mgr. d'Esgly, the curé of Saint-Pierre-d'Orléans, who was also the Bishop's coadjutor, was denounced to the American authorities by Joseph Petrus Langlais.[89] In the course of an argument about the presbytery, a Champlain butcher called Beaudoin asserted that he recognized "neither the authority of the Bishop nor that of the Vicar-General, and that he would complain to the American commander at Three Rivers." At Cap-de-la-Madeleine a certain Dorval affirmed that "the Bishop of Quebec and the Vicar-General of Three Rivers had been paid to preach in favour of the King's party."[90] When the pro-rebel parishoners of Saint-Pierre-les-Becquets reported to the American command that Father Louis "refused them the sacraments," an aide-de-camp rebuked the priest with "a reprimand and threats."[91] As he was coming out of the church at Saint-Nicolas, where the curé had just preached a sermon on the duty of obedience to the prince, Denis Fréchet commented audibly: "What does our curé mean now? What is he meddling with? Has he too turned Englishman?"[92] The habitants of Rivière-Ouelle seized their curé, M. Parent, and took him to Saint-Jean-Port-Joli, where they finally set him free.[93] Two or three curés from the parishes in the vicinity of Pointe-Lévis were taken as prisoners to the camp at Quebec, and were released only after they had promised to change their conduct.[94] Several of his parishoners threatened to complain to the Americans of the conduct of M. Sarault, the curé of Saint-Charles, but they did not carry out their threats.[95] Finally, General Wooster himself ordered that priests on the Ile d'Orléans who dared to refuse absolution to pro-rebels should be arrested and taken to the American headquarters.[96] In short, there was evidence in numerous parishes of real rebellion against the doctrine and even the freedom of the Church.

Only a very small number of the clergy, no more than three or four in all, openly disregarded the Bishop's instructions. The Abbé Louis de Lotbinière agreed to act as chaplain to volunteers serving in the American army besieging Quebec. This "new scandal," wrote Mgr. Briand, would "surprise no one," since it was perpetrated by a priest whose conduct had always left much to be desired.[97] The Abbé de Lotbinière was also influential in the parishes of Nicolet, Bécancour, and Saint-Pierre-les-Becquets.[98] As already noted, Father Floquet became chaplain of Hazen's regiment and was given a part of the Jesuits' house in Montreal.[99] Not only did he give absolution to Canadians enrolled in the American army, but he administered communion to those who had been denied the sacrament by other priests. This conduct so angered M. de Montgolfier that he withdrew an invitation which had been received by Father Floquet to preach at Notre-Dame, and was on the point of interdicting him.[100] M. de Montgolfier expressed disapproval of another Jesuit, Father Huguet,[101] but his offence was less heinous in that he had been led astray by Father Floquet and that his misdemeanours were minor ones.[102] It should be noted, however, that Father Huguet was also better placed to escape the vigilant eye of the Vicar-General. As pastor of the Indians of Caughnawaga, he lived among his flock, and one may be sure that he did nothing to interfere with the activities of these faithful friends of the Americans. At L'Assomption, the home of Thomas Walker, the Abbé La Valinière went to "extravagant" lengths in his support of the rebels, thereby incurring the extreme displeasure of the Vicar-General. M. de Montgolfier later advised him to return to France and appointed another curé. This action was taken "in order to call back to the path of duty a large number of persons in several parishes, and also to put a curb on the activties of ill-disposed priests, if there should still be any such."[103] One more name, that of the Récollet father Claude Charpentier of Longueuil, is to be added to the list of priests guilty of "indiscreet" zeal for the American cause. We may assume that there were also other minor offenders since, in a letter to the Bishop, the Vicar-General of Montreal refers, without naming them, to a few other curés in his jurisdiction whose conduct in this respect merited "some reproach."[104]

9

DETERIORATION OF THE AMERICAN SITUATION

Military and financial difficulties of the occupying army. Dispatch of reinforcements. Instructions from Congress to its delegates. Change in the attitude of Canadians. Appeal of Sanguinet to their loyalty. Organization of a counter-offensive. The clash at Saint-Pierre-du-Sud. Reinforcements for the American army before Quebec. Excesses of the occupying troops. Congressional delegates in Montreal.

THE FAILURE of the American assault on Quebec had created repercussions affecting the situation in general. As the future now appeared uncertain and even threatening for the invaders, a practical-minded population could not but be conscious of the wisdom of remaining strictly neutral. Canadians remembered that in 1760, although Lévis had won a victory against Murray under the very walls of the city, he had not been able to recapture Quebec. They also remembered that in the following April an English fleet had raised the siege and forced the French army to retreat. In an atmosphere in which uncertainty as to the present awoke memories of past experience, "virtually all" members of the clergy maintained an attitude of inflexible opposition to the invaders, and continued to refuse absolution to unrepentant friends of Congress. Ecclesiastical imperatives were expressed in still more forcible terms, as the Church preached that even now it was "not too late to take up arms against the enemy."[1] The Americans soon perceived that the hopes they had placed in the rural population and in Canadian volunteers would not be realized. Wooster reported that there was "little confidence to be placed in the Canadians," who were "but a small remove from the savages," and who were inclined to align themselves with the strongest party.[2] American officers also observed that Canadian recruits, from both the Montreal and the Quebec regions, were poor material, and that they had enlisted less with the intention of fighting than to get the enlistment bonus and a share of the booty after the capture of Quebec.[3] A hundred men who had deserted the previous autumn were taken into the forces again in March, 1776.[4] How could one have any confidence in such supporters?

In the rural districts civil collaboration was also falling off. Even those habitants whose sympathies lay with the invaders were beginning to show a certain reluctance about helping them. For some time now, the Americans had not been meeting their engagements either to recruits or to the farmers who provided labour and provisions. Sometimes they gave receipts for produce received or services rendered, and then refused to honour their receipts;[5] sometimes they paid their debts with paper money which the Canadians hated.[6] The paper money was soon offered at a discount and its value fell rapidly. As early as December, 1775,[7] it had ceased to command confidence,[8] and soon people simply refused to accept it.[9] At Three Rivers, the habitants, whose labour had not been paid for, declined to undertake further work.[10] When a friend of the rebels, after placing "all his possessions" at the service of Congress, was refused payment in cash, his case was cited as "an example of bad faith" on the part of the Americans.[11] The loyalists naturally made the most of every incident of this kind and kept repeating that the Americans were making fools of their partisans and had not the least intention of paying their debts. These taunts could not fail to have a disturbing effect in the parishes, especially since they were accompanied by the observation that there were only 1,200 men in the army of invasion and that it could not hope for reinforcements.[12]

There were still other factors working against the invaders. They had exhausted the resources of their great banker, James

Price, as well as Hazen's recruiting fund, and they were now suffering a famine of specie.[13] Canadians serving in their army at Quebec refused re-engagement, and went home as soon as their time was up. The Americans had only 600 men to garrison Montreal and the forts at Saint-Jean and Chambly,[14] while Arnold was maintaining the siege of Quebec with an army of seven hundred.[15] His only help came from 200 Canadians who mounted guard at Pointe-Lévis and the Ile d'Orléans, and thus cut off communication between Quebec and the rest of the province.[16] These numbers spoke for themselves, and the Americans knew quite well that, at least for the time being, the fortress which had repulsed Montgomery's assault stood impregnable behind its walls with its winter store of provisions laid in.[17]

Between January and March modest reinforcements, about 400 men a month, succeeded in reaching Quebec[18] to fill the gaps left by desertions and by the departure of time-expired volunteers. But a smallpox epidemic, sweeping through an army, with few facilities for caring for the sick, once more drastically reduced its fighting strength. Meanwhile, in the province, the tendency to neutralism, which had favoured the invaders, was gradually weakening, and the heroic measures prescribed by Wooster as a cure aggravated the malady. The imprisonment of militia officers in Montreal and the arrest and persecution of priests aroused deep resentment.[19] The excessive partisan zeal of Gosselin and his co-workers in the Quebec area was equally unpopular.[20] In a word, the situation of the Americans, in both the poltical and the military sphere, continued to deteriorate.

When it became evident that American hopes for conquering Canada were crumbling, Congress at first reacted vigorously, but other and more imperious preoccupations pushed the Canadian question into the background. Reinforcements for Canada were moving slowly and in small detachments when, on February 12, a Canadian, Prudent Lajeunesse, appeared before Congress. He informed the assembly that if its letters had made little impression on the people of Canada it was because they had been presented to most Canadians by the priests and the *bourgeois* who had explained them in their own way, that is, in a way which would prejudice their hearers against the Americans. The same interpreters had read articles from New York royalist newspapers affirming that the rebels meant to suppress the Catholic religion and to appropriate the property of Canadians. Lajeunesse suggested that, in order to counteract the British propaganda being disseminated by the clergy and the nobility, Congress should send some of its own members to Canada. These envoys would explain by word of mouth the nature of their quarrel with England, and would demonstrate to priests and seigneurs that their intention was not to harm them in any way, but simply to put Canada in possession of its full liberty. Unless Congress adopted some such plan, the American cause would continue to meet with difficulties. Lajeunesse also mentioned one of the difficulties already in existence, the profound mistrust of Canadians for paper money.[21]

On February 15, acting on this advice, Congress decided to send a delegation to Canada. It appointed a commission of three members, Benjamin Franklin, Samuel Chase, and Charles Carroll, and instructed it to add an associate member, Charles Carroll's brother, the Father John Carroll.[22] The two Carrolls, who had been brought up in France, spoke perfect French, and would be able to present the American case effectively and sympathetically to the clergy and the seigniorial and professional groups. Two days later, Congress ordered that a consignment of cannon and cannon balls be dispatched promptly to Quebec, and that sleighs be rented for the transport of troops.[23] On February 26, in a move designed to counteract the influence of the *Quebec Gazette*, the French printer Fleury Mesplet was engaged to go to Montreal and set up his press at the Treasury's expense.[24] On March 6, the delegates again gave consideration to the military situation and appointed General Thomas to command the army in Canada,[25] but it was not until March 20 that Congress approved the instructions, embodying the already familiar themes, to be given to its commissioners.

Their prime mission was to make known the fact that Amer-

ican troops had invaded Canada only to defend the freedom of
the Thirteen Colonies and to make it possible for the Canadians
to win their own freedom. Since the two countries were bound
by a common interest, the defeat of Canada's neighbours must
inevitably result in the enslavement of Canada herself, while
their victory would guarantee to Canadians a government of
their own choice. The desire of the Colonies was that Canada
should choose her own form of government, but also that she
should join them in a union in which uniform laws would at
the same time respect local differences and be adapted to the
needs of each province. Finally, Canadians must be convinced
that fears of an alliance between France and England were
groundless. On the contrary, all signs indicated that France was
"favourable to the colonies."[26]

The commissioners were not, however, to limit their discussion to general principles. They were to recommend the adoption of the colonial method of determining the public will,
through conventions and committees.[27] They were also to expose the insidious designs of the Quebec Act, and to explain
the principles of a free government through which Canadians
would govern themselves.[28] Above all, they must "promise to
the whole people, solemnly . . . the free and undisturbed exercise of their religion, and to the clergy the full, perfect, and
peaceable possession and enjoyment of all their estates." It was
to be clearly understood "that the government of everything
relating to their religion and clergy should be left entirely in
the hands of the good people of that province."[29] As for present
conditions, the commission was to make it its business to smooth
out the difficulties which had arisen between Canadians and
the army of occupation,[30] and it was given full authority to make
regulations for the good of the country.[31] It was also to encourage trading with the Indians, to protect external trade,[32]
and to insure the circulation of American money in Canada.[33]

On March 20, Congress approved this tardily-conceived programme and the following day it authorized a French nobleman,
the Chevalier de Saint-Aulaire, to raise a company of *coureurs*

de bois in Canada.[34] Four days later, "being of the opinion that the reduction of Quebec and the general security of Canada [were] objects of great concern" it directed the Commander-in-Chief, General Washington, to dispatch four battalions to Canada with all possible speed.[35]

In a situation in which every day counted, Congress lost precious time in deliberation while the shift in Canadian opinion became more definite and more significant. The arrival of a few small bodies of reinforcing troops did not suffice to inspire confidence in pro-rebel partisans' tales of an army of 7,000 Americans — 20,000 according to the bolder propagandists — marching to Quebec from the south.[36] These assurances did not stifle the dawning conviction that the Americans could not capture Quebec, and that in the spring, just as in 1760, an English fleet would win the victory. Fearful of suffering the ravages resulting from a military campaign, Canadians were becoming resentful of a foreign occupation which, dragging on without any hope of a successful outcome, disturbed the country, and paralyzed its normal activities.[37] For some time now, in Montreal, members of the clergy and the nobility had been disseminating loyalist and anti-rebel propaganda.[38] There was even a scheme to take advantage of the weakness of the American forces and launch an offensive. A corps of Canadians and Indians would have been raised and would have acted in conjunction with the British garrison at Oswegatchie (La Galette).[39]

In time, the loyalists became bold enough to circulate a letter in which the notary Sanguinet adjured his erring compatriots to reconsider their decision, and not to incur the punishment justly due to rebels guilty of betraying their allegiance. How, he asked, could they allow the *Bostonnais* to tyrannize over them?[40] Were they waiting for the invaders to indemnify themselves by making Canadians pay taxes? Were they not tired of working without pay? If Quebec was taken, they would become "slaves to be sold in the market with women and children, as is only too common" in the British colonies.[41] And the ardent polemicist went on to further flights of oratory: their fathers had

129

made their name feared in the Colonies; to what depths had the descendants of these brave ancestors fallen when those who could call themselves subjects of a King accepted "as tyrants . . . a band of *hinquis*" (Yankees) .[42] Their faint-heartedness was the only strength of an enemy who would not scruple "to burn and sack" their houses.[43]

Sanguinet's letter, while reflecting a certain confusion in the thinking of the people, also reveals an increasing uneasiness and the desire to be rid of the invasion. Immediately after Montgomery's defeat, the idea of launching an attack against Arnold's forces had come up. Carleton's aide-de-camp, Lanaudière, had sent a message to a M. Mauge from Varennes, exhorting him to redeem Canadian honour by leading a force of 200 men in an attack on the *misérable canaille* investing Quebec. But Lanaudière's messenger was taken prisoner on December 31 and the note was handed over to Arnold.[44]

A more serious attempt was made in March, 1776. On March 14, between two and three o'clock in the morning, Jean-Baptiste Chasseur from Saint-Vallier beached his boat at Quebec and stepped ashore with two companions. He brought 200 pounds of flour and six pairs of turkeys, and he was the bearer of important news. He informed Governor Carleton that 200 men from the south shore were ready to march against the Americans and that the farmers, who were becoming very impatient, were anxious to see the end of the paralyzing occupation. Chasseur agreed to take a whole packet of mail to M. de Beaujeu, the seigneur of the Ile-aux-Grues. Among the documents were an amnesty in favour of pro-rebels and the copy of an intercepted letter in which Arnold described the difficulties of the besieging army before Quebec.[45] De Beaujeu had already received a commission authorizing him to raise men for the royal cause, and a circular for distribution to curés and captains of militia.

The project for taking offensive action was not a new one. In the preceding autumn Cramahé had informed Augustin Roy, known as Lauzier, and François Lefebvre, known as Duchouquet, both of Sainte-Anne-de-la-Pocatière, that they would be informed as to "action to be taken." With the co-operation of Father Porlier of Saint-Thomas de Montmagny and the Abbé Bailly of the Quebec seminary, who was staying in the neighbourhood at the time, a movement to surprise the American post at Pointe-Lévis was organized under the leadership of Riverin and Féré. On March 20, the leaders decided to carry out the mission entrusted to them and to make their attempt. "Even if it should cost us our lives," they resolved, "let us obey; we shall perhaps fail, but we shall preserve our parishes from the stain of rebellion."[46] On March 21, orders were sent to the parishes as far as Kamouraska. At Sainte-Anne-de-la-Pocatière, the British flag was hoisted between Lauzier's house and the presbytery, and M. de Beaujeu at once dispatched a form of amnesty for pro-rebels who abjured their error. The document was signed by M. de Beaujeu and countersigned by the Abbé Porlier. At the same time, Deacon Jean-Marie Fortin was sent over to the north shore where, thanks to the influence of Mgr. d'Esgly, he succeeded in rounding up a "substantial party" of volunteers.[47]

On the morning of March 23, de Beaujeu set out with 106 militiamen, fifty from Kamouraska, four from Rivière-Ouelle, twenty-seven from Sainte-Anne-de-la-Pocatière, and twenty-five from Saint-Roch-des-Aulnaies. Their progress was slowed down by bad weather, and the habitants in the parishes through which they passed, most of them neutralist, "sought only to discourage them," but they reached Saint-Thomas during the night of the twenty-fourth. A second detachment under Captain François Pelletier had left Sainte- Anne on March 23, and the rear guard was ready to leave at four o'clock in the morning of the twenty-fifth.[48] These two groups counted about 172 men.[49] In the meantime, the royalist advance guard of forty-six men,[50] with its commanders Couillard and de Gaspé, and its chaplain, the Abbé Bailly, had reached Saint-Pierre-du-Sud, and hoisted the British flag over its headquarters in the house of Captain Michel Blais. However, the pro-rebel leaders—Bellerive from Beaumont, Gosselin from Sainte-Anne, and Lièvre from Pointe-Lévis—had warned the Americans on the twenty-third, and Arnold had dispatched a detachment of eighty men under Major John Dubois. On its way to Saint-Pierre, this force was joined by about 150 Canadians from the surrounding region, who had been recruited by Pierre Hayot.[51]

Completely taken by suprise, the royalist advance guard barricaded itself in Blais' house, which was attacked by Dubois' forces with cannon and musketry fire. Three men were killed and several others were wounded,[52] and the beleaguered survivors soon realized that they were in a hopeless situation, and must surrender to the enemy's superior strength. A few escaped, but thirty-eight were taken prisoner, among them the Abbé Bailly, who had been slightly wounded. The Americans also captured the British flag.

The skirmish had brought pro-rebel Canadians face to face with Canadian loyalists; men from the same parish found themselves in rival camps, and families were divided, with sons on one side and fathers on the other. In their rage at this attempt to frustrate their hopes, the furious pro-rebels might have made good their threat to massacre their compatriots, but fortunately the Americans intervened to avert any such disaster.

Thinking that Beaujeu's expedition had been undertaken without any legal authority, Major Dubois went to the presbytery at Sainte-Anne-de-la-Pocatière to complain to Father Porlier, but the curé showed him the official orders signed by the Governor. On the promise to offer no further armed opposition, some of the loyalist prisoners were released, but twenty-one were sent to the camp at Quebec under Canadian guards who treated them roughly and jeered at their misfortune in being captured.[53] Thanks to Dionne, and especially to Hayot, neither the Abbé Porlier nor the Abbé Bailly was molested, and the proprieties were respected. For Hayot made it clear to the Americans that they would ruin their case "if they went to extremes, and especially if they kidnapped priests." Although the skirmish at Saint-Pierre had resulted in victory for the Congress party, some of its repercussions were unfavourable to the American cause, and the pro-rebel fathers and mothers heaped reproaches on their curé: "That's what happens," they said, "when you churchmen meddle with things which do not concern you."[54]

This minor victory for the rebel party had little effect on the feeling in the country which was becoming more and more anxious for the arrival of the British forces. However, the long-delayed American reinforcements reached Quebec first. On March 30, Arnold had 2,850 men under his command, the largest number since the beginning of the siege. But of this number, 790 were more or less unfit for service, most of them victims of smallpox. Moreover, the morale of the army in general was at a low ebb, and Hazen was convinced that the 500 Canadians in his and Livingston's regiments would declare against the Americans if the Canadian people did so.[55] The besiegers had only three light batteries, one at Pointe-Lévis, one at Butte-à-Neveu on the Plains, and the third at the ferry landing. Their store of ammunition consisted of three or four tons of powder and ten or twelve tons of cannon balls and bombs, but as they had no engineers, any attempt at bombardment would be futile and their batteries could be demolished by the guns on the ramparts. Wooster had been promoted General, and was now in command of the army, which, under his orders, was engaged in building two fireboats to be directed against the ships in port as soon as the harbour should be free of ice.[56]

Meanwhile, the feeling of antagonism towards the invaders was becoming constantly more bitter. American officers had to admit that the Canadians, who should no longer be regarded as friends, were just waiting for a favourable chance to join their enemies. They also recognized the reasons for the change of attitude. The clergy, who were the guardians of the people's souls and directors of their conduct, were unanimously, although not always openly, opposed to the American cause; and the clergy had been slighted, sometimes even ill-treated, by the occupying forces. Moreover, the habitants had sometimes been roughly used; on several occasions forced to carry out instructions at the point of bayonet. In exchange for their produce they had been given illegible or unsigned notes, half of which were later repudiated by the commissariat. As a result of this treatment, the farmers now regarded the labour and supplies which they had furnished to the American invader as a dead loss and the United Colonies and their Congress as bankrupts.[57]

To this general picture, Colonel Hazen added a few specific examples of "flagrant abuses" of which the soldiers had been guilty. Troopers had forced their way into a priest's house and had taken his watch away from him. A man who insisted on being paid a debt of about twenty shillings owing to him was attacked and wounded in the neck by a bayonet thrust. Women and children were terrorized and forced, at bayonet point and without any prospect of payment, to supply horses to private soldiers.[58]

As one wave of bad news after another reached Philadelphia from Canada—inadequacy of the invading force, smallpox, abusive treatment of Canadian recruits, growing antagonism of the people—Congress made heroic efforts. It dispatched reinforcements: between January and April 1,200 men, in small groups of between fifteen and a hundred,[59] joined the besieging army before Quebec.[60] At the same time, Congress voted large sums of money: 64,358 dollars to Price and Heywood, and 300,000 dollars to General Schuyler.[61] It also instructed its commissioners to publish a letter to Canadians, expressing the "resentment" of Congress towards its soldiers who had caused damage or hardship, and its desire to insure that Canadians should be protected. The letter also promised that the damage would be repaired and the guilty punished.[62] Finally, on April 24, Congress ordered that reinforcements and supplies be sent to Canada: ten fresh battalions, 4,000 barrels of pork, 10,000 pairs of shoes, five tons of powder. On April 29, it requested the New England colonies to send to Schuyler as much specie as could be collected.[63]

Also on April 29, two months and a half after their appointment, the congressional commissioners reached Montreal, where they were greeted with cannon salvos and military honours.

Arnold was at the landing stage to meet them with other military officers and prominent citizens, and was later host at his residence in the Château de Ramezay. After the *vin d'honneur* and reception for town notables, the ladies, most of them Canadians, were presented to the distinguished visitors and drank a cup of tea with them. The day ended with an "elegant dinner" and a concert.[64]

The commissioners and Father Carroll were lodged in the house of Thomas Walker. Father Carroll, who had brought a letter from a Philadelphia Jesuit, Father Farmer, presented himself to Father Floquet. He had at least one meal in the Jesuits' house, and he was given permission by M. de Montgolfier to say mass there.[65] He had a number of interviews with Father Floquet, not in the Jesuits' house, since this would involve them, but in the garden of Du Calvet, who also took part in the conversations.[66] Father Carroll had been rather hesitant about accepting this particular mission, because he considered that for "ministers of religion" there was a certain danger in "taking an active part in political affairs." Canadians appeared to him to be no more disposed to oppose the Colonists than to help the British, and he did not feel he had any right to advise them to abandon their neutralism for active participation. On the one hand, they had not the same reasons as the Americans for rebelling against England, and, on the other hand, they had presented no remonstrance and taken no steps to obtain a reform of their present constitution. It was his opinion that they would be justified in resorting to arms only if other means of obtaining reform had been tried and had proved unsuccessful.[67]

Since the Canadian clergy, firm in its strict interpretation of the doctrine of obedience, refused to receive him, and since an impartial examination of the facts had led him to the conclusion that no pressure should be brought to bear on the Canadian people, Father Carroll refrained from active participation in the propaganda campaign, although the presence of a priest among the congressional spokesmen lent a considerable weight of moral support to the commission. This result, how-

135

ever, fell far short of justifying the conviction of General Lee, based on a conversation with Price, that a Jesuit among the delegates would be worth "battalions"[68] to the Colonial cause. In point of fact, neither Father Carroll's mission nor that of the printer, Fleury Mesplet, met with any success. Mesplet installed his press in the basement of the Château de Ramezay, but before he had time to print anything the face of events had changed.

The commissioners' first report betrayed their consternation at the conditions which greeted them in Canada. The credit of Congress had fallen so low that, if they had not had a friend to pay for it, they could not have hired a *calèche* in Montreal. They could not procure the smallest service unless they agreed to pay immediately, in gold or silver. The general feeling that a rebel defeat was imminent, and the Americans' failure to redeem their promises had combined to ruin every vestige of confidence in them. Eight thousand men and 20,000 pounds were required immediately. Without them it would be impossible to continue the war,[69] since it was impossible to maintain discipline in an army whose soldiers were not paid well and promptly.[70] Furthermore, the people who had been despoiled by undisciplined and penniless troopers had conceived such a violent hatred of Colonials that they were ready to drive them out of the country at the first news of the arrival of the British army. The American debt in Canada had risen to 14,000 pounds, in addition to Price's many unpaid accounts of which the total amount was 64,358 dollars.[71] In a situation which was already critical and which was becoming disastrous, the one effective measure which the commissioners managed to take was to grant trading permits to a few merchants in exchange for their promise not to give any sort of aid to the King's troops.[72]

10

THE INVASION ENDS IN DISASTER

Activities of the besieging army before Quebec. Arrival of the English fleet. Rout of the Americans. Departure of congressional delegates from Canada. Plan of the Colonies for further action. English victory at Les Cèdres. American reinforcements. The battle of Three Rivers. Retreat of the invaders. French officers captured. Violence and looting. Departure of Canadian pro-rebels to the Colonies.

THE CONGRESSIONAL commissioners had arrived in Canada five months too late. The game was now being played out, not on the Richelieu or before Quebec, but on the St. Lawrence, and the trump card was the English fleet. Alerted the previous autumn by dispatches from Carleton and Cramahé, the Colonial Secretary, Lord Germain, had equipped the powerful fleet which sailed for Canada in March with more than 10,000 British and German troops under the command of General Burgoyne.[1]

Early in April, the irascible muddler Wooster had been appointed to command the American army besieging Quebec. Wooster knew that English ships were speeding across the Atlantic under full sail. The danger was coming closer every day and he was most anxious to take advantage of the reinforcements in men and material being sent to him by Congress. However, as it seemed a hopeless venture to lead 3,000 ill-trained troops in an assault against the walls of Quebec, he undertook to reduce the fort by bombardment. Acting on his orders, the batteries of Pointe-Lévis, the River Saint Charles, and the Plains opened fire on the city. As supplies of both powder and balls

137

were limited, the cannonade, which was noisy rather than effective, could not be maintained, and a much heavier answering fire from the ramparts soon forced the gunners to abandon their batteries.

The Americans then decided to try an attack by the river. They prepared a fire-ship to be sent in among the sixty boats anchored in the *cul-de-sac*. They hoped that, as well as destroying the boats, the fire would spread to the sheds on the wharves and thus facilitate an attack on the Lower Town. In order to encourage his soldiers and his Canadian partisans, Wooster allowed it to be known that an attack was to be made as soon as the ice disappeared. At seven o'clock in the evening of May 3, the fire-ship was launched in a favourable north-east wind, but Quebec's batteries opened fire on it, and its crew, after lighting the fire, set it adrift too soon. It was still some distance from the wharves when the current caught it and carried it out to the middle of the river where its grenades and bombs exploded harmlessly. The ship itself ran ashore and burnt in the Beauport shallows.[2]

Two day later, fires lit up the night sky from Kamouraska to Saint-Michel to signal the approach of English ships coming up the river. On May 5, a council of war, summoned by Wooster's successor, General Thomas, had decided to abandon the siege the very next day, and it was on that next day that the first British sail was sighted from Quebec. The whole town hastened to the ramparts to see the ships as they approached: a solid frigate, well-named *Surprise*, followed by a second frigate, the *Isis*, and the sloop *Martin*. When the ships reached the wharf, 100 men from the 29th Regiment and eighty sailors disembarked and marched to the citadel, with flags flying, and accompanied by cheers from the populace. At noon Carleton gave the order for a sortie. A detachment composed of 180 soldiers from the reinforcing troops and 720 regulars, sailors, and militiamen from the garrison marched straight on the enemy's camp. As they came out of the town the Americans fired a few rifle shots, but when, after taking their positions in battle order on the Plains, the English soldiers advanced at the double to attack, the Colonial army broke and fled in confusion. General Thomas set the example of headlong flight, while his men, without waiting to fire guns already loaded, abandoned artillery, ammunition, provisions, baggage, and papers. Some of the fugitives threw away rifles and uniforms which impeded their flight. After a pause at Pointe-aux-Trembles during the night, the army pushed on the next day and finally halted at Deschambault, forty-five miles from Quebec.[3]

Still faithful to his policy of winning over the rebels by leniency, Carleton refrained from pursuing the fugitives. On the other hand, he sent out detachments to round up about thirty Americans who had not been able to escape and who had hidden. Some of them were wounded, and some had smallpox. In the course of their search through the suburbs and the surrounding country, the troops captured a few pro-rebel Canadians who had taken up arms and given active support to the enemy, and freed a number of loyalists who had been taken prisoner. They also brought in 300 wagon loads of provisions and baggage and five carts loaded with rifles.[4]

On May 10, Carleton issued a proclamation ordering militia officers to search the parishes for sick and wounded rebels in need of medical care. These men were to be assured that they would be released as soon as they had recovered.[5] A second proclamation, dated May 12, forbade men who had left Quebec in order to avoid military service to return to the town without permission from the Governor.[6]

As several regiments had arrived with the fleet they could now assume responsibility for the defence of Quebec. On May 23, on Carleton's orders, Colonel MacLean assembled the citizens and militia on the Place d'Armes and thanked them for the valuable service which they had rendered during the siege. The troops then took over regular guard duty.[7] On June 1, Carleton had under his orders ten regiments of infantry, a battalion of Scottish recruits, and four companies of artillery; a fighting force of 5,111 men.[8]

On May 9, Montreal learned that the Americans had been routed at Quebec. The news struck terror into the hearts of the New Englanders, who began immediately to evacuate the town. By May 12, there were only about 150 soldiers left,[9] with "no money, either paper or specie, to pay for anything." Franklin had left by boat with Mrs. Walker and Mrs. Price at eight o'clock on the morning of May 11. Chase, the two Carrolls, and Price left on the twelfth, and they were followed by a number of English merchants, among them Wells, McCarty, Meredith, Tucker, Heywood, and Bindon. The merchants "had been great partisans and propagandists for the American cause and their poisoned discourses had been largely responsible for deceiving the Canadian habitants."[10]

On May 22, four days after Congress had sent a consignment of gold to its commissioners, its members were stunned by the news of the disastrous defeat of their troops at Quebec. It was the end of all their hopes, but in a fine spirit of justice and courage they dispatched a letter to General Schuyler that very day. The first aim of the Colonies, said the letter, must be to protect the Canadians, and the English must also be prevented from enlisting the support of the Indians. Moreover, Congress would send the money required, up to 100,000 dollars, to pay its debts and restore its credit in Canada. The great objective, if the drive on Quebec was not renewed, should be to protect the frontier. In case of evacuation, the commissioners were to place on the army payrolls and promise protection to any pro-rebel partisans desiring to leave the country.[11]

On May 23, Congress appointed General Washington chairman of a committee of five members to study the Canadian situation. The following day it recommended "that the commanding officer in Canada be informed that the Congress are fully convinced of the absolute necessity of keeping possession of that country, and that they expect the forces . . . will contest every foot of ground." Accordingly, the Congressmen ordered that the dispatch of troops be hastened. They also urged that communication between Deschambault and Saint-Jean be kept open in order "to prevent the enemy's passing to the upper country."[12] Finally, at the beginning of June, it was agreed to send 6,000 men to reinforce the army, and to enlist 2,000 Indians in an effort to maintain a footing in Canadian territory.[13]

About the same time, the English launched an offensive from the west. Montreal was the target and the attack had been in preparation for months. In March, a Canadian loyalist, de Lorimier, after escaping from Montreal, had reached Oswegatchie on the upper St. Lawrence and proposed that the commander of the fort, Captain Forster, should lead an attack against the Americans. He then set out on a recruiting campaign from which he returned in May with a few hundred Indian warriors.[14] Meanwhile, on April 2, at the first rumour of activity at Oswegatchie, Arnold, who was in command in Montreal, had sent an advance guard of sixty men to Carillon on the Ottawa and a contingent of two hundred under Major Bedel to the fortified post at Les Cèdres, forty-three miles above Montreal.[15] On May 12, Major Bedel returned to Montreal, leaving Major Butterfield in command of 400 men, including about a hundred Canadians.[16]

On May 18, the British detachment of soldiers, Canadians, and Indians, appeared before Les Cèdres. Forster summoned the Americans to surrender, and warned that the Indians would give no quarter if the fort was taken by storm. The summons was rejected, and the defenders made preparations to fight off an attack. But Butterfield's terror of Indian tomahawks proved stronger than his will to resist, and he capitulated the following day.[17]

On May 16, Major Sherburne had left Montreal with 140 men to reinforce Butterfield's contingent, and on May 20, when they were within four miles of Les Cèdres, 100 members of the group, including the leader, were attacked by a detachment of sixty Indians and thirty Canadians under the command of de Lorimier. After a sharp engagement, the Americans retreated, but they were caught in the rear by a party of Canadians from Vaudreuil commanded by Montigny. The Americans then surrendered to de Lorimier who led them back to Les Cèdres, where Forster and Sherburne signed a cartel for an exchange of prisoners.[18]

Continuing his advance towards Montreal, Forster entrenched himself at Quinze-Chênes, between Les Cèdres and Vaudreuil. There, on the evening of May 26, a skirmish took place between his forces and an army of 700 men which Arnold had led out from Montreal. The next day, an English officer came forward under the protection of a white flag, and presented to Arnold the agreement on the exchange of prisoners signed by Forster and Sherburne. Arnold was reluctant to accept it, but when it was made clear to him that in the event of an attack Forster would be powerless to prevent the Indians from massacring their prisoners, he agreed to sign a new exchange cartel. After handing over all his prisoners except the 115 Canadians who had been captured at Les Cèdres and who were not included in the agreement, Forster led his troops back to Fort Oswegatchie.[19]

In the centre of the province, the American army was still in retreat from Quebec. It had made a brief halt at Deschambault to reassemble its forces, but, faced with a shortage of provisions, it pressed on towards Three Rivers, while its commanding officer, General Thomas, established his camp on the south shore, at Sorel.[20] Incompetent officers and short-term troopers combined to create conditions of disorder and confusion which grew worse every day. Officers and soldiers whose time had expired two or three months after their arrival in Canada abandoned their comrades and took the road home, regardless of orders, discipline, or possible consequences of their desertion. In their frenzy to evade service, recent recruits from New England inoculated themselves with the smallpox which was rampant in the army.[21] At the same time, the commissariat was in a state of complete disarray. For want of money to pay for provisions, the troops at Sorel were left for two days without meat. Starved for bare necessities, riddled with disease, the army was embittered by the conviction that it had been neglected and sacrificed.[22] At the same time, its commanding officer, General Thomas, struck down by illness, was obliged to hand over his command to Wooster, whom he had himself replaced.

Before leaving Montreal, the commissioners wrote to Congress to urge the immediate recall of a general so totally incapable of commanding the army and conducting the war. In their judgement, Wooster's continued presence in Canada would do the Colonies no good, and could even be harmful to their cause. To their frank and unflattering opinion of the Commander-in-Chief, they added an equally frank picture of conditions in the armed forces. Confusion was everywhere, unpaid soldiers had lost all sense of discipline, and the army was short of everything: meat, bread, tents, shoes. In Montreal, where no one was willing to sell anything even when payment was guaranteed by commissioners representing Congress, fifteen barrels of flour had had to be seized by force to feed the starving garrison. What would conditions be like when thousands of soldiers arrived from the Colonies without provisions or money to buy them? The army coffers contained only 1,100 dollars in paper money, while the army owed three times that amount to the soldiers and 15,000 dollars to the farmers.[23]

Meanwhile, a new Commander-in-Chief, Brigadier-General John Sullivan, was appointed and reinforcements continued to arrive by way of the Richelieu. By mid-May, the American forces in Canada had reached a total of 7,000 men, although two weeks later 1,800 were incapacitated by smallpox. On May 30, a council of war which Wooster had called at Chambly decided that the army should maintain its position in Canada and establish its headquarters at Sorel.[24] Shortly afterwards, General Thompson, who was temporarily in command of the fort, learned that 800 British soldiers and Canadians from Quebec were encamped at Three Rivers, and conceived the idea of launching a sudden attack on the post before it was organized for defence. The operation would halt the enemy's advance and at the same time it would restore the confidence of the American troops.[25] At this juncture, General Sullivan arrived on the scene, approved the project, and appointed Thompson to lead 2,000 men in the expedition which was set for June 6.

After crossing the river, the little army assembled at Pointe-du-Lac, and on the night of June 7, set out on the seven-mile march to Three Rivers, which it hoped to take by surprise. Since they did not know the country, the soldiers forced the Canadian Antoine Gautier to guide them through the forest. But Gautier, on the pretext that he had mistaken the road, lengthened their march by a whole series of detours. Meanwhile, Captain Landron of the Pointe-du-Lac militia took advantage of the delay and made haste to Three Rivers, where he gave the alarm at four o'clock in the morning. While these events were going on, the sloop *Martin*, with several warships and troopships, dropped anchor before the town. Alerted by Landron, General Fraser, the officer in command at Three Rivers, immediately ordered the troops to disembark, arranged them in battle order, and set up batteries. When the Americans, worn out from their long march, came within sight of the town the English troops suddenly opened fire with musketry and cannon. After a brief fusillade, the exhausted soldiers turned and fled along the river, pursued by fire from the ships. In the course of their flight they lost their cannon and left behind 200 prisoners.[26]

Still faithful to his policy of complaisance towards the rebels, Carleton, who had arrived to take command, did not attempt to surround the American force. Instead, he recalled the troops guarding the Rivière-du-Loup bridge, and called a halt to the pursuit. To the great surprise of all concerned, the Americans who had not been captured were allowed to regain their *bateaux* and return to Sorel. Among the prisoners were General Thompson and Colonel Irvine, captured at Pointe-du-Lac by Captain Rainville, the militiaman Chabot, and a few other Canadians.[27] On June 13, when the wounded and fugitives had been rounded up by militia officers, Carleton sent all the prisoners back to the Colonies by boat. The only condition imposed upon them was that they should give their word not to serve again against the mother country.[28]

144

Heavily laden troopships were now arriving from Europe. Four thousand German auxiliary troops under General Riedesel and 5,000 soldiers under the Commander-in-Chief, General Burgoyne,[29] disembarked in Quebec. Under instructions from Carleton to drive the Americans out of the province, Burgoyne wasted no time. The army was given its marching orders, and by the evening of June 14 the advance-guard was in camp at Sorel. The enemy forces under Sullivan had evacuated Sorel during the day, and at the same time the troops from the Montreal region had crossed the St. Lawrence on their way to Saint-Jean. On the fifteenth, when the English ships reached Varennes, the skeleton garrison which had been left in Montreal hastily abandoned its post, after first setting fire to two piles of wood in the hope of starting a general conflagration. When the fire had been brought under control, the citizens gave the keys of the town to the Superior of Saint-Sulpice, M. de Montgolfier, who in turn delivered them to M. Dufy, the militia Colonel. M. Dufy immediately called out his men who performed guard duty until the arrival of the royal troops on June 17.

Setting out from Sorel, the English army was joined by "numerous Canadians" on the way, and reached Saint-Jean on June 18. Burgoyne could have engaged the Americans immediately, but Carleton had ordered him to defer his attack until the arrival of the troops from Montreal. However, when the Montreal contingent arrived, the Americans had fled to the nearby post on Ile-aux-Noix. Before evacuating Saint-Jean, they had set fire to the fort and burned any boats or provisions which they had not been able to take with them. Of the 7,000 men encamped at Ile-aux-Noix, almost half were suffering from smallpox or were otherwise incapacitated for service, and as the place was obviously unhealthy, it was abandoned. On July 2, the whole American army retreated to Crown Point, thus leaving Canada free of the presence of enemies.[30]

On August 4, Carleton released another group of prisoners on parole in the hope that they might once more become loyal subjects;[31] for he was still convinced that these men were victims of insidious propaganda rather than rebels.[32] Among the prisoners released were two French officers, one of whom, M. de Bonvouloir, France's first unofficial secret representative to Congress, had come to Montreal to plead the Colonies' cause with the Canadian gentry. Although he succeeded in forming a friendship with the Hertel family, his mission was completely unsuccessful, and he was captured in June. On his release, he was allowed to go to the West Indies.[33] The second officer, the Chevalier de Saint-Aulaire, had gone to Canada with the intention of raising a regiment of *voyageurs*. He was sent to London, where he arrived in September, 1776.[34]

At Saint-Jean, the English found themselves faced with a fort in ruins, and without the *bateaux* and small craft which they needed if they were to proceed up the Richelieu and carry the war into the enemy's country. Moreover, an American fleet of fifteen sails barred the Lake Champlain route. As a first move in preparation for offensive action, a whole fleet of boats had to be built, and their construction kept engineers, carpenters, and labourers busy in the shipyards all summer.[35]

Thus, in spite of the skilful strategy, the wise measures, and constant activity which Congress had lavished on Canada for more than a year, the Canadian front had literally crumbled: after Quebec, Les Cèdres and Three Rivers! On June 11, when Chase and Carroll, back in Philadelphia from Montreal, reported to Congress, the delegates who listened to their description of the political and military situation in Canada were bitterly disillusioned men. Six days later, still unaware that the final evacuation had taken place, Congress made a supreme decision: to send General Gates to Canada with two fresh battalions, and to equip a fleet on the frontier waters of Lake Champlain.[36]

On June 21, Washington was instructed to investigate the conduct of the troops in Canada and to bring to trial officers "accused of cowardice, plundering, embezzlement of public monies, and other misdemeanours."[37] On July 19, after studying the report of the committee appointed to look into the matter,

146

"The Mitred Minuet," an American cartoon depicting colonial propaganda against the Quebec Act

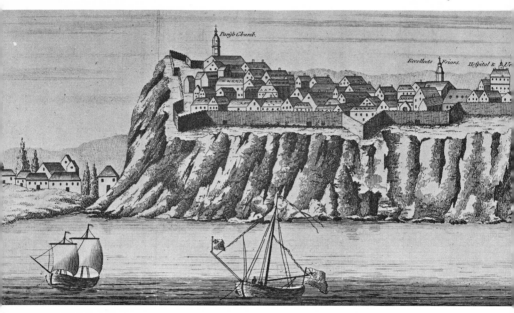

Parish Church.

Recollects Friars. Hospital &

Three Rivers

Congress decided that, in view of thefts of baggage and the murder of two American prisoners by Indians from the English detachment, the Forster-Arnold cartel could not become effective until after the murderers had been turned over to the American authorities.[38] An investigation into the causes of the Canadian fiasco[39] had convinced Congress that the whole affair should be wound up. Accordingly, on August 10, it ordered that 59,962 dollars be paid in specie to Price and Heywood, the bankers of the American forces, and that accounts for pay be settled with several Canadian officers and men who, after serving as volunteers in Canada, had retreated into the Colonies with the army.[40]

Although the first bitterly disappointing reports had thrown Congress into a state of dismay, it had not yet heard the full story of the disorderly retreat with its accompaniment of extortion, looting, violence, and vandalism. On May 14, the Americans in Montreal seized barrels of flour from the warehouse of Mocquin and Lemoine, with vague promises that they would "pay soon."[41] In this campaign of plunder, the commander himself was the chief culprit. On June 5, Arnold ordered quantities of merchandise of all sorts to be seized in his name. An officer presented a requisition signed by the General, but refused to surrender it to the merchants.[42] On the order of Captain Scott, the goods were then sent to Albany, where profits from their sale were pocketed by Arnold.[43]

In the rural districts officers and soldiers looted farms and abused farmers so shamelessly that General Woedtke had to post an order instructing Canadians to bring complaints to him.[44] At Senneville, M. de Montigny's house was sacked and burned; at Sainte-Geneviève, rebels ransacked the church and several houses; at Lachine, Arnold gave the order to empty M. Champion's store of its stock; the curé of Pointe-Claire was robbed of his most precious possessions.[45] Soldiers rifled M. Gugy's house at Machiche,[46] and those of M. de Tonnancourt and M. de Normanville in Three Rivers.[47] Excesses committed by pro-American Canadians were particularly shocking.[48] "Our

147

lives are not safe," wrote one citizen of Three Rivers, "since the Canadians have arrived; they are like madmen, intent only on pillage and murder."[49] When Heywood and Price fled, after the attempt to set Montreal on fire,[50] they left behind unpaid debts to the amount of 30,000 pounds, most of them contracted for provisions bought from a variety of persons all over the province.[51]

As the rebel army retreated, it left bitter memories behind it. The failure of the American adventure also drove into exile a certain number of Canadians who had openly espoused the cause of the invaders. One hundred and twenty-four men in Hazen's regiment followed the American army,[52] among them Captains Clément Gosselin and Jacques Robichaud, and Lieutenants Germain Dionne, François Monty, Laurent Olivier, and Pierre Boileau.[53] Ninety-seven of these refugees formed a Canadian detachment in Hazen's regiment. Although badly paid, they continued to serve under Colonel De Russy until the end of the year and were distinguished by their conduct and courage.[54] On October 10, probably in the interests of propaganda, Congress liberated Canadian prisoners who at the time of their capture were not bearing arms. The release, from which only Saint-Luc de la Corne and Rouville were excluded, was conditional on a promise not to serve in the British forces nor to provide them with information.[55]

11

POLITICAL, MILITARY, AND RELIGIOUS ORDER RESTORED

Rally of volunteers to the royal cause. Sanctions against pro-rebels. Inquiry into damage caused by the occupation. Carleton's policy in matters of discipline: indulgence and severity. An episcopal mandate. Pro-rebels required to retract publicly. Pro-American priests. Mandates stigmatizing disloyalty. Religious sanctions.

THE AMERICAN forces continued to retreat, while the British authorities took up the task of restoring order and discipline. As soon as the siege of Quebec was raised, enemy stragglers were rounded up and brought in: wounded, smallpox victims, fugitives who had been left behind in the flight. Carleton allowed them all to return home. At the same time the troops captured a few habitants from the country districts and the immediate vicinity of Quebec who had gone over to the enemy.[1] Even in these cases of flagrant disloyalty and rebellion, the Governor remained faithful to his policy of clemency. After a brief period of detention during which each of them promised to respond to the first call to service under the British flag, the rebels were allowed to return to their families. At the same time the commissions of militia officers were renewed, and they were instructed to put their men to work repairing the roads and bridges.

Many of the men from the country around Quebec were armed with all speed and fought with the King's forces at various points.[2] Habitants from the neighbourhood of Beau-

149

harnois and Vaudreuil fought with de Lorimier at Les Cèdres and at Quinze-Chênes. They were joined later by another contingent of Canadians, and the combined force entered Montreal with a detachment of 300 Highlanders and Indians under Sir John Johnson.[3] Before the end of May, Carleton was able to post about 300 Canadians at Three Rivers to observe the enemy's movements.[4] Canadians captured several American officers at Pointe-du-Lac and helped to repulse the attack on Three Rivers.[5] Early in June, 150 militiamen were attached to Riedesel's Germans,[6] and when Burgoyne advanced on Saint-Jean "a number of Canadians" marched at the head of the army.[7] At the end of June, when the enemy had been put to flight, Carleton released the militiamen, after thanking them for their zeal in the service of their country,[8] and warning them that they must hold themselves in readiness to answer the call whenever their services were required.[9]

Canadian volunteers had answered the Governor's call to arms in Montreal and had stood with Beaujeu at Saint-Pierre. The fact that loyalists later rallied to the British flag in greater numbers than pro-rebels to the American cause proves that there was a considerable loyalist element in a good many other parishes as well. When, with the retreat of the army of occupation, the loyalist element could give free expression to its feelings, it became apparent that these feelings were shared by the people in general. Captain Digby reported that, after all they had suffered during the winter, the joy of the people when they learned that a large body of troops was coming to their aid was indescribable.[10] Another officer filled in the shadings and presented a more accurate picture showing the clergy and "the better part of the people" loyally attached to the government, and the habitants inclined to be neutral or to join the strongest side, but willing to help the army when asked to do so.[11] M. de Montgolfier also bore witness that, now that they could appreciate the advantage of living "in tranquillity under an equitable government," all the parishes appeared "to have become decidedly more reasonable." At least, added the prelate, that was true of most

150

of the habitants.[12] There still remained a refractory element, however, especially in the neighbourhood of Quebec. Individuals who had been in league with the rebels were closely watched by the Governor, and an episcopal mandate condemned those who refused to admit their error and recognize their duty.[13]

Although Carleton had been consistently lenient towards American sympathizers, he now considered it most important not only to re-establish royal authority in the rural districts, but to punish with public disapproval and sanctions the conduct of the men who, when called up, had refused to obey the King's orders, or who had openly sided with the invaders. Accordingly, in May, 1776, he appointed a commission of three members: François Baby, Gabriel Taschereau, and Jenkins Williams. The commissioners were instructed to assemble the militia in each parish and to require the surrender of all congressional commissions. They were then to cancel the commissions of officers who had failed in their duty to the King, and to grant new ones to men more worthy of the honour. Finally, they were to disarm any subjects suspected of disloyalty, to inquire into their conduct, and to report to the Governor.[14]

The commission set to work promptly and between May 22 and July 16 it visited all the parishes, on both sides of the river, from Three Rivers to Kamouraska. The inquiry revealed that the great mass of the people had been imbued with the desire and the determination to remain neutral. Their neutralism tended to be friendly rather than hostile towards the invaders, and this tendency had been encouraged by the failure of the British authorities to take any positive action. The commission further established that actively hostile and vigilant pro-rebel minorities had taken over the direction of most of the parishes and had used the threat of American intervention to impose their will on the neutralist majorities. Finally, it found evidence in all the parishes, of the existence of a loyalist minority, usually passively inactive though supported by the clergy, which professed the doctrine of fidelity to the King and the lawful authority.[15]

151

On June 25, five days after his entry into Montreal, the Governor appointed a second commission, of whom the members were Saint-Georges-Dupré, Edward William Gray, and Pierre Panet, to make a similar inquiry in the Montreal district. Documents relating to the conduct of militiamen give evidence that the commission visited at least some of the parishes in the region, but its minutes have been lost.[16]

On July 30, the Governor created still another commission composed of Judges Adam Mabane, Thomas Dunn, and Jean-Claude Panet. This commission was instructed to investigate and assess the damage caused by royal and rebel troops and the value of goods sold or provided to the Americans. After considering the report, the government granted compensation in a certain number of cases.[17]

Immediately after the liberation of Quebec, Carleton called up the militia and sent detachments to join the army marching on Saint-Jean. He also insisted that the farmers should be treated with strict justice.[18] An order of June 15 stipulated that provisions and services should be paid for in cash and on the spot. Acknowledgement that such goods and services had been provided no longer sufficed.[19] When complaints reached the Governor's ears that transport drivers and boatmen were harassing farmers and looting farms, he ordered the brigades on the Richelieu to patrol the parishes and prevent any bullying.[20] As for the armed forces, M. de Montgolfier reported that they behaved "calmly and in a spirit of discipline" and that there was "absolutely no complaint" about them anywhere.[21] To prevent abuses, even on the part of the officers, captains of militia were instructed not to supply horses or carriages except on immediate payment and on presentation of an order from the Brigadier-General.[22]

Since the retreating Americans had blocked the roads and destroyed the bridges, the Canadians had to be called in to repair them. They provided the labour for these tasks and also the transport for food and ammunition for the army. Pro-rebels serving prison terms were freed of their irons and put to work.[23]

The work force was made up of 1,200 men who were called in rotation and who worked without pay.[24] When this system of corvées met with resistance, officers were ordered to arrest defaulters and bring them in as army prisoners.[25] Those who refused to obey the orders of militia officers were sent to do forced labour on the fortifications of Ile-aux-Noix. Habitants who failed to denounce, or who helped, American spies were also sent to the island with their hands chained, but those guilty of minor offenses were released promptly on promise of good conduct.[26] The Governor might be willing to forget defections under the American occupation, and to allow militiamen to repair past errors by present obedience, but he was inflexibly severe in his attitude towards new offenders. Insubordination was punished by prison,[27] but the sanction was not often required, for the passage of German soldiers and the presence of troops at Saint-François-du-Sud had made "everyone docile," even the purest "Yenkis."[28]

Carleton's severity, motivated and justified by earlier resistance to authority, was also tempered by a number of wise provisions. Habitants were exempted from military service and corvées during the harvest.[29] Transport work was interrupted for the ploughing season and put off to the winter, when the snow made hauling easier. In order to spare those who had already given their share, heavier contributions were required from parishes where past demands had been lighter.[30] The Governor was on the whole well satisfied with the effort of the labour force,[31] and he was anxious to know whether Canadians would be equally reliable in military service. On September 23, he instructed the military commanders, Dufy in Montreal, de Tonnancourt in Three Rivers, and Voyer in Quebec, to have their captains draw up lists of the men ready to answer the call to serve in the army.[32] Two thousand volunteers signed up,[33] and the Governor was delighted with this excellent result. He sent his thanks to the commanders, and explained that for the moment he did not require the services of the militia. He had simply wanted the people to express their feelings and thus provide a lesson for the delinquents.[34]

This show of good will did not, however, destroy the mental image of the Canadian which had been substituted in the course of the invasion for Carleton's earlier impression. He expressed his new conviction in September, 1776, in a letter written from Chambly to the Colonial Secretary: "As to my opinion of the Canadians, I think there is nothing to fear of them, while we are in a state of prosperity, and nothing to hope for when in distress. I speak of the people at large; there are some among them who are guided by sentiments of honour, but the multitude is influenced by hopes of gain, or fear of punishment."[35]

When the time came to go into winter quarters, Carleton announced that the German troops would be billeted in the district of Three Rivers, and he warned the habitants that they must not expect to be treated with the same consideration as if they had given evidence of the zeal and devotion to duty which they owed to their King.[36] He was careful, however, to ensure that loyalists should be well treated by the troops. In December, he instructed district commanders not to quarter soldiers on men who had served during the campaign. If necessary, they were to find new billets for troopers who were already placed. The same men were to be exempt from corvées, and they were not to be asked to provide servants, horses, or carts. For it was only just that these burdens should fall chiefly on the cowards who, by refusing to defend their country, had created the need for them.[37] Another order provided that men who had served should receive back pay and a bonus of four dollars each.[38]

People in the Montreal region appear to have been less fortunate than those in Three Rivers. Sanguinet reported that citizens, even good loyalists, had reason to complain of the troops who were quartered on them, and by whom they were "ill-treated and molested . . . without obtaining justice."[39] In the country, although there were official declarations of a spirit of good will, there were certainly abuses, especially in parishes which had shown sympathy for the rebels. This becomes evident when one examines the instructions issued to the Dupré-Panet-Gray commission. The commissioners were directed to investigate complaints concerning corvées and billets, as well as the conduct of soldiers, and they were ordered to pay for everything that had been supplied to the army. These matters were dealt with in at least two meetings of the commission, at Berthier and at Lavaltrie, in March, 1777. The German troops were known for their brutal treatment of civilians, and two of their superior officers, Brigadier Gall and General Riedesel, were summoned to Berthier and instructed to put an end to abuses on the part of their troopers.[40]

At the height of the religious crisis many Canadian Catholics were in open revolt against their Bishop, and curés had been forcibly detained by their parishioners. Now, although the invaders had been driven from Canadian territory and the royal administration was once more functioning smoothly, the religious crisis was still unresolved. On May 12, 1776, only a few days after the end of the siege of Quebec, Mgr. Briand issued a mandate in which he reviewed the complex circumstances of the invasion. After praising the courage and fortitude of the officers, soldiers, and militia who had defended the capital, the Bishop rendered thanks to Providence for the salvation of "the last bulwark of the province and the religion of our fathers." He then expressed the hope that the victory, opening the eyes of "those of our brothers who had been blinded by error and falsehood," would lead them back "to the paths of truth," and would make them "obedient to the voice of their pastors, and more submissive to the powers established by God to govern them." That evening the cathedral was lit for vespers with a thousand candles. The celebrant chanted a *Te Deum* which was followed by a solemn Office of the Blessed Sacrament.[41]

Mgr. Briand now faced the thorny and difficult task of bringing back into the fold those erring Catholics who had ignored monitions and refused to listen to the voice of their Bishop. In many cases parishioners who had not submitted to the conditions laid down by their pastors had thereby been prevented from fulfilling their paschal obligations. At Saint-Charles-de-Bellechasse, for example, since the withdrawal of the Americans, although the pro-rebels had been looking very crestfallen and saying very little, only the children and about twenty women partook of Holy Communion on Easter Sunday.[42] On the point of doctrine, the Bishop had all the inflexibility of a true Breton. Following his instructions, the curés admitted to the sacraments "only those who, having displayed an attitude of rebellion or indifference, confessed their fault and publicly renounced it both by word and deed, and who were prepared to expiate it in any way which might be considered suitable."[43]

For some time the Bishop did not appear to be satisfied even with public recantation and penance. "For," he declared, "in addition to the crime of rebellion and disobedience, there is the damage suffered by the kingdom and by many individuals."[44] Instructions were actually issued which would have excluded the culprits from the sacraments until an evaluation of material damage had been made,[45] but when the Bishop consulted the Governor on this point, they agreed that the best means of reclaiming the sheep who had gone astray was "not to cut them off from the sacraments, but to facilitate access to them." Although the proposal for recovering material damage was abandoned, the spirit of Christian clemency did not entirely wipe out latent resistance, nor did it entirely prevent scandalous incidents. In one instance, at Saint-François-du-Sud, two fathers, former pro-rebels, forestalled refusal of the sacrament by not presenting their children to the priest for baptism, and by having the symbolic sprinkling performed by a layman.[46] On July 25, Mgr. Briand replied to this act of defiance by excommunicating the two offenders. This measure proved effective and a few weeks later the two parents declared themselves willing to submit to the Bishop's conditions.[47]

Mgr. Briand was equally intransigent in his treatment of priests who had given proof of American sympathies. The chief culprit was the Jesuit, Father Floquet, the friend of Montgomery, Wooster, and Hazen. Convicted by his own confession of "several faults," he was placed under an interdict which was not lifted until the end of the year, after he had written a letter of submission to the Bishop.[48] A second Jesuit, Father Huguet of Caughnawaga, and the Récollet father, Claude Charpentier, curé of Longueuil, were castigated by M. de Montgolfier, the Vicar-General of Montreal, but no other sanctions were applied against them. As he considered the Abbé La Valinière, the curé of L'Assomption and Walker's friend, to be among "the very guilty", M. de Montgolfier submitted this case to the Governor, who left him free to deal with it.[49] Accordingly, the Abbé La Valinière was virtually confined to the distant little parish of Saint-Roch-des-Aulnaies, and in 1778, was ordered to return to France.[50] A few other priests, whose former attitudes appeared to have been "deserving of reproach," tried to show that they had been "constantly faithful to the government." After considering M. de Montgolfier's opinion that "their conduct" appeared to constitute "adequate recantation and reparation,"[51] the Bishop agreed tacitly to forget their offences.

Among the Canadians who had been deaf to the admonitions of the Bishop during the invasion, there were still some who appeared to be in no hurry to make their peace with the Church. In the summer of 1776, the number of those who had not met the Bishop's requirements was so considerable that Mgr. Briand issued another mandate "on the subject of rebellious subjects during the American war." Addressing himself to these stubborn cases with a bluntness born of pastoral solicitude, he reminded them that insidious American propaganda was the prime cause of their political and religious downfall. They were "too intelligent," he observed, "not to perceive the gross deception and the iniquitous lies" which had been used to seduce them. And since they now recognized them, why did they not reject them? Even delayed repentance was better than no repentance at all, and although the Governor was known for his clemency, stubbornness in wrongdoing could not be condoned and must ultimately be punished. Only fools could refuse to believe in the final triumph of the Empire.[52]

157

Once again the Bishop expounded the doctrine of the Church, and repeated that their own interest, both temporal and spiritual, lay in the acceptance of their duty. In the temporal sphere, since the English régime had brought peace and prosperity, the King had a right to expect gratitude from them, and their defection called for just punishment.[53] As for the Colonies, the Bishop, as "their father in God" whom they hated, but "who had never desired anything but [their] good," asked leave of his flock to show them how these Colonies had behaved towards the province. Jealous of the favours granted by Parliament to the Canadians, the Colonists "had made every effort . . . to prevent them." Having failed in that attempt, and knowing that Canadians "had no knowledge of politics," they had then attempted to spur them on to revolt, and even to "a kind of apostasy of religion." The Colonists represented the Quebec Act as a return to the "slavery" which placed Canadians "at the mercy" of their seigneurs and the nobility. "They promised you exemption from seigneurial dues, and you were pleased at this injustice. They promised that you would pay no more tithes, and you did not spurn with horror this impious and sacrilegious ingratitude towards God."[54] These, concluded the Bishop, were the iniquitous and sinful promptings with which the rebels had succeeded in deceiving Canadians, making them unworthy to enjoy the rights of British citizens and liable to confiscation of their property and even to banishment.[55]

The prelate then considered the matter as it related to the spiritual well-being of his flock. At the instigation of the Colonies, pro-rebel Canadians had broken their sacred oath and had served as the instrument of death and material losses which must be repaired before pardon could be granted. If Quebec had fallen, they would have been faced with Protestantism, and the Protestantism of the New Englanders was "the most cruel enemy" of Catholicism. With their "crass ignorance" of their faith and their determination not to listen to their spiritual guides, how could Canadian Catholics hope to withstand such a force?[56] And what remained of the faith of Catholics such as these? Those who had said publicly that "the religion of the *Bostonnais* was good," who had flaunted their Protestantism and refused to heed the voice of the Church, had fallen into schism and doctrinal heresy.[57] They would claim, as they had already done, that it was not the business of priests to meddle with war. That might be so, but it was the business of priests to judge whether a war was a just or an unjust one, as it was their business to judge the obedience due to a sovereign.[58] Mgr. Briand's ringing phrases defined and stigmatized the faults of the pro-rebels: disobedience to authority, violation of oaths, crimes of theft and violence, denunciation of priests, betrayal of confessors' counsels, advice to curés to disobey episcopal mandates.[59] Those who had committed such faults, especially those guilty of acts of violence and those who had voiced their protest in churches, had made themselves liable to excommunication, as had all those who had encouraged or approved such acts, or who had "stolen, looted, assassinated, burnt, betrayed, or seized their brothers by force." As he reached the end of this severe castigation, the Bishop assumed a gentler tone to remind his erring children that, as their "father," he desired only to make them aware of the enormity of their crime, and to bring them to repentance and contrition. Their curés could pardon those who repented, and it was to be hoped that their experience of error would make them more submissive to their pastors.[60]

This passionate exhortation, full of bitter disappointment and fatherly emotion, stirred and awakened many consciences, and Mgr. Briand was gratified to note that "the habitants were coming back gradually to the Church." But he remained inexorable on the question of doctrine. The conditions which he had laid down must be met. "I stand firm," he wrote in September, "the rebel must retract publicly before being admitted to the sacraments, even at the hour of death."[61] The Bishop's unwavering firmness on this point was demonstrated at a solemn ceremony which took place in Quebec on Tuesday, December 31, 1776. On that day, in response to an episcopal mandate, solemn high mass was celebrated in the Cathedral and the Bishop himself, in pontifical vestments, sang a *Te Deum* in thanksgiving for the raising of the siege of Quebec and other victories won during the year just ending.[62] Twelve Canadians who had been condemned to prison for bearing arms against the King, and who had made a public confession of guilt in the prison the day before, were led to the church door with ropes about their necks. There, after the ceremony, they confessed their guilt, and craved pardon of God and their King. They were then sent back to their villages to repeat the ceremony of humble recantation at their own parish churches.[63]

Faithful to his task of bringing the lost sheep back into the fold, the Bishop continued to exhort them to return to their religion and their duty.[64] The work of reconciliation went on slowly but steadily, helped in many cases by the understanding with which the curés mitigated the harshness of the sentence imposed. The Abbé Cardin of Saint-Joachim explained to the Bishop a method which must have been followed by other priests as well. If there was no conclusive proof that a suspect had "been directly implicated in revolt," he was admitted to the sacraments. The Bishop's mandate permitted the use of such means to reclaim those victims of "fear" or "enticements" who had only appeared to espouse the rebels' cause, and the curé assured the Bishop that he had not abused this permission. No offender was admitted to the sacraments without having made known his repentance by a "sufficiently public recantation." But the Abbé Cardin did not insist upon public confession at the church door because, although some culprits would have accepted this sentence, others would have rebelled against it. For, as the shrewd curé observed, while some of these pro-*Bostonnais* were true Christians "who had been . . . misled and blinded," most of them were not the best Christians in their parishes, and "did not attach as much importance as they should to the sacraments." In his parish, there remained only three or four offenders who were unwilling to make their confession in the presence of witnesses, but he felt that some offenders were more guilty than others. Some appeared to him to have become attached to the rebel party "out of vain fear, or for political reasons, to pander to the said party in case it should prevail." He therefore proposed to accept a confession and apology made in the presbytery in the presence of witnesses. However, in the case of Lespérance, a stubborn rebel, he would require that, whether his confession took place in the semi-privacy of the presbytery or at the church door, he should carry a candle.[65]

In spite of the general movement of reconciliation, there remained a hard core of intractable rebels. Father Gatien of Lotbinière had to report the activities of Antoine Lapointe who continued to dissuade men from the King's service. Lapointe was arrested and condemned to prison, and on his release he threatened to be avenged on his curé and his militia captain.[66] Other culprits steadfastly refused to recant, even when they were at the point of death. In the course of the years a number of tombstones appeared in fields on the south shore. They commemorated rebels who had refused to acknowledge their error and had been refused Christian burial. It is reported that one rebel, when urged on his deathbed to recant, replied to his curé: "You sound like an Englishman," and with these words turned his face to the wall and died.[67]

12

SARATOGA AND A PROJECTED INVASION

*Creation of courts of justice and a "privy council."
Battle of Lake Champlain. Ordinance governing militia service.
Burgoyne's expedition. Military service and labour. Surrender
of Saratoga. Canada's place in the American constitution. Project of an invasion led by La Fayette. Carleton's preparations
for defence.*

DURING the summer of 1776, Carleton made use of the interval
while boats were being built in preparation for an invasion
of the American colonies to carry out the provisions of the
constitution established by the Quebec Act. In July, he appointed judges for the new courts: Adam Mabane, Thomas Dunn,
and Claude Panet in Quebec, and Peter Livius, William Owen,
and Gabriel Taschereau in Montreal.[1] On August 8, acting
on his own interpretation of the authority vested in him, he
set up a sort of "privy council," to which he appointed the
Lieutenant-Governor, Cramahé, and four English members of
the legislative council, Thomas Dunn, Hugh Finlay, Adam
Mabane, and John Collins. To this council, in which there was
no representative of the French population and which had no
legal basis, he delegated some of the functions reserved to the
legislative council, and it was this smaller council which, under
the Governor's direction, really administered the affairs of the
country.[2]

Early in October, a fleet of ten vessels was ready, manned
and equipped, at Saint-Jean, and Carleton gave the order for
an attack on Arnold's vessels barring the invasion route to the

162

American Colonies. On October 11, action was engaged at Ile Valcourt, and before nightfall several of Arnold's fifteen boats had been sunk. The rest of the fleet slipped away in the dark, but the English ships pursued them, and when they caught up with them again two days later the Americans could not hold out against the heavy cannonade to which they were subjected. Five boats were beached and burnt and the remaining three succeeded in reaching the shelter of Crown Point. Then, after setting fire to the houses and fortifications there, the Americans withdrew, with arms and baggage, to Ticonderoga.[3] As Ticonderoga was strongly fortified and defended by an army under the command of General Gates, and it was too late in the season to enter on a new campaign, the troops were ordered back to winter quarters at Saint-Jean.[4]

In January, 1777, Carleton finally gave effect to the essential article of the Quebec Act by convening the legislative council. The opening took place on January 21, at the Governor's residence, the Château Saint-Louis, and the session lasted until April. The council adopted sixteen ordinances, of which the most important provided for a new judiciary system. The others formulated regulations for business and for the administration of the country.[5] The ordinance which preoccupied the people more than any other was the one dealing with militia service. It was a direct result of the war and it bore the mark of the Governor's personal intervention. "In the hopes of rendering Canada of use to Great Britain by its military strength as well as by its commerce," Carleton proposed to bring Canadians to "that state of deference and obedience which they formerly paid their ancient government."[6] In the chaotic conditions resulting from the invasion, the militia ordinance appeared to him to be the most efficacious means to this end; for he was convinced that these people had been governed with too loose a rein, and had imbibed too much of "the American spirit of licentiousness and independence . . . to be suddenly restored to a proper and desirable subordination."[7]

The ordinance, adopted on March 29, 1777, made militia

163

service obligatory for every male between the ages of sixteen and sixty. Anyone guilty of evading his obligation was fined five pounds for the first offence. A second offence was punishable by a fine, a month in prison, and withdrawal of the right to possess a firearm. In peace time, failure to take part in military exercises was punishable by a fine. The Governor or the Commander-in-Chief could mobilize the militia as circumstances required. The penalties for evading service in time of war were a fine of ten pounds for the first offence and, for the second, a fine and two months in prison. The habitants were required to take turns in providing carts and horses for the King's service, for which a set price was paid. Militia officers were ordered to arrest deserters and agents of the rebel colonies. Anyone guilty of giving any sort of help to a deserter or a rebel was liable to a month in prison and a fine of ten pounds in towns and five in rural districts, for the first offence. For a subsequent offence, the fine and the prison terms were doubled. The following categories of persons were exempt from military service and also from the obligation to provide transport: high officials, former seigneurs, the gentry, officers on half-pay, the clergy, seminarians, and persons engaged in the public service.[8] Provision of sanctions, as well as specific definition of obligations under this ordinance, prove that Carleton had at last recognized the futility of leniency. Strong measures were necessary if he wished to reawaken to a sense of its duty a population infiltrated by propaganda at once skilful, insidious, and subversive.

Others means of coercion having failed, England now resolved to send an expedition against her rebellious colonies by way of Canada and Lake Champlain, and in May, 1777, General John Burgoyne returned to Quebec to command the invasion force. The Governor immediately issued an order for three militia companies of 100 men each to be called up. He kept this draft of Canadians to a minimum "in order to reconcile them by degrees to what under the French government was deemed an indispensable duty." The three companies of militia were sent to Montreal, where they were lodged in the Récollet monastery, and forbidden to go out, "as if they had been prisoners." Irritated by this restriction, and disturbed by the rumour that they were engaged to fight, the men at once began to seek opportunities to desert.[9] To Burgoyne's report (May 26) of these desertions, Carleton replied that they did not surprise him. There were no more of them than he had expected, and they were as numerous in Quebec as in Montreal. He explained that the militia ordinance was a "trial" towards "bringing things into order," a task which would "require . . . time, temper, and management." As in the present emergency coercion was also required, he ordered that two married men should be called up from the parish of each deserter,[10] and by this painful means the three companies were brought up to strength. Those commanded by Captains Monnin and Boucherville were attached to Burgoyne's army,[11] while the third, under Rouville was sent to join the detachment of Colonel St.-Léger which was about to attack Fort Stanwix.[12]

Two militia companies were far from satisfying the needs of General Burgoyne, who now requested a thousand drivers for transport duty.[13] Fearing that the demand for such a large number of labourers might provoke a refusal, Carleton enrolled only 175 volunteers. To these he added a contingent of 500 men from the Quebec region who showed a "better spirit" than he had anticipated.[14] During the month of June, Burgoyne, who was making his way from Saint-Jean towards Ticonderoga, became more and more impatient as one difficulty after another impeded his progress, more and more urgent in his demands for fighting men and corvées.[15] Consequently, Canadians "continued to be ordered up for work . . . which was not paid for." They also had to provide means of transport and sometimes give temporary lodging to troops;[16] and since they all hated military service and forced labour, many of them deserted at the first opportunity.[17] When the army reached the frontier, in July, the trickle of deserters became a torrent. When they reached Ticonderoga, only 400 remained of a work force of 800, while the fighting strength was being reduced[18] at the rate

165

of a dozen desertions a day.[19] The deserters in this case were acting on the principle, recognized by Canadians ever since 1775, that they could not be forced to serve outside Canada.[20]

This time the Governor dealt firmly with all acts of insubordination. Arguing from the principle that by the terms of feudal tenure[21] both the seigneur and the tenant were bound to furnish labour and military service to the King, he insisted on the strict application of the law, with punishment for deserters, fighting men, and labourers alike.[22] Instructions were issued for soldiers to be quartered in the houses of offenders.[23] When the habitants of L'Assomption refused to submit to requisitions, a detachment of German troopers was ordered to conduct the chief culprits to prison in Montreal, while troops quartered in the village[24] stole clothes from the houses where they were lodged and chickens and rabbits from the farmyards.[25]

For men unaccustomed since the conquest to military service and corvées, 1777 was a hard year,[26] the more so since the burdens were not distributed evenly. Parishes in the populous centre of the province were "harassed," while the more distant parishes were virtually exempt from requisitions.[27] According to one witness, there were certainly abuses, "rough treatment, and hard unpaid labour for men and horses."[28] On the other hand, in applying the law, Carleton was as considerate as possible. He reduced the corvées of city-dwellers to a minimum,[29] and in special cases services were paid for.[30] He made an exception for artisans[31] and for voyageurs engaged on trading expeditions,[32] and, in order to relieve farmers, he suspended corvées during the harvest period.[33] He sent blankets and shoes to men attached to the army.[34] He ordered that irregularities and oppressive acts should be punished,[35] and he established patrols of observers to prevent such abuses[36] and to draw up a scale of allowances for workers.[37] Finally, he ordered that militiamen and workers should be free after the first of November.[38] In spite of all these mitigating provisions, there was no radical change in the custom of the age, and the corvées continued to be a heavy charge, as they had been throughout the French régime.[39]

Meanwhile, in New York and Philadelphia, the Canadian situation continued to present a problem. Burgoyne might be a mediocre tactician, but he was a brave soldier, and Congress kept an anxious eye on the frontier where he had assembled an army of 8,000 men. In July, the Congressmen were dismayed at the news that Burgoyne's force had appeared on Lake Champlain and that the key post of Ticonderoga had been evacuated.[40] However, when the English army penetrated farther into enemy country, it was harried by elusive guerilla bands and detachments of militia which succeeded in cutting its supply lines to the Richelieu valley. St.-Léger and his force had failed in their attempt to capture Fort Stanwix, the German auxiliaries had suffered defeat at Bennington, and the British troops were on reduced rations. Finally the day came when the army found itself bottled up in Saratoga, without hope of relief, and surrounded by the Colonial forces. On October 17, 1777, a decisive date in the American struggle for independence, General Burgoyne surrendered to General Gates, with 6,000 men, flags, arms, and baggage. The threat of an invasion from Canada had been destroyed.

On November 4, Congress, transported with enthusiasm at this first great victory, moved a vote of thanks to General Gates, his officers, and his army.[41] Among the thousands of English prisoners, there were about thirty Canadians from Captain Monnin's militia company. A special article in the terms of capitulation dealt with them and showed that the Americans were already preparing the political ground for the future. The article stipulated that Canadians accompanying the English army, in whatever capacity, would be permitted to return to their country. They would be conducted to the post on Lake George, and they would be required, as English soldiers were, to promise that they would take no further part in hostilities.[42]

On November 15, in the course of framing a draft constitution for the new state which the Colonies had decided to set up,

Congress, still conscious of the importance of bringing Canada into the union, inserted a discreet formula which could be interpreted as an invitation to join the confederation. A clause in the text reserved a special place for her: "Canada acceding to this confederation and joining in the measures of the United States shall be admitted into and entitled to all the advantages of this union, but no other colony shall be admitted into the same, unless such admission be agreed to by nine states."[43]

By leaving the frontier without protection, Burgoyne's defeat reawakened the Colonials' hopes of conquering Canada. On November 29, Congress appointed a committee of three members: William Duer, James Lowell, and Francis Lightfoot Lee, whose instructions were to have the Articles of Confederation translated into French, and to prepare an address inviting the people of Canada to join the other colonies. The committee was to present a plan for facilitating the distribution of the address and fostering affection for the United States among Canadians.[44] The climate was favorable for a new invasion of the neighbouring province; enthusiasm for the enterprise was general and on every hand the opinion was expressed that "there could not be an easier or more profitable undertaking."[45] Congress was soon infected with the fever. On December 2, the Duer-Lowell-Lee committee presented its report. It proposed that the Colonies should build a strong citadel on Lake Champlain and provide it with a garrison of 1,700 men, that they should raise a regiment in Quebec with the aid of the Canadian prisoners, and that they should appoint a chaplain who would help to recruit volunteers, and who would use his influence to bring Canada into the American union.[46] To these first proposals, a second committee added a recommendation that Congress give its attention to the destruction of the English fleet at Saint-Jean.[47]

Towards the end of 1777, the idea of invasion became more definite. The plan was discussed throughout the country, and the Board of War, which had just been created with Gates as chairman, favoured it. Since Saratoga, Gates had been emerging as a rival of Washington, and he and his friends saw in the invasion project an opportunity to ignore and isolate the Commander-in-Chief. In order to exploit the prestige of his name and his nationality, it was agreed to entrust the command of the expedition to the Marquis de La Fayette[48] who, with all the enthusiasm of his twenty years, had come straight from Versailles to place his sword at the service of Congress. On January 22, 1778, Congress adopted a resolution recommending that the Colonies organize an "irruption into Canada" and that measures be taken to assure the successful execution of the plan. The next day, La Fayette was appointed to command the expedition.[49] So far, Washington had not been consulted, and when he learned indirectly of the War Board's scheme, he called it a "child of folly."[50] In pursuance of its plan and with a care for making the counsel of experienced tacticians available to its young leader, Congress detached Generals Conway and Stark to accompany the expedition, which also included seven French officers destined to take command "of the Canadians whom they might enlist in Canada."[51]

La Fayette was full of enthusiasm for the idea of reconquering "New France," but he also saw that his enterprise was beset with many difficulties. He asked General McDougall to help him overcome these obstacles to success. For, he wrote, "when I am among Canadians, I shall have to be very French and talk a lot about French blood in order to win their hearts. I should like to have with me [an American] of sound judgement with an ardent love for his country, so that I may be in a position to counteract the suspicions which are unfortunately so widespread in a free people." He then asked for a larger number of French officers and soldiers as well as the service of Colonel Hazen's Canadian companies.[52] He even offered to guarantee the cost of the expedition by giving his properties as security, and he proposed to borrow five or six thousand guineas, to be spent in "gifts and pious offerings to priests' charities, etc."[53]

It was not long before La Fayette discovered that the invasion project was a screen for the personal intrigues of "two or three rascals," and since the Board of War did not clearly dissociate itself from these manoeuvres, he threatened to return to France and to take the French officers with him.[54] After having clarified his own position, he proceeded, according to instructions, to his headquarters at Albany, where he arrived on February 17. He soon discovered, however, that he had been grossly deceived as to preparations for the expedition which he was to command. Its organization was a nightmare of blunders, folly, and deception. Instead of 2,500 soldiers, there were 1,200 half-clad men. Not only had the General no uniforms for his troops, but he had only half the meagre sum of money which he had been promised. In these circumstances two experienced officers, Schuyler and Arnold, advised definitely against the undertaking. Hazen considered that the force was inadequate for the task, especially since the enemy was reported to be stronger than they had thought. Hazen's Canadians declared themselves ready to march but none of the other troops wanted to face a winter campaign.

Colonel Stark certainly deserved some of the blame for the lack of preparation, and Gates' inefficiency was quite inexcusable in "a future Commander-in-Chief of the American forces." La Fayette gave the explanation of the whole affair when he wrote that the expedition had been undertaken "to satisfy the ambition of one man,"[55] Gates himself. Proof of the truth of this explanation is to be found in the supplementary instructions which, in order to cover himself, Gates wrote "from memory," claiming that the earlier ones had been "lost." These instructions reveal the object of the expedition as limited to the destruction of the English boats at Saint-Jean.[56]

The directives issued by Congress indicate how uncertain this body was as to possible Canadian reaction to a new invasion. If Montreal or Saint-Jean were captured, La Fayette was to issue a proclamation inviting the Canadians to join the American army. However, if it seemed wiser to expect them to remain neutral, he was to solicit their neutrality in a manifesto. But, if the Canadian people showed no interest in an alliance with the Americans, La Fayette was to withdraw after destroying the boats on the Richelieu. Finally, if they did desire to establish their independence, he would urge them to accept the resolutions approved by the Colonies, to adopt continental currency, to send delegates to the Continental Congress, and to recognize the statutes of the Union.[57]

With the failure of the intrigue in favour of Gates, all these diplomatic instructions lost their reason for existence. Henceforth, it was merely a question of saving face. On February 24, Congress asked the Board of War to inform La Fayette that, if the strength of his force was inadequate for the projected operation, he was to take whatever action seemed best in the circumstances and not to expose his men to great risks. A few days later (March 2, 1778) Congress put an end to the whole affair. La Fayette was praised for his zeal and devotion, an order was issued for the suspension of the "present irruption into Canada,"[58] and the only result of the ill-conceived project of invasion was the ruin of Gates' reputation.

North of the frontier, Carleton had not been inactive, although Burgoyne's defeat had left an anxious population with the feeling that it was abandoned and defenceless. Adopting a scorched earth policy, the Governor ordered Brigadier MacLean to burn the forts at Mont-de-l'Indépendance and Carillon and the houses along the invasion route as far as Ile-aux-Noix.[59] He posted detachments of troops at possible points of entry into the country, reinforced all defence works, and established patrols to prevent the enemy from approaching the frontier.[60] In January, 1778, on learning that preparations for invasion were again going forward in Albany, he posted troops along the Richelieu, between Sorel and Saint-Jean,[61] and at the end of January militiamen were ordered to hold themselves in readiness. In case of an invasion, the salvation of the country would depend on the promptness with which they answered the first call to arms. Instructions were issued to arrest all suspects, and specifically anyone travelling without a passport. At the same time, orders were issued for the payment of gratuities to men who had

171

served in the campaigns of 1776, and their dependents: sixteen dollars to sergeants, twelve to wounded militiamen, eight to all other combatants, four to non-combatant members of the labour force, forty to widows, and sixteen to wives of prisoners, who also received a number of articles of clothing.[62]

In March, repatriated prisoners spread the rumour that the American army was preparing to attack the Canadian province. This time circumstances were quite different from those which had obtained in 1775. Reassured by experience and by the strength of the English forces, the Canadians were ready "to take up arms against the *Bostonnais*" if the latter again crossed the frontier.[63] Carleton went to Saint-Jean himself and at the same time sent orders to Tonnancourt and Longueuil to call up one-third of the militia in the districts of Three Rivers and Montreal. The call-up was answered promptly and the men were ready to march, when it was learned that the American expedition had been put off.[64] However, the false alarm had served to convince the Governor that, with the exception of Mascouche and Terrebonne, most of the disaffected parishes appeared to have changed greatly for the better.[65]

According to Sanguinet, a great news-gatherer, thirty-one militiamen from Mascouche refused to obey orders from their captain, "a bad-tempered drunkard, who treated his men unjustly." The captain complained to the commander in Montreal, who sent a detachment of soldiers to Mascouche. The soldiers robbed a number of houses and "violated several girls and women,"[66] but they also arrested the objectors, who appeared before a military commission presided over by Colonel Sevestre and Major Dupré. Twenty-three of the prisoners, those who were guilty of the lesser offences, were sent back to Mascouche and ordered to express submission to their captain. Charges were laid against the eight others, leaders in the revolt, but it was stipulated that they would appear before a criminal court, rather than the more severe court martial.[67]

13

THE FRANCO-AMERICAN ALLIANCE

Carleton succeeded by Haldimand. Anti-British policy in Versailles. Effect of the Franco-American alliance on Canadians. The Governor's activities and difficulties. Canada's place in France's self-interested foreign policy. Invasion recommended by Washington. Instructions to Admiral d'Estaing. Intervention of La Fayette. Opposition of Washington. A letter from La Fayette. Jautard's intrigues. D'Estaing's manifesto to Canadians. Its influence. Subsequent reaction.

AFTER the dissipation of the invasion threat in March, several months went by without incident. Then two events brought important modifications in the Canadian situation. The appointment of Burgoyne to command the army of invasion had been a severe blow to Carleton's pride and ambition, and he asked to be relieved of his position. His letter reached the Secretary of State in July, 1777, and in August, Lord Germain advised General Frederick Haldimand of his appointment as Governor of Canada and Commander of the military forces in that country.[1] Haldimand embarked for Canada in September, but his ship was delayed so long by contrary winds that in order to avoid the risk of ice in the St. Lawrence, it put back to England. In the spring of 1778, the new Governor set out again and, after a crossing which lasted eight weeks, reached Quebec on June 27, 1778.[2]

A Swiss Protestant soldier of fortune, Haldimand had fought under the flags of Sardinia and Holland before entering the British army in 1754. He had served under Amherst and spent

173

five years in Canada, three of them (1762-1764) as Governor of Three Rivers. His was not only an energetic and forceful personality, but a wisely intelligent and generous one, and his knowledge in his own profession was equalled by his knowledge of men. He promptly executed boldly-conceived plans, and an unusual capacity for work made it possible for him to be well informed on all aspects of a question. Imbued with the spirit of justice and humanity, he found pleasure both in books and in nature. As a man of the world he was fond of society, and as a diplomat he eschewed all racial and religious prejudice.

Before the new Governor arrived in Canada, a second event had changed the face of things. On February 6, 1778, France signed an alliance with the American colonies in revolt against the mother country. The alliance, which had been foreshadowed ever since the outbreak of hostilities, had come as the immediate consequence of the victory of the Colonial forces at Saratoga. Ever since the Seven Years' War had been brought to an end by the disastrous Treaty of Paris, France had been waiting for an opportunity to reduce the power of England and to restore her own prestige, and when the American Revolution broke out, her Minister of Foreign Affairs, the Comte de Vergennes, immediately considered the possibility of an American alliance. As early as August 7, 1775, he dispatched a secret emissary, the Chevalier Achard de Bonvouloir, to America. Driven by an imperious desire to humble the age-old enemy, Vergennes charged his envoy to inform the Americans, confidentially, that the King had no intention of reconquering his former colony, that France "was not even considering" such an idea.[3] For the time being, Louis XVI would merely permit Beaumarchais to act as his intermediary in supplying arms, while La Fayette and his companions, and others like them, could go to America and offer their services as volunteers.

The Colonies, whose forces were pitted against the vastly superior strength of the British army, were quick to appreciate the value of French material and military support. In July, 1776, a committee of Congress discussed a project of alliance with

France, a project in which the principle of future American policy with respect to Canada was also laid down. The Colonies could not forget the terror inspired by the devastating Canadian raids on their frontiers, nor their resentment at being cut off from the Ohio valley by colonists from Quebec. Their fear of seeing France once more established as their neighbour was quite as great as their fear of a British triumph. Thus the eighth article of the project of alliance proposed that the King of France should undertake never to attempt the recapture of Labrador, Nova Scotia, Acadia, or Canada.[4] In January, 1778, when, with a confidence born of their victory at Saratoga, the Colonies sent a delegation to the French government, one of the articles of their proposals for a treaty dealt with the same question. It stipulated that France should not invade Canada or any other country in America, or under any pretext acquire possession of any of them. The fixed idea of the Americans was a determination not to share with any foreign state American territory then under the jurisdiction of Great Britain.[5] The Franco-American treaty was signed in February and ratified by Congress on the fourth of May. Article V contained the famous stipulation that, if the United States conquered any British territory, that territory would become a part of the United States, and Article VI added the further stipulation that the King of France renounced *forever* the right of possession of any such territory.[6] These conditions, which were kept secret, destroyed in advance any hope which might be cherished by Canadians that for them the war might be the prelude of restoration to France.

Less than two months after the ratification of this treaty, Haldimand took up residence in the Château Saint-Louis. His most pressing task was to take stock of the situation, and he had been busy gathering information for some time. He had spent the interval since his appointment going through official correspondence, and he arrived in Quebec with a whole series of questions to be discussed with Carleton.[7] Once established in his post, he extended his investigation in every direction.

As Commander-in-Chief, he had under his order 4,409 British soldiers and 2,109 German auxiliaries. He had also, on paper, 462 American loyalists, and a militia force of 403 English and 17,714 French-Canadians. At Saint-Jean and on Lake Champlain there was a fleet of thirty-six war vessels and thirty-nine *bateaux* for transport.[8] Forts, both large and small, were in a very precarious state. The fortifications of Quebec were falling into ruin, and defence works at Ile-aux-Noix, Saint-Jean, and Chambly were quite inadequate.[9] Haldimand quickly realized that, while the clergy, the gentry, and some of the *bourgeois* in the towns gave their support to the government, he could not count on the other classes, especially in the event of a war with France, or if the English troops were forced to withdraw from the American colonies. The British population in Canada still counted many who favoured rebellion, and "who were indefatigable in their efforts to poison the minds of the Canadians and to swerve them from their duty and allegiance."[10]

News of the French alliance spread quickly. French papers, which the Americans were careful to send to Canada, attested to its authenticity and its importance,[11] and a few months later Haldimand observed that the event had produced an "inconceivable" change in the attitude of Canadians. "They were beginning to recognize their error; but when they heard of the arrival of a French fleet on our shores, they could not conceal their interest in the success of French arms."[12] Even those Canadians who were most closely attached to the government had been touched by an influence which was all the more powerful since they considered that the country was wide open to invasion, and that the British forces were quite inadequate for its defence.[13]

Although he was disturbed by this evidence of disaffection, the Governor hoped he could prevent the Canadians from "doing anything foolish," and even force them to do their duty.[14] Acting more promptly than his predecessor, he at once took steps to provide against the possibility of invasion.[15] Guards were established at all possible points of entry and parties of scouts were on constant duty.[16] In July, he republished the law authorizing the arrest of any person guilty of, or suspected of, treason,[17] thus protecting the country against the renewed danger of rebel agents bearing false news.[18] In carrying out his task, he could count on the services of influential Canadians. Commissioners Saint-Georges-Dupré in Montreal, Godefroi de Tonnancourt in Three Rivers, and François Baby in Quebec, kept a close watch on roads and transports, and three officers, Joseph de Longueil, J. F. Deschambault, and C. Lanaudière kept the militia in fighting trim.[19] The Governor could also count on support from the staff of three companies of volunteers[20] and the militia officers, while on Lake Ontario, Captain Bouchette commanded the Canadian crew of the brig *Seneca*.[21] Thus the defence organization covered the whole country.

One serious problem was still unresolved. Military provisioning depended upon corvées, and the habitants resented the obligation to provide a service which they found onerous and for which they were badly paid. They ignored orders to provide transport, even though such refusal entailed legal charges and fines.[22] The parishes were furious at having to transport provisions to the up-country posts or to haul firewood or comply with some other requisition,[23] and workers deserted at the first opportunity. The parishes of Saint-Martin, Sainte-Rose, Quinze-Chênes, and Vaudreuil were notorious in this respect.[24] Haldimand ordered that troops should be quartered on the recalcitrant parishes. He also ordered that a distinction be made between dutiful subjects and those who had failed in their duty, and that persons who had given proof of goodwill should have the best treatment possible.[25] In the Saint-Jean region, thanks probably to competent supervisors, corvées presented no problem. Colonel MacLean explained that particular pains had been taken to create no difficulties for the farmers, and that as a result those who were assigned, with their horses, to carry out a corvée came back from the job quite satisfied.[26] In Lachine also, supply corvées were carried out without difficulty.[27]

South of the frontier, the rebel colonies did not abandon the idea of bringing Canada into their union. During the negotiations with France, the congressional delegates "had proposed that the King undertake to promote the conquest" of the country. But although Louis XVI was willing to agree not to re-annex New France, he was not inclined to make any contribution towards its conquest by another country. Moreover, while France was glad to embarrass England by helping the Colonies, the object of her policy with respect to Canada was not the aggrandizement of the United States. On the contrary, the possession of Canada by England constituted "a useful source of anxiety to the Americans, which [would] make them conscious of their need for the friendship of the King and for an alliance with him."[28] The removal of this anxiety was not in the King's interest. The secret design of France, in giving up any possibility of reconquest and preserving Canada for the English, was to perpetuate a subject of opposition and animosity between England and the United States, and thus oblige the latter country to maintain friendly relations with France and resort to her for aid against their common enemy. After the ratification of the treaty, the Americans, who were completely unaware of France's attitude, returned to their project of invasion with greater confidence and greater enthusiasm than ever. In July, 1778, they gave serious consideration to the possibility of invading Canada during the following winter or spring. They had no doubts as to the success of such a venture and a fresh motive for action was their fear that "if England preserved Canada and Florida she would become dangerous for the United States during the peace."[29] Accordingly, in September, Washington submitted a questionnaire to General Bayley. Among the points on which he wished to be informed were the following: What was the strength of military forces in Canada? Were there any Canadians under arms? Were they volunteers or conscripts, and how many were they? What was the feeling of the people, and, more particularly, of the clergy, on the American question? Would the Canadians choose to join the Independent United States of America? On September 12, after receiving the infor-

The Death of General Montgomery

An east view of Montreal, an engraving by P. Canot, after the water-colour by T. Patten

mation for which he had asked, Washington recommended a plan of invasion, but he added the prudent restriction that the invasion should not be undertaken until the enemy had prepared the way for it.[30] In reply, Congress informed the Commander-in-Chief on September 16 that it fully approved his decision.[31] In short, the project was postponed to a more opportune moment.

At the beginning of July, 1778, a French fleet under Admiral d'Estaing had anchored in Boston harbour. A clause in the Admiral's instruction ordered him not to seek to establish himself anywhere on the American continent and to refuse to "contribute anything more to the conquest of Canada than a cruise or attacks upon outposts." The clause authorized him, however, in the event of a successful outcome to the projected invasion, "to issue declarations in the name of the King assuring Canadians and Indians of the King's protection if they ceased to recognize the sovereignty of England." France disclaimed any interest in reconquering her former colony for herself, and if the vague and ambiguous phraseology of d'Estaing's instructions appeared to suggest that she would support the American claim once the conquest had been achieved, it was because she believed such an outcome unlikely.[32]

Still ignorant of these secret instructions, and obsessed with the idea of acquiring Canada, Congress asked La Fayette, who had first suggested an invasion,[33] to sound out d'Estaing as to the possibilities of support for the expedition.[34] A letter was dispatched to Franklin in Paris, instructing him to solicit the co-operation of France, and finally, it was decided to send La Fayette himself to Paris to petition the King for a favorable answer to Franklin's request.[35] Public opinion in France, less forgetful of old ties than the ministers, was deeply interested in the idea of a possible reconquest of Canada. The idea, which was being openly discussed in February, 1779, had been in circulation in the seaports of France since 1774, when a memoir on the subject had been submitted to the government.[36]

Meanwhile, emissaries from Canada had reached Philadelphia. They bore messages couched in terms which revealed that "the large number of distinguished persons" whom they represented were British pro-rebels soliciting the help of the United States "to throw off the English yoke." They declared that the savages were ready to join the Americans as soon as they saw "white coats," (French uniforms), and that they themselves were on their way to see the French fleet with their own eyes. The messages emphasized the sympathy of Canadians for France, "the boundless affection which they had preserved" for the French nation. A successful expedition would assure a free Canada whose government would be in the hands of the French population. As a result, the fur trade and trade in general would fill the coffers of France with "wealth more solid" than the possession of Canada could ever bring her.[37] Congress still yearned after Canada, and with all these influences at work the project of invasion was again revived. D'Estaing, whose resistance gave way before the persuasive arguments of La Fayette, composed a "Declaration Addressed in the Name of the King to All Former French Subjects in North America." The manifesto, dated October 28, 1778, was printed on board the flagship *Languedoc*. Copies were then sent to Washington to await a favourable opportunity for dispatch to Canada.[38]

The new project of invasion adopted by Congress required a considerable force. One army would penetrate into Canada by the Saint-François valley while two other detachments would march on Detroit and Niagara. At the same time a French fleet would sail up the St. Lawrence as far as Sorel.[39] Following a resolution of October 22, the plan was submitted to Washington[40] who commented on it in a letter of November 11. He pronounced the scheme "not eligible" for the moment. If the English troops did not withdraw from New York and Rhode Island, these territories would have to be liberated, and in that case it would be impossible to provide men and provisions for a Canadian expedition. Moreover, a storm or an English fleet could prevent the junction of the French fleet with the American army. It must also be remembered that an advance by way of the Saint-François presented many serious difficulties. In a word, the plan was too complicated and too ambitious, and in any case the first essential task was to drive the enemy out of the Colonies. This task must be accomplished before Congress could embark upon any other undertaking.[41]

These were official reasons, intended to satisfy public opinion. Washington's real motive for refusal was revealed in a confidential letter to the President of Congress. He feared that possession of a former colony "would be too great a temptation to be resisted by any nation actuated by the common motives of national policy." If the French did succumb to the temptation to hold Canada for themselves, they would be masters of the fur trade and the Newfoundland fisheries. Still more serious, they would possess "the facility of awing and controlling" the United States.[42] Thus France's secret intentions had their counterpart in the Colonies' mistrust, diplomatically concealed, of their ally.

Washington's letters made a deep impression on Congress. At the same time, Gérard, the French minister taking part in the negotiations in Philadelphia, was instructed to remain vague on the question of the Canadian operation, and neither "to condemn nor to approve" it.[43] On December 5, in this atmosphere charged with apprehension, uncertainty, and secrecy, Congress adopted Washington's advice to postpone the invasion of Canada to a later date.[44] The plan still had its advocates, however, among them La Fayette and a certain number of important leaders. Finally, on January 1, 1779, a further report recommended that the expedition be put off until such time as circumstances should permit of more efficacious co-operation between the allied forces. The report was adopted, and La Fayette was duly informed of this action.[45] For the moment, the project was abandoned. This did not mean, however, that Congress had given up the hope of possessing Canada, in whole or in part, at some future date. On February 2, just a month after it had decided against an invasion, it instructed its delegates in France to claim, in any peace negotiations, all Canadian territory east of a line running from Lake Nipissing to the

Mississippi.⁴⁶ These instructions, practically unchanged, were renewed on August 14.⁴⁷

As the Americans cast covetous glances towards Canada, Haldimand maintained a vigilant watch. For months he had known that an invasion was in preparation and that American agents were infiltrating the country. In May, 1779, seven Colonial envoys passed through Baie Saint-Antoine and went on to Quebec. Two Canadians, Traversy from Saint-François, and Charles Champagne from Nicolet, as well as Indian messengers, travelled through the province assuring Colonial sympathizers that the Americans were about to return in considerable numbers. Meanwhile the Governor kept militia detachments on a war footing, and ordered farms and mills at Rivière-aux-Oignons to be destroyed so that they should not provide the enemy with provisions in case of an invasion.⁴⁸ Although propagators of tendentious news were being arrested and put in irons,⁴⁹ pro-rebels continued to announce an imminent invasion and to report that Traversy had left orders to buy wheat and cattle for the future invaders.⁵⁰

The news of the French alliance and the rumour of invasion were followed by reports of Admiral d'Estaing's proclamation to Canadians. Although the proclamation had been ready since the end of October, 1778, the Admiral was still keeping it in reserve in mid-November.⁵¹ On December 5, Gérard presented it to Congress,⁵² which body decided that it should be circulated in Canada. Two weeks later, on December 18, La Fayette wrote a letter inviting the Indians to unite with the French to drive out the English. For the King of France, he explained, having proclaimed his support of the Canadians, had also formed an alliance with the Americans, and desired to unite Canada and the Colonies.⁵³ Soon the American agents seized on the theme, and before long Canadians were telling one another that when spring came they would see a French fleet sailing up the river. The agents insisted brazenly that Canadians were under no obligation to take up arms to repulse invaders for, although France had ceded the soil of Canada, she had not ceded the inhabitants, who therefore continued to be French subjects.[54] Successive waves of news and rumours from the south, penetrating into the far corners of the province, stirred the deepest emotions of the people, who finally believed quite firmly and generally that a French fleet would come in the spring.[55]

Towards the end of winter, a brief sensation was created by an extraordinary proclamation, supposedly signed and counter-signed by Louis XVI and Washington respectively. In a style at once rhetorical, dogmatic, and coercive, "Louis de Bourbon, . . . King of France, Navarre, America, Canada, and other terri-tories," forbade Canadians to take up arms for the English on pain of "total and entire destruction of their property, and exile of their persons and their families." For, continued the pro-clamation, no punishment could be too severe for the criminal guilty of "completely forgetting his religion, denying his King, and forsaking his own happiness."[56] The proclamation, an obvious fabrication, whose author, Jautard, betrayed himself by the magniloquence of his style, was printed in Montreal on the presses of Fleury Mesplet. Both Mesplet and Jautard were Frenchmen in the service of the Colonials, who had remained in Montreal after the departure of the American army. They had founded the Montreal *Gazette* and they had already been guilty of violating previous promises by insulting the clergy and the bench in their journal. As a result of this fresh act of de-fiance, and in order to forestall others, the Governor issued orders for their arrest and imprisonment.[57]

D'Estaing's proclamation does not appear to have reached Canada during the winter. Its distributors were apparently wait-ing for the opening of navigation in order to send their consign-ment by water. Whatever the reason, the first copies did not appear at the church doors until the beginning of May, 1779.[58] They were brought in by Clément Gosselin and were distributed throughout the province, along with the letter from La Fayette to the Indians, by François Cazeau and his helper, the ex-Jesuit, Father Germain.[59] Before their arrest, Mesplet and Jautard had undertaken to circulate copies in Montreal.[60] D'Estaing's "manifesto" was accompanied by a declaration from Gérard, France's Minister to the United States, attesting that it had been published by order of the King of France to inform "nations which remain attached to his Majesty" of his friendship for the Americans and the help which he was granting to them.

The document was somewhat lengthy and diffuse, but its first sentence struck a cord of national pride in the hearts of Canadians of all classes: "You are French, you have not ceased to be French." After this clarion call, the manifesto went on to declare that although the war had separated them from what they held most dear, their mother country, it would be a crime for them to arm themselves against her.[61] For the King, entry into the war was unavoidable, and, if he asked Canadians to give proof of continuing attachment to their country, it was only in order to insure their happiness. He could promise that neither French arms nor those of her American allies or the Indians would inflict any damage on their country.[62] D'Estaing reminded the gentry that a French nobleman could serve only one King. He then declared to the French in America that they would be worthy of the King's favour "when they dared to become the friends" of his allies. The companions in arms of Lévis and Montcalm could not make war against the families of their former leaders.[63] The clergy was well aware that the Catholic faith must be able to rely on a protection which held no threat for the future, and incidentally, nowhere did the representatives of religion constitute a body more useful to the State than the priests of Canada.[64] Addressing itself to the mass of the Canadian people, the proclamation affirmed that a monarchy professing the same religion as they, following the same customs, and speaking the same language, would constitute for them a unique source of commerce and wealth. At the same time it would be better for all Canadians to be allies of powerful neighbours rather than the subjects of distant strangers who might treat them as a conquered people. Alliance with the United States could not fail to assure their future happiness, and Canadians who repudiated the authority of England could count on the protection and support of their former monarch.[65]

The proclamation was skilful, sometimes moving, but vague and general in its terms. To former subjects, who had fought to the end out of pride and attachment to the mother country, it brought neither the warmth of fraternal feeling nor the solace of hope. It announced neither the will to reconquer, nor the desire for reunion, not even a decision to send out a fleet. To brothers in blood and religious faith it offered only a cold invitation to alliance with a foreign Protestant power.

The diplomatic vagueness of its language did not prevent the manifesto from exerting a profound influence. Haldimand noted at once that the Admiral's message had added considerably to the difficulties of the moment.[66] The Franco-American alliance and the presence of a French fleet in American waters had brought about a profound change in the spirit of a weak and ignorant population, unable to foresee that they would become the slaves of the Americans if they became their allies.[67] As a result of a manifesto full of arguments designed to lure people of French blood, the government admitted that it was "surrounded by enemies," and that it could hope for little help from the province.[68]

Undoubtedly a change had come about; a chain of circumstances had created a reaction of French loyalty in the Canadian people. The clergy which, with the exception of the Jesuits,[69] "had generally conducted itself so loyally in 1775 and 1776," suddenly lost its zeal for the English cause. The change affected not only priests who had come from France, but natives of the province as well.[70] Although the French proclamation had been posted at the doors of churches with the knowledge of several curés, almost none of the latter sent copies to the authorities or reported the appearance of the placards. The only exceptions were the Abbé Porlier of Saint-Ours[71] and the Abbé Cherrier of Saint-Denis, both known as "most reliable" servitors of the government.

The presence of French troops in America and reproaches

185

addressed by the Bishops of France to their anti-rebel Canadian *confrères*[72] had so profound an effect that a few curés joined the ranks of the rebel partisans. One of the most fervent converts, the Abbé Gatien of Lotbinière, received the colonial agents with open arms and gave them every possible assistance. He dared not lodge them in the presbytery, for that would have been an act of treason, but he proclaimed energetically his attachment to the American cause.[73] As for the Abbé La Valinière, who, in 1776, had shown himself to be a "perfect rebel" at heart; the Governor and the Bishop were agreed that it would be wiser to dispatch him to France. He would serve as an example to his fellow priests to be more prudent and circumspect in their reactions to the Franco-American alliance.[74] Spies were sent out to observe the conduct of the curés, and one of these spies told a most unlikely story of a priest who, with five Indian companions, had called at Fort Edward on his way to the Continental Congress.[75] As a means of stemming the tide of French sentiment among the clergy and their charges, Haldimand conceived the idea of bringing priests from the Italian province of Savoy where the people spoke French but did not owe allegiance to the King of France. Such a move, he wrote, might inspire the Canadian clergy to a greater effort towards the loyalty which would win them the favour of the government.[76]

A mercenary in the service of a foreign power, Haldimand was incapable of judging the feelings and conduct of men except in relation to their utilitarian interests. He applied to the *noblesse* and the upper classes the measuring rod which he had used with the clergy, and argued that they had obtained more from the British government than they could hope to get from the French régime. He was surprised that after the conclusion of the Franco-American alliance the Canadian *élite*, with only a few exceptions, should manifest so little gratitude towards Great Britain. They ought to realize, or so it seemed to him, that if the province were conquered, Canadians would be ruled and exploited by the United States with no more substantial benefit than a very small proportion of their trade.[77] He did not understand that, in 1779, it was no longer simply a question of an Anglo-American quarrel. The atmosphere was profoundly modified by the miraculous presence of French forces right on the borders of Canada. Doubtless the partisans of 1775 and 1776 did become more fervent than ever, but it was not the American cause which rallied the people. One observer estimated that if the rebels invaded the province "without being accompanied by French forces," there would be "more spectators than actors among the Canadians."[78] Unless they saw the fleur-de-lis of France even the warmest rebel partisans would refuse to take up arms while the British held command of the river.[79]

In this climate the attitude of the people gradually became clarified: they all believed that a French fleet was coming and they awaited its arrival with joy. "Should a French ship or two make their appearance, Bougainville or any other French officer known to them, come with four or five hundred French or other men clothed in white, they most probably would take their part and appear in arms against us."[80] This was the opinion of Haldimand, who also "apprehended" that "any considerable misfortune . . . would raise the whole country. . . . And this opinion is not founded upon distant and precarious intelligence, but upon a precise knowledge of the general disposition of the inhabitants."[81] Confirmation of the Governor's impression is to be found in a statement made by a captain of militia and twelve other men "from different parishes below and above Saint-Charles." Less prudent than some of their compatriots, they informed the American scout Whitcomb that "provided the French would send a fleet into the river they would to a man take up arms in favour of the rebels."[82]

By 1779, American propaganda had inculcated the concept of political liberty in Canadians and converted them to the idea of opposition to the established authority. For, in spite of Haldimand's vigilance, the flow of propaganda kept on, at a slower pace but unremittingly. Winter and summer, emissaries and partisans, with a wary eye open for possible detection, spread rumours of an invasion, while agents eluded the authorities and circulated throughout the province.[83] In May, Traversy from Saint-François, Charles Champagne from Nicolet, and the Indian Jean Vincent Miron from Lorette went right into Quebec,[84] while Captain Clément Gosselin, Lieutenant Jean Goulet, and two private soldiers, Pierre Cadieux and Noël Bélanger, all members of Hazen's regiment, made various forays into Canada.[85] Agents such as these constituted an efficient American intelligence service,[86] while a Canadian, Longueville, formerly of Saint-Charles, served as a messenger to Congress.[87]

On the other side, Haldimand knew that Hazen had cut a road from Newbury on the Connecticut to the frontier, and that Whitcomb, Taylor, and Canadian partisans were working with the Saint-Charles captain of the militia and twelve of his men.[88] News from England echoed the rumour of a projected French naval expedition to the St. Lawrence,[89] to be carried out in conjunction with an American invasion.[90] Some of Montcalm's old soldiers and a group of disloyal subjects, almost all from south shore parishes, were busy spreading false news and disturbing rumours.[91] To combat their activities, the Governor kept scouts at the frontiers and on the highroads. He had lists drawn up of rebel partisans, their families and property, and of Frenchmen, soldiers, and others, established in the country.[92] He also kept a close watch on the Montreal cabals of which the two leaders, Mesplet and Jautard, had already been arrested.[93]

Not all Canadians, however, were carried away by this new wave of emotion and propaganda. D'Estaing's vague manifesto gave no evidence of a project, or even the intention, of reconquest, and as the hope of a French expedition became dimmer with every passing day, many disappointed Canadians preferred to lay their odds on present security and British superiority. In an uncertain situation they tended distinctly towards loyalism, and refused, after the experience of the American occupation, to align themselves with the Colonial rebels. Thus, in July, 1779, even after French troops had been incorporated into the

American army, twenty-nine Canadians who had been captured at Saratoga chose to remain prisoners rather than accept Hazen's urgent invitation to join his regiment.[94] At Three Rivers, in mid-winter, when a detachment was being formed to hunt down deserters, so many volunteers presented themselves that a great many who were determined to join had to be refused.[95] All things considered, it was difficult for Haldimand to attach any serious blame to the Canadians who were so deeply stirred by the call of France, and who, twenty years after the conquest, could not forget their mother country in favour of their age-old enemy.

14

FRENCH, AMERICAN, AND CANADIAN ATTITUDES

Discovery and destruction of a spy network. La Fayette's proclamation. France's policy of abstention. Canada's relations with the Continental Congress. Expectation and hope of a French expedition. Attitude of the clergy.

THE AUTUMN and winter of 1779 passed without bringing to Canada either a French fleet or an American army. On the other hand, Haldimand's posts and patrols did not arrest the movement of Canadian partisans and American emissaries between Canada and the Colonies.[1] In February, 1780, Pierre Berthiaume of Verchères came back from Cohoes with letters announcing an imminent invasion by the Saint-François route,[2] while other couriers brought news of English defeats and French victories.[3]

In his determination to identify the key figures in the network of correspondents the Governor had recourse to spies and *agents provocateurs*.[4] In April, 1780, a certain James Kenny was betrayed into the hands of the authorities by his Indian guide. Kenny was an employee of Charles Hay, a Quebec merchant, who, with the Abbé Gatien of Lotbinière as intermediary, was in communication with his brother Udney Hay, Quartermaster-General in Albany.[5] In 1775, the two Hays had refused to take part in the defence of Quebec and had left the city during the siege. François Cazeau, a rich French merchant who had been instrumental in the distribution of d'Estaing's proclamation, and who was working with Charles Hay, sent Kenny to carry certain information to the rebels. He had also offered, in the event of

190

an invasion, to raise men in the parishes of Châteauguay, Ile Perrot, and La Prairie, and to seize stores of wheat and equipment at Lachine. Kenny was apprehended at the end of March,[6] and Haldimand's orders for the arrest of Hay and Cazeau were carried out on April 10.[7] Thus several links in the chain were broken.

Although Congress had decided in January, 1779 against invasion, the project of conquest came to life again the following year. The presence of Hazen and his Canadian officers, and the construction of a road from Cohoes to the frontier encouraged the idea of an expedition. Moreover, there existed in almost every quarter "a general tendency . . . towards an attempt against Canada." According to La Luzerne, France's new representative in Philadelphia, "the eastern states did not limit their desire to setting Canada free;" they also aspired to conquer it, not to keep it, but to be in the position of masters when the time came to "dictate" frontier lines. For Canada would be a trump card in the hands of the Americans when peace terms were being discussed. La Fayette had always cherished an ambition to liberate his Canadian compatriots, and, since the idea had once more become a popular one, he became its active advocate.[8] Massachusetts, which viewed the independence of Canada as its own safeguard, was altogether in favour of the project. The Massachusetts delegate, Samuel Adams, supporting it in Congress, declared that the expedition would realize the deepest desire of his heart.[9] But when the plan was submitted to Washington, he neither accepted it nor rejected it completely. For the moment, the project could serve a useful purpose by worrying the Canadian authorities. Fear of invasion would tie down Haldimand's troops, and the Canadian people could not but be deeply affected by the presence of French troops beside the Americans. Washington therefore wrote to La Fayette in May, 1780 to suggest that he issue a false proclamation bearing his own signature and inviting Canadians to unite with the Franco-American troops in order to bring their country into the American union. To add another complication to the stratagem, Washington proposed to issue a second apocryphal notice proclaiming the arrival of French troops and exhorting the population to take up arms.[10]

La Fayette himself composed the proclamation. Speaking in his own name, and free of all political responsibility, the young officer allowed his enthusiasm full play, and as he struck the note of remembrance of the mother country his tone was more frankly emotional than that of d'Estaing. It was love of Canadians he wrote, and the desire to liberate them, which had moved the King of France to detach a fleet and an army to America. Now the time had come when Canada, restored to herself, could unite with the thirteen American states. Canadians had not ceased to glory in the French blood which flowed in their veins. Under the constitution which they would give themselves, clergy, nobility, and people would see their religion, their privileges, and their customs flourish. No longer would they suffer the scorn of a foreign master. For the King and Congress knew that love of liberty would rally them under the French flag. Still following Washington's suggestion, La Fayette then announced that he would command the American army which would accompany the French troops marching to deliver Canada. In the name of the King, he invited the *noblesse* and the inhabitants in general to join the armies and to provide them with whatever help they might require. The present message urged Canadians to "break their fetters;" when General Rochambeau arrived at the head of the French troops, he would publish "a more particular invitation to join Canada to the Confederacy of the United States."[11]

Before composing his spurious proclamation, La Fayette informed the French minister La Luzerne of his intention, and explained that the trick was designed to deceive Haldimand. Some copies of the document, which was to be printed secretly, would be allowed to fall into the hands of the English authorities in New York, while the rest of the edition would be burnt on the arrival of the French troops.[12] Meanwhile, Washington also instructed Benedict Arnold to have 500 copies made.[13]

Everything went according to plan; the copies reached the headquarters of General Clinton in New York, and Clinton lost no time in sending an English copy to Haldimand.[14]

As for Arnold's copies, a certain number of them must have reached Canada by way of the rebels in New York. For in the course of the summer, in order to forestall any premature manifestation, La Fayette sent two emissaries, Clément Gosselin and Amable Boileau, to warn the inhabitants of the province to "do nothing" until the Franco-American forces should give the word for them to declare in their favour.[15] The existence of copies of the proclamation in Quebec would explain the fact that the rebel partisans Du Calvet and Pilon were soon sending their communications from Montreal direct to La Fayette.

Protected by his instructions from the contagion of La Fayette's enthusiasm, La Luzerne refused to commit himself, even verbally, in any such adventure as a Canadian expedition, and the letter in which he reported the matter to the Minister of Foreign Affairs, the Comte de Vergennes, is imbued not only with prudence but with a deep sense of honesty. "It would be wrong to incite former subjects of our Kings to throw off the yoke of England unless they could be sure of maintaining their independence." Not only were there political advantages in leaving the English in possession of Canada and keeping the American colonies dependent upon French support, but also it would "be odious to offer the lure of independence in order to incite Canadians and Acadians to rebellion." For some of the Colonial leaders were unwilling to guarantee that Canada would continue to be independent. These men proposed to have Canada available for exchange in case any states of the Union should still be in English hands when the treaty came to be signed.[16]

Congress was finally convinced by the French argument that it was more important to deliver the states occupied by English troops[17] than to invade the neighbouring province, however "glorious" or "easy" the conquest of that province might be.[18] At the same time, Washington, who had lost none of his fear of repossession of Canada by France, continued to advise that Congress abandon the idea of "any foreign expedition."[19] But the invasion party remained undefeated. On August 30, the people of the Connecticut valley held a meeting to urge the acquisition of Canada as a measure of protection for their frontiers. The conquest, they claimed, would be an easy one since Canadians now desired it themselves; it would give 30,000 soldiers to the Union, and it would "destroy the effects of the Quebec Act."[20]

On that same date, August 30, 1780, the Comte de Rochambeau, commander of the French troops which had just disembarked, presented a message to the Canadian Indians who had come to greet him at Newport. The message was an invitation from the King of France, who was still their father, to join the Americans and their French allies against the English.[21] The King's message was carried back to Canada and duly distributed among the tribes.[22] At this juncture, Washington himself, finally convinced that France was sincere in her engagement not to recapture Canada, made proposals to La Luzerne for the organization of a Canadian expedition. The proposal was repeated several times, and each time the minister gave a diplomat's answer: "The King was no less desirous than the United States of restoring the liberty of a province whose people were French. . . . But his Majesty wished to postpone this conquest until such time as he had delivered the United States from the oppression under which they groaned."[23] As the southern states were still in the hands of the English, the answer, couched in diplomatic language, was a decision to postpone the matter indefinitely. The Minister of Foreign Affairs signified to La Luzerne that his answer was in complete accord with the opinion of the government of France.[24]

After the autumn of 1780, the project of a Franco-American expedition ceased to figure in military plans. The rumour was kept alive, however, since the Americans saw in it an instrument for opening a breach between Canada and England, retaining

British forces within Canada's frontiers, and removing any temptation they might have to cross the frontier.

On the Canadian side, Major Carleton organized an active service of espionage along the border.[25] Agents operating from a base at Saint-Jean posed as English deserters or American emissaries,[26] but vigilant Canadian partisans kept close watch on the movements of the English scouts and made it very difficult for them to catch the rebels' couriers.[27] Finally Azariah Pritchard, a skilful counter-spy who had a brother in the American army, discovered the "head of the snake" in Montreal. It was a certain Dr. Pilon who had a son serving with the rebels, and who "corresponded constantly" with Hazen. In June, 1780, Pilon had a group of agents ready to set out[28] as soon as they received the plan of the Quebec fort which was to be supplied by the French Protestant Du Calvet, who, since 1775, had held a commission as an American officer.[29] Pilon confided to Pritchard a dispatch reporting, among other things, that in the event of an invasion Canadians who were unwilling to fight would remain neutral "provided the colours . . . were white," that is, provided they were the colours of France.[30] A few weeks later, on August 13, one of Pilon's messengers was intercepted[31] and his dispatches were handed over to Major Carleton.[32]

Over a period of years Du Calvet had maintained a correspondence with agents on the other side of the border. In 1779, he had undertaken to supply provisions to the invaders,[33] and he had been in contact with the pro-rebels of the Chambly river and their leader, Dr. Lalaine of Saint-Mathias. He held conferences in Montreal with Pilon and the American agents, and he maintained a secret store of weapons for a hundred men.[34] He also collaborated with Pilon to compose letters to Washington and La Fayette, and to Congress. The writers offered their services to an army of invasion. They requested commissions signed by La Fayette and they promised help in men and supplies.[35] The names of Washington and La Fayette were cut out of the letter to Congress, and the slip of paper containing them was concealed in a ball of lead which could easily be thrown away if the bearer should be captured.[36] But a member of the counter-intelligence service turned the letters themselves over to Pritchard who sent them on to Major Carleton.[37]

Armed with these documents, General MacLean in Montreal immediately signed an order to apprehend Pilon and Du Calvet. When he was arrested on September 26, 1780,[38] Pilon admitted that he had written the letters.[39] Du Calvet, who was on his way to Quebec, was arrested in Three Rivers the following day.[40] He was incarcerated in Quebec, but Cramahé ordered that he should be treated "with complete humanity" and that he should be allowed to receive "refreshments and provisions at his choice from the innkeeper Le Moine." He could not communicate with the outside except with the permission of the Governor,[41] who allowed it to be understood, however, that he wished "the private interests" of Du Calvet to suffer as little as possible from his imprisonment.[42]

Two other accomplices, Pierre Charland and Louis Nadeau from the Richelieu country, had been locked up as a result of having offered their services to the Americans.[43] François Breton in Lorette[44] and François Germain in Cap-Santé[45] were apprehended for having given hospitality to American agents. Warned by these arrests, the pro-rebel partisans became extremely circumspect. Their meetings in Montreal, which they had been in the habit of holding in Pilon's house in the Saint-Laurent suburb, were moved to the house of a man called Metcalf. Promoted as a result of the move to leadership in the band, Metcalf was a most generous host, although no one knew the source of the money which paid for his hospitality.[46]

The arrests had little effect, however, on the psychological climate. Emotion born of La Fayette's proclamation once more revived the hope and the belief that a French fleet would appear in the St. Lawrence.[47] In June, 1780, at least two men, Gérard and Boileau, were so completely convinced that this would happen that they set out for Quebec, meaning to go down the river to meet the ships and deliver dispatches to their officers.[48] Even as late as September, Baptiste Labonté and Jean Goulet came back from the Colonies and reported that the French and the Americans would soon be in Canada.[49] When news of an invasion reached Montreal, "the whole town, *generally* was pleased."[50] To this atmosphere of expectancy must be attributed the attitude of several militia captains who refused, during the course of the summer, to summon men for corvées,[51] as well as that of certain men who, when called for military service, cited a non-existent provision and claimed that they were not obliged to obey orders, "since the twenty-one years of the capitulation had expired."[52] There is no doubt that the hope of French intervention revived and increased the activity and boldness of the pro-rebels. American agents knew they would be sheltered in certain houses at Saint-Jean, Saint-Mathias, and Verchères. The men of Saint-Pierre-les-Becquets affirmed boldly that they were "all good rebels." Habitants in Lachine, Ile Jésus, Terrebonne, and Sainte-Thérèse stated frankly that they were resolved to support an army of invasion. Several parishes in the Quebec region, Deschambault, Cap-Santé, les Ecureuils, Saint-Antoine, and Sainte-Croix sheltered agents and transmitted their messages. The miller of Pointe-aux-Trembles opened his door to anyone who rapped on the window and gave the password: *Bostonnais*. While awaiting an opportunity to pass on correspondence, the Abbé Gatien placed it for safe keeping in the tabernacle of his church at Lotbinière.[53]

The messages from d'Estaing and La Fayette, and the prospect of seeing the fleur-de-lis once more in the St. Lawrence fanned the spark of French patriotism, more or less ardent according to circumstances, which every Canadian cherished in the bottom of his heart. Afraid to reveal a hope so uncertain of realization, the French population remained discreetly silent on the possibility of reconquest of the country by France. But the English observed and commented upon the effects of this hope. One officer reported that "the inhabitants [seemed] universally to have lost all their allegiance to the government which [protected] them."[54] The people were so deeply moved by the report of a French fleet "nearby" that they were inclined "to rebellion."

197

In the event of an invasion, the authorities should be prepared for an increasing number of treasonable acts.[55] According to Haldimand, people confidently expected that a French fleet would reconquer the country. His pragmatic point of view made it difficult for him to understand that their national sympathies could make them forget their favourable political situation, but it was his opinion, nevertheless, that a French invasion would spark a revolt in a great part of the province.[56]

The feelings which were now being restrained would burst out when the great day came. But how did the people react to the existing situation? Du Calvet and Pilon talked of raising 200 men to support a purely American invasion,[57] but there were only fifty or sixty names on the list that Pritchard saw.[58] Pierre Charland promised to raise a hundred men in six days, but he recruited no more than thirty volunteers, and they were unwilling to bear arms.[59] Pilon did not dare to claim that the people would rise; his dispatch stated merely that "those who were unwilling to participate, would not oppose."[60] Obviously, the American cause could not even count on friendly neutrality.

But what would happen if there were French troops with the Americans? The evidence suggested that a large number of Canadians would co-operate with them, but that, as long as the outcome was in doubt, the majority would take no active part in the struggle. Pierre Charland realized that the attitude of the people was one of expectancy rather than ardent aspiration. He thought the French flag "might rally 600 men, and that, as the habitants seemed disposed to favour the French, they would all be generally helpful." Dr. Lalaine considered that it would be a good thing if the French came, for they were "compatriots,"[61] and there was no doubt that in every parish a number of habitants would forsake their British allegiance at the approach of a French army.[62]

On the other hand, the government could count on the loyal services of leading Canadians, the Babys, the Lanaudières, the Tonnancourts, the Saint-Georges-Duprés, and the most influential militia officers. The zeal of the *noblesse* was perhaps somewhat less ardent than before the Franco-American alliance, but most of them would remain faithful "to their duty and their honour,"[63] for they knew that the Quebec Act was a sacred charter granted by the King and Parliament and guaranteeing their religion and their laws.[64] Most militia officers gave zealous service,[65] and militiamen collaborated in the capture of rebel agents.[66] If he were faced with the prospect of a purely American invasion, Haldimand could be sure of support from the Canadian *élite* and most captains of militia. The question as to what might be the effect of French flags and French martial music remained unsolved.

For the moment, the question did not arise; Congress had to think of defending its own territory, and now that the troops in Canada had been reinforced by 1,000 British soldiers, there was little prospect of success for an invading army.[67] So, although hearts were stirred by the idea of a return of the fleur-de-lis, the Canadian people continued to be torn between French patriotic sentiment, fear of American domination, and loyalty to a government which had recognized all their rights. One particularly disturbing factor in the situation was France's attitude. Far from promising that Canada would be restored to her, the mother country was abandoning her former colony to the mercy of the American invader. In such a complex situation, the Canadian could only wait resignedly and allow events to decide for him. The French fleet was not ready to sail, the American army had not crossed the border, while in Quebec the British flag flew above a fortress manned by thousands of British soldiers.

What was the attitude of the clergy in this new situation? The zeal of their British loyalty was certainly somewhat cooler than it had been.[68] Haldimand reported that, after d'Estaing's manifesto and La Fayette's letter, a good many priests had altered their opinions and that in the event of an invasion, they would adopt another rule of conduct.[69] A number of them were already active in the American cause. The Abbé Gatien used his church at Lotbinière as a post-office for the handling of rebel mail, while his *confrère* in Bécancour gave hospitality to American agents and supplied them with provisions.[70] Haldimand suspected certain priests, the Jesuits among them, of corresponding with the French generals in the United States.[71] On the other hand, Mgr. Briand had full confidence in his clergy and in its "zeal for the King's service."[72] He also paid tribute to M. de Montgolfier's work and the "zeal and activity of the Montreal Seminary." Moreover, at this date (1780), curés were still refusing absolution to pro-rebels. One such example is that of the curé of Sainte-Geneviève, who refused to administer the sacrament to Joseph Pouchet, known as Lavigne.[73] The Bishop himself remained unshakable in his loyalty. In January, 1781, a circular letter instructed curés to urge farmers to thresh and store their wheat in order to keep it out of the hands of the enemy. At the very moment when the hope of French intervention was being revived, he reminded his clergy that there were still rebel partisans in the country, and pronounced this rousing directive: "It would be a most monstrous insult if I were to believe you capable of violating your oath of fidelity to a government under which we have been happy up to this time. Be on guard then, and if you discover traitors do not hide them, but expose them as you have sworn to do."[74] Canadians had sworn loyalty to the English authority. As Mgr Briand interpreted the doctrine of the Church, they had only one duty: loyalty to the established order.

15

THE LONG ROAD TO PEACE

Range of Canadian opinion. Anti-American and pro-French feeling. Loyalty of the clergy. Project of invasion put off by Americans. Persistence of Haldimand's anxiety. Suggestion of invasion renewed by Washington. Peace parleys. Treaty of Paris. Departure of Haldimand from Canada. Canada and the Peace.

IN SPITE of messages from d'Estaing and La Fayette, reports from spies, and rumours from every source, the year 1780 went by, as the year 1779 had done, without a single French officer crossing the Canadian border, and without a single French sail being sighted on the St. Lawrence. However, American agents continued their policy of announcing an imminent invasion, and thus kept Haldimand's forces immobilized behind their own frontier.[1] In order to be ready for any eventuality, and to make it impossible for invaders to live off the country, the Governor issued a proclamation (January 15, 1781) ordering farmers to thresh their wheat so that it could more easily be stored in a safe place.

After two years of waiting, Canadians were beginning to lose faith in stories of a French intervention constantly delayed. The latent exultation of the first days was giving way to a growing incredulity. The people who, in December and January, heard reports of Saint-Aulaire coming back with French troops, observed sceptically that the enemy could not invade Canada during the winter.[2] Hopes for the miracle were becoming fainter every day, but if French troops did come with an invading army there was no doubt as to the reaction of the people. They would be unanimous in their refusal to fight,[3] since, as everyone said, "the French belong to our nation."[4] Haldimand did not even expect them to remain inactive. He was convinced, on the contrary, that if French soldiers were present in the country a large number of Canadians would take up arms, and that most of them would serve as guides, provide supplies, and give every possible assistance.[5]

On the other hand, if the rebels should cross the frontier without accompanying French troops, several parishes declared themselves ready to fight against them, and for two excellent reasons.[6] The first was the painful memory of the American occupation. The second, and much more important reason, was the presence of imposing British forces under the orders of an "active" general. This fact had a profound significance for Canadian opinion.[7] It explains the action of the French-Canadian citizens of Montreal who, in January, 1781, joined their British co-citizens to present addresses bearing hundreds of signatures, expressing their desire to participate in the defence of the country.[8] In February, the English and French citizens of Quebec also offered to fight off invaders,[9] and Three Rivers followed their example.[10] Haldimand did not place much faith in such official declarations, but he took care to publish them in the *Quebec Gazette*, for "the merchants in the towns [gave] the tone to the traders in the country who had but too often been the instruments of retailing sedition and rebellion to the ignorant inhabitants."[11]

In contrast with these declared loyalists, a number of Canadians in the country districts, and even in Montreal, maintained their resolve to remain neutral and their hostility to military service. "It was not their business," they said, "to fight."[12] Their one desire was to be left in their own homes, and many of them argued that they were not bound by any oath of allegiance.[13] Furthermore, there was a strong current of dissatisfaction in certain parishes where subjects who had remained loyal in 1775 had received no better treatment than pro-rebels.[14] Another cause of discontent lay in the rough treatment to which habitants had been subjected by the German troops. English officers had sometimes had to intervene in disputes over billets or requisitions, and they were not always successful in preventing the mercenaries from bullying farmers and even attacking curés.[15]

A few parishes, of which Saint-Ours was one, were animated by a definitely hostile spirit. Individuals in these parishes paraded their "anti-English" sentiments and remained in communication with the rebels, generally through members of their families serving in the United States.[16] Although correspondence between the Colonies and their English and French partisans had slowed down after the arrest of the Du Calvet group, it was still carried on from Sainte-Anne, Saint-Jean,[17] Saint-Ours,[18] and a number of other parishes. Metcalf of Montreal and Pierre Chicoine of Saint-Charles[19] were very active, and in November four suspects were arrested, as well as three men known to be correspondents.[20] Two of the suspects were released on bail,[21] because, as Haldimand wrote, "the liberty of the subject being by our laws very sacred, it is necessary that suspicion should be well founded to justify imprisonment."[22] The procedure of allowing suspects to remain free on parole, which was the Governor's own idea, combined the advantages of not filling up the prisons needlessly and not separating the accused from their families and their business. At the same time, the government was protected from the possibility of disloyal activities on their part.[23] Accordingly, a number of suspects were released on their own personal bail, while in other cases, bail was provided by a third party.[24]

Expectancy, uncertainty, and conflicting waves of influence all combined to create a complex and disturbing atmosphere in which a large majority of the people were hostile to a purely American invasion, a small minority favoured the rebels, and virtually all felt an instinctive impulse to fight under the French flag, if the fleur-de-lis should appear on the Canadian horizon. Even the gentry and the clergy, although they were strongly opposed to any American influence, and although they were sensible of the advantages of the current régime, felt the emotional appeal within them. For if Canada were restored to France, the past would be reborn and they would once more know the delight of living among brothers in race and religion in a society unhampered by any foreign presence.[25]

But by the middle of 1781, the country's leaders had abandoned all hope of a French reconquest. They had observed that d'Estaing's manifesto, even though it held out the possibility that France might recapture the country, did not suggest that Canada would be restored to the mother country, but rather that it should join the American confederation.[26] When the French forces left Boston to march against the English positions in the south, the news spread quickly to Quebec and brought with it the realization that there was no place for a Canadian expedition in Rochambeau's plans.[27] Whatever their inmost feelings may have been, the members of the nobility did not falter in the accomplishment of their duty, and the clergy continued to exhort its charges to act as loyal subjects.[28] Haldimand recognized the value of this support from the parish priests, and from the Sulpicians, "the most useful and zealous" in their service to the government.[29] Among the curés of country parishes who were particularly helpful in supporting government measures were the curé of Chambly, the Abbé Demers of Saint-Pierre-les-Becquets, and the Abbé Porlier of Saint-Ours.[30] The Bishop held firmly to the doctrine of obedience to the established authority, and even as late as 1782, he required that a rebel who had expressed the desire to recant, should kneel at the door of the church with a votive candle in his hand, and ask pardon for his sin.[31]

The winter of 1780-1781 went by without any pretence at preparations south of the border for a Canadian campaign. The absence of any kind of activity might justify the Canadian opinion that a winter expedition was not being undertaken because it would meet with insurmountable obstacles. With the return of summer, however, rumours were once more set on foot, while the rebels gave colour to the tales of their agents by beginning to build boats on Lake Champlain. Alarmed by these preparations, Haldimand continued to urge on the Secretary of State the necessity for sending out more troops, for he remained convinced that, without the means of "forcing them to do their duty," he could not count on the Canadians.[32] Lord Germain tried to allay his fears with information which had been gathered by British intelligence agents. According to this information, La Luzerne had been instructed to advise Congress against undertaking any project of invasion until after the southern colonies had been liberated.[33] For the policy of Louis XVI and his ministers was still to leave England in possession of Canada. With such a weapon trained on them and threatening their independence, the United States would be entirely dependent upon French help and would therefore maintain their friendship and their trade with France.

Lord Germain had been correctly informed. In the autumn of 1781, when Washington suggested to the French minister the idea of a Canadian expedition or at least a Canadian diversion, La Luzerne reminded him that the policy of the King of France was to liberate the United States before helping them to make conquests, and that it would be particularly unwise to undertake any such adventure at a moment when the difficulties which they were experiencing might lead the southern colonies to treat separately with England.[34] After allowing this new suggestion of invasion to drop, Congress appeared to lose all interest in the Canadian situation and even in its Canadian sympathizers, and on October 18, 1781, it adopted a resolution stipulating that Canadians who had been receiving help in return for past services would not receive pay or rations after December 31, 1781.[35]

Naval construction on Lake Champlain had not been the only cause of Haldimand's anxiety. He was also alarmed by Guichen's naval victory over Rodney in April, 1781, and Rochambeau's military victory over Cornwallis at Yorktown on October 19. Would not the victorious French troops now join an American expedition into Canada, and would they not have the support of the Canadian population, perhaps even of the clergy? A letter written by the Abbé de Lotbinière in Paris on March 6, 1781 had announced that an invasion would be launched in fourteen or fifteen months. And once the southern provinces had been reconquered, France would no longer be able to persist in her refusal to participate in the expedition.

In the spring of 1782, although he had no specific basis for his fears, Haldimand was still anxious. He was conscious of a ferment of pro-French sentiment.[36] Some Canadians gave credence to the fantastic rumour that the Pope would free them from their oath of allegiance to England if they recognized France as their mother country. To the familiar tales of invasion and concentration of American forces in Albany were added new ones of Canadians being supplied with arms by France and of a projected French naval attack on Halifax.[37] All these stories are, of course, evidence of the activities of American agents and British and Canadian pro-rebel partisans.[38] At the same time some individuals openly expressed anti-British feelings. A considerable number of men refused to obey the order for corvées.[39] When Rodney had his revenge on the French fleet and the English citizens of Montreal were celebrating his victory, the people in the Saint-Laurent *faubourg* refused to put lights in their windows, and fought with English sailors who tried to force them to follow the accepted custom.[40] Such incidents were hardly reassuring, and Haldimand kept himself informed of the temper of the people by maintaining a network of secret agents throughout the country.[41]

The Governor took the opportunity offered by these various symptoms to explain to the new Secretary of State, Lord Shelburne, his system of surveillance. In a country surrounded by enemies, populated by former French subjects and British citizens of whom many were in sympathy with the rebel colonies, he kept suspects under observation but at the same time maintained the fiction that he knew nothing of their intrigues. In a few particularly flagrant cases, however, he ordered arrests in the interests of the country's safety. He did not bring the suspects to trial, but detained them temporarily. Then, when the proper time had come, he released them. Although it was suggested that they might be sent to Halifax, he preferred to keep them in prison in the province, where they could look after their personal affairs.[42] This system of arrest and detention broke important links in the chain of communication with the rebels and at the same time reduced political agitation and subversion to a minimum.[43]

In the American colonies two years had passed without any military action directed towards Canada. However, after the failure of his project for a Canadian campaign in 1781, Washington returned to the attack in 1782. On May 1, he drew up on paper the plan of an expedition of enormous strength, considering the time and the circumstances, for he was convinced that the annexation of Canada was a matter "of great concern" to the United States. He proposed to conquer the country with an army of 8,000 men supported by a naval force of 2,000. Hostilities would begin in September, when the roads would be in good shape and supplies plentiful, and when it would be too late in the year for England to send reinforcements by sea. The invasion would follow the Richelieu route, and collaborating French troops would prove to Canadians not only that France was an ally of the United States, but that their mother country was an active partner in the Canadian expedition.[44]

Washington's grandiose plan came too late to be submitted to Congress and the French minister. In October, 1781, with the disastrous defeat of Cornwallis by the Franco-American troops at Yorktown, Great Britain lost all hope of coming out victorious from the long struggle. Moreover, continuation of the conflict would entail still greater losses and was likely to make irreconcilable enemies of her former colonies. On February 22, 1782, General Conway proposed in the House of Commons that hostilities should be brought to an end, and on March 4, Parliament adopted a resolution in favour of peace.

Haldimand, who had taken no military initiative since 1778, was considering the possibility of creating a diversion on the frontier, when a letter of June 20 from Carleton, now Commander-in-Chief of British forces in America, informed him that henceforth, in view of the possibility of peace, all operations must be confined to measures of defence.[45] Three days after the arrival of Carleton's letter, Haldimand received one from the Secretary of State. Shelburne's letter, which had been written on April 22, contained the information that although a French fleet was expected to sail from Brest with the possible objective of an attack on Quebec, the government had decided to refrain from further offensive action as well as from any act indicative of an intention to reduce the colonies by force.[46] The reception of this letter, in August, 1782, closes the chapter of military operations and plans in Canada.[47]

Although Haldimand was convinced that Rodney's naval victories had made it impossible for the French fleet to take part in any Canadian invasion, he continued to take precautions against the improbable possibility of an American invasion by strengthening the fortifications of Quebec and Ile-aux-Noix.[48]

There was no longer any ground for Haldimand's fears. Lord North had resigned on March 20, 1782, and Lord Rockingham had become Prime Minister. One of the first acts of the new Secretary of State, Lord Shelburne, was the appointment of a British representative, Richard Oswald, who at once opened negotiations with the American plenipotentiaries. Negotiations continued until November 30, 1782, when the two parties reached an agreement and signed preliminary articles, a copy of which reached Haldimand on April 26, 1783. The definitive treaty of peace between Great Britain and the newly-established United States was concluded on September 3, 1783.

In actual fact, the war had practically ended in June, 1782, when Carleton arrived in New York with instructions to limit his activities to defensive measures. On April 23, 1783, Congress adopted a resolution expressing its gratitude to Canadian officers and soldiers who had served with the American forces, and its intention of rewarding their "virtuous suffering in the cause of liberty." It proposed to offer them grants of land,[49] but it was not until fifteen years later, in 1798, that a law sanctioned land grants to refugees from Canada and Nova Scotia.[50] A tract of land was selected in the region of the present city of Columbus, Ohio, but these lands were not attributed definitively until 1801. The state of New York moved more rapidly than the Union. In the autumn of 1783, Colonel Hazen and the little group of Canadians in his regiment were settled on land on Lake Champlain,[51] and a law of May 11, 1784 distributed lands in the northern part of the state to Canadians, 1,000 acres to officers and 500 to other refugees.[52]

The arrests of Hay, Cazeau, Du Calvet, and Pilon had been officially approved by the Cabinet. The date of their liberation from detention had been left to the discretion of the Governor,[53] who released them on May 2, 1783.[54] Haldimand embarked for England on November 16, 1784, at the end of his term of office. He had governed the country with a firm and just hand through years of difficulty and danger, maintaining public order, respect for the law, and the integrity of Canada's frontiers. The excellence of his work is a measure of the quality of a man who has too often been judged by the false, unjust, and spiteful portrait drawn by the traitor Du Calvet.[55]

The Peace brought to an end the longest war that North America had experienced up to that time. For Canada's clergy and gentry, it ended the haunting nightmare of a choice between fighting against their brothers from France, who offered them liberty under the dubious protection of the United States, and betraying their allegiance to the country which had recognized all their national and religious rights. For all classes of the population it extinguished the star of a hope scarcely visible above the horizon, the hope that the children who had not forgotten their mother country might be restored to her. After years of turmoil, uncertainty, and upheaval, including a long period of invasion and occupation, peace finally took possession of the country. It restored civil liberty and religious harmony, and made the way free for political evolution and the development of independent trade. Canada resumed once more her march towards a destiny of labour and confidence, of expansion and hope.

A view of Quebec, the capital of Canada, taken from the rock on Point Levi, an aquatint after the original by Wm. Peachey (James Peachey)

A south-west view of St. Johns, a water-colour by J. Peachey, after the original view by J. Hunter

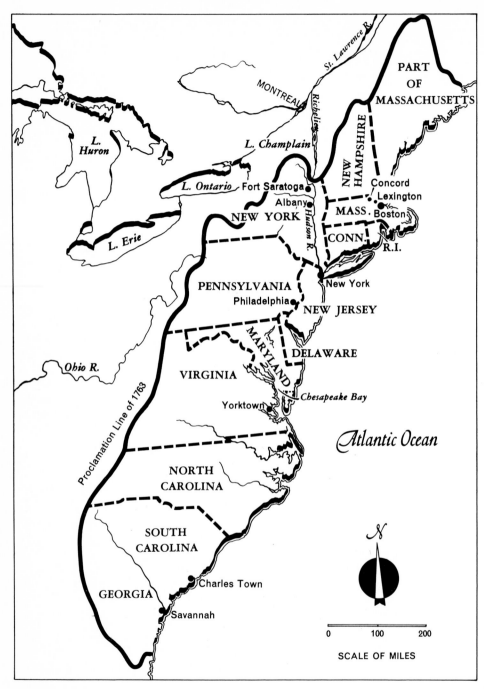

Canada and the American Colonies, 1774

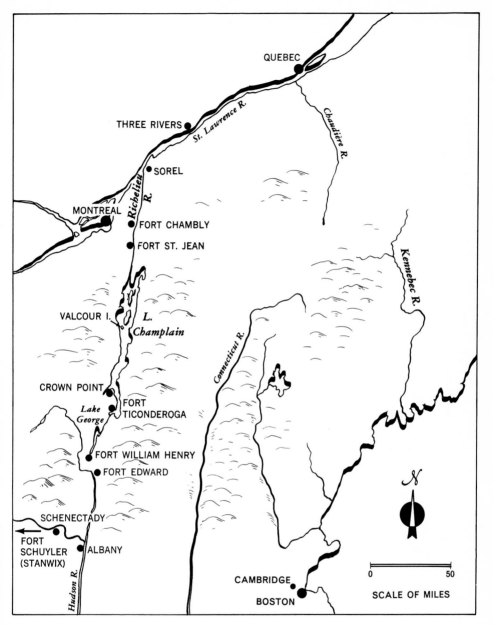

Centre of conflict during the American invasions of the
Province of Quebec

A view of Quebec from the south-east, an aquatint by J. F. W.
Des Barres, from *The Atlantic Neptune*

CONCLUSION

THE CONQUEST and the Treaty of Paris marked the end of a régime which had endured for a hundred and fifty years. Henceforth Canada was a British colony, and, after the influx of immigrants from the American colonies and Great Britain, a colony with two distinct populations, one French and the other English. The 60,000 country dwellers and the 15,000 townsmen who made up the former group were equally inexperienced in political affairs. Under an absolute government the smallest details of their individual and collective lives had been directed from Versailles, and after the departure of the French officials they felt no incentive to take any political action themselves. The only unified authority surviving from the former régime, the clergy, followed the counsel of prudence and confined its activities strictly to the religious sphere, while the very modest influence exercised by the seigneurs was due entirely to their relations with the British military hierarchy. A small number of notaries, and an even smaller number of doctors constituted a professional *élite*, but its members, like the population in general, lacked experience in public affairs, and their professional status conferred no special prestige upon them. The same limitations applied to the commercial *bourgeoisie*, a small group of men of modest fortune. The people of Canada were united in the bitterness of defeat, attachment to the mother country, and in the desire for religious freedom. They shared the hope that French law might be re-established and the fear of government by an elected assembly dominated by the Anglo-Protestant minority.

211

The English group comprised two classes. The first was made up of officers and public servants, generally tolerant and broadminded, who gravitated around the Governor. Most of them established friendly contacts with the Canadian seigneurs, with whom they were socially congenial. Their professions fostered in them a preference for direct administration by the governing authority, and indifference towards the idea of popular participation in government. The second and more numerous group of English settlers included merchants, business employees, small artisans, and tavern keepers. In this class the relatively large number of subjects from the semi-autonomous American colonies were great democrats and small politicians, accustomed to a régime in which an elected assembly could be the instrument through which they asserted their own personal interests.

Immediately after the conclusion of the Treaty of Paris, this second group began to play an active role in a political movement whose direction was soon in the hands of the experienced and aggressive American colonists. After the introduction of English law, the English group petitioned for the creation of an elective assembly from which Catholic Canadians would be excluded and which would therefore reserve all legislative action to their own group. Such religious ostracism was common in an age when France denied all political rights to Protestants, and when Catholics were denied the same rights both in England and in the British colonies. But while the denial of political capacity might find some justification in certain circumstances, in Canada it was supremely unjust since it deprived the population of a country almost universally Catholic of all political rights.

Thanks to the remarkable spirit of justice which animated Canada's first two governors, the agitation for a Protestant assembly ended in failure. The Anglo-American proposal was vehemently opposed by Murray, and his successor Carleton brought about its defeat. Adopting a decision dictated by strict justice and political foresight, Parliament passed the Quebec Act, whose terms guaranteed to Canadians religious freedom, French law, and access to public office. England thus refused to place 75,000 French Catholics under the domination of 3,000 English Protestants.

Such was the situation when the insurrection broke out in the American colonies. The Americans feared that an English army reinforced by Canadian militia might invade their territory from the north, and in the Quebec Act the Continental Congress at once recognized a two-edged weapon of propaganda which could be used both in England and in Canada. In a letter circulated in England and written in the fanatical style of the age, Congress accused the Act of legalizing in Canada a religion which bred impiety, murder, and bloodshed, and which was outlawed in Great Britain and in British colonies. At the same time, a letter addressed to Canadians exhorted them to rise above religious differences and to unite with the Americans to win their political liberty. The appeal met with an immediate and favourable response from the Anglo-Americans in Canada, bitterly resentful of the Quebec Act and its failure to grant them an elective legislature.

These malcontents, natural allies of the revolting British colonials, were also in a position to shelter emissaries and distribute messages, and they became willing partners in a campaign designed to incite Canadians against the government and the Church. Their propaganda represented the Quebec Act as a dangerous and revolutionary instrument which recognized the clergy's right to tithes and the seigneurs' to rents, and which made it possible to create new taxes and to call up men for military service. United in opposition to this movement of opinion, the ecclesiastical hierarchy and the *bourgeois* and seigniorial *élite* preached gratitude and fidelity to a government which had given satisfaction to the aspirations of the people of Quebec. The great mass of the population occupied a position between these two camps. They refused to serve as a buckler for conquerors who lacked the strength to defend themselves, and they had no desire to become involved in a revolt which did not concern them, and which they regarded as a family quarrel. They therefore maintained an attitude of neutrality.

213

The most passionate neutralists went so far as to give vocal expression to their feelings in the church itself when the Bishop and his clergy preached the obligation of obedience to, and defence of, the established authority. In their opposition to the anglophil exhortations of their pastors, these insubordinate sons of the Church even attempted to influence ecclesiastical consciences.

Attitudes became more rigid and the conflict of opinion assumed an active form when, in the summer of 1775, an invading army from the Colonies received help from Anglo-Americans and Britishers. A Canadian minority also gave assistance to the invaders, but a larger minority demonstrated its loyalty by offering to serve in a defence force, while the people of Montreal and Quebec defended their cities when they were attacked. With the arrival of an English fleet and English troops in the spring of 1776, the Americans were forced to withdraw their army, but a well-established network of spies continued to carry out their mission of subversion. National sentiment offered a fresh stimulus to their campaign when France, after signing an alliance with the Colonies, sent troops to America and messages to the King's former subjects leading them to believe that French troops might invade Canada. But the messages were disappointing and specious: they urged Canadians to support the cause of the rebellious colonies, but gave no indication of any intention on the part of the mother country to send a French army to reconquer her lost colony. This confused and unstable situation persisted until the end of 1783.

This brief review of the circumstances in which the ideas and behaviour of the opposing groups were manifested, will serve as an introduction to the examination of the motive forces underlying them. The explanation of the crisis in Canada, political as well as religious, resides, in the last analysis, in the policy of the American colonies. At first sight the extreme violence of colonial opposition to the Quebec Act may seem surprising. It can be explained, however, by reasons of propaganda, diplomacy, and interest. In an age of religious intolerance an act legalizing Catholicism was a powerful instrument of propaganda. Not only in the colonies, but in England, it could be a means of bringing anti-papist feeling to bear against George III and his ministers. What a shocking contrast for an Englishman to see the government of his country persecuting Protestant Massachusetts at the very moment when it was lavishing favours on the minions of Rome! The contrast offered a magnificent theme for the vituperative eloquence of Puritan pulpits. One preacher foresaw, as a consequence of the Act, papist legions from Canada participating in the subjection and perversion by fire and sword of loyal British subjects in America and England.

The new charter was also a precious weapon for American diplomacy. By pointing out to them that the Act was an outrageous denial of their rights as British citizens, Congress could win over the Anglo-Americans, and even a number of Britishers, in Canada. Now that Catholicism and French law were installed in Quebec, the only course open to British subjects was to take their stand under the rebel flag and to play their part in the conquest of the province. Membership in the union would give Canada representative government and freedom from the scourge of the Quebec Act.

The Colonies had also their own special reasons for hostility towards the Quebec Act. Memories of Canadian and Indian raids against their frontier villages still came to haunt the dreams of New Englanders with visions of massacre and fire. In the current struggle, a Quebec faithful to England presented the threat of other such raids. The Canadian militia could reinforce a British army, and Quebec would provide an open door through which an invading army could penetrate into the Colonies. Boston and New York, hemmed in on one side by a land force and on the other by the Atlantic fleet, could be crushed between two offensives. It was therefore imperative for America to be assured of the support, or at least the neutrality, of the people of Canada. This necessity explains not only the Colonials' condemnation of the Quebec Act, and their political propaganda in Canada, but their invasion of the country and subsequent abortive invasion projects.

In Canada the situation resulting from the Quebec Act was much more confused and complex. Within each of the two distinct populations, divergent opinions created smaller groups. English civil and military officers, and all British subjects connected in any way with the administration of the country, were intransigent in their attitude towards the rebellion. Bound by tradition, as well as by their office and their oath, they were unswerving in their fidelity to the flag.

The example set by public servants was followed by the majority of the businessmen of Quebec. In Montreal, on the contrary, the revolutionary cause was supported by most of the English merchants and by almost all the colonials, who also provided the leaders in the movement. These pro-rebels probably did not constitute the majority of the British population, but they included many of its most active and enterprising members. Two main motives inspired their decision to align themselves with the rebels: the American origin of the leaders was a powerful influence in favour of the Colonies, and the political and business interests of the British group in general led them to support a party which was opposed to the official and military class. A further motive lay in the failure to maintain English law and to introduce representative institutions. Since the government refused to grant their petitions, the malcontents would have recourse to rebellion as the only means of achieving their aim.

These were the motives which led certain elements in the British population in Canada to deny their allegiance and to raise the standard of revolt against the King and his representatives. With the support of the rebels south of the border, and in collaboration with them, they kept up a constant stream of clever and unscrupulous propaganda and sowed seeds of unrest, insubordination, latent and finally armed, revolt, Their appeals and their support encouraged the Americans in their projects of invasion. Without the intervention of these rebellious British elements, Canada would probably have known neither political division nor religious insubordination; she might possibly have been spared the invasion and the troubles which accompanied and followed it. The chief responsibility for the crisis must then be attributed to Anglo-Americans in Canada, colonial immigrants, and their British partisans.

In order to explain the behaviour of Canadians at this critical time, one must distinguish between the groups which together made up the population: clergy, *élite*, and common people. But we must first observe that in the second half of the eighteenth century patriotism was not, either in individuals or in nations, the deep, inviolable feeling which it was later to become. Powers conquered provinces and territories by force of arms, or ceded them by treaty, or exchanged them as compensation, at the will of kings and plenipotentiaries, and with no thought for the inhabitants. One day a war made Russian subjects of Poles, and a few years later, as a result of further hostilities, these same Poles were transformed into Prussian or Austrian subjects. And each country imposed its own laws without any regard for the customs and religion of its new subjects. New France itself presented the case of the Acadians who, transformed into British subjects in 1713 by the Treaty of Utrecht, were expelled from their country forty-two years later because they refused to swear absolute allegiance to the King of England. It is in the light of these facts and of ideas current at the time that one must examine the policy of England towards the people of Canada, the designs of the American colonies, and the conduct of the different classes of Canadians.

The country's *élite* included former officers and members of the minor nobility, seigneurs of simple as well as of gentle origin, a small number of professional men, and the most important merchants. The members of this class were bound together by family ties and by social and business contacts. They constituted the head and the conscience of the province, but their precarious position as French-Catholic subjects of an Eng-

217

lish-Protestant power tended to make them move very circum-
spectly in the political field.

When the Treaty of Paris had confirmed the conquest, they
had bowed to an inexorable decree of fate and accepted their
new status. Their reconciliation with the British was facilitated
by the attitude of Canada's first two English governors. Both
Murray and Carleton chose their friends and collaborators from
the Canadian *élite* rather than from the Anglo-American clan.
Moreover, in the eyes of this group of Canadians, their acceptance of the new régime was justified by the Quebec Act with
its guarantee of all religious and political rights. When the
revolt broke out, and the Colonies bombarded Quebec with
protestations of brotherhood and invitations to solidarity they
refused to be taken in. After its vehement denunciation of
papism in its Letter to the People of Great Britain, Congress
could have no message for them. They realized that by abstain-
ing from military service they would make themselves pawns
in the Americans' game, and they also foresaw the political
future which would be theirs in the event of an American
victory. For these reasons they rejected any suggestion of com-
promise with the rebel colonies. So strong were the ties of
gratitude, policy, and foresight binding them to England that
their loyalty suffered no more than a faint tremor when France
became a partner in the combat. The first instinctive surge of
emotion at the thought of a possible return to the mother
country was quickly suppressed when it became evident that
France was asking her former colony not to come back into her
fold but to accept the protection, more interested than sympathetic, of the American federation.

At the head of the second group, the clergy, were that in-
domitable Breton, Mgr. Briand, and his dogmatic Vicar-General,
M. de Montgolfier. Under their direction the Church in Quebec,
recognizing the good of religion as its unique goal, performed
the painful operation of severing the ties which bound it to the
kingdom of France. Perish the motherland, if only the faith
survive! In order to remain Catholic, as the papal nuncio declared

to Mgr. Briand, the Church in Canada must cease to be French. When the Quebec Act promised the Church all its religious rights, how could the Church refuse to be loyal to England? The Bishop therefore required of his flock that they be faithful British subjects. He based the duty of loyalty in the first instance on the principle of obedience to the established authority and respect for the oath of allegiance. Loyalty was also an expression of gratitude towards a government which, by an act of justice unknown in that age of political and religious intolerance, had given generous recognition to the rights of a conquered people. The prelate continued to insist that all the members of his clergy follow strictly the line of conduct which he had laid down for them and for himself. Even in the midst of rumours of a French invasion, he did not deviate by a hairbreadth from his conception of loyalty based on canon law and on the primacy of faith over nationality. With very few exceptions, his clergy followed his example, although for many of them it must have been hard to stifle the hope of France's return to Canada. Carleton was well aware of the work accomplished by the Bishop. "It was the Catholic clergy," he wrote, "who saved the Province of Quebec for the King."[1]

The third group included the great mass of the people of Canada, and especially the country people, who constituted four-fifths of the population. It must be remembered that they had lived until very recently under an absolute régime and that they were quite ignorant of matters political. Their natural instinct would have been to follow the guidance of their civil and religious superiors. But at this particular moment they found that they had become the object of very special solicitude on the part of Congress and its partisans in Canada. It was flattering for the countryman, who until that time had counted for little in public life, to be made judge and arbiter of his own destiny. Moreover, the habitants had always been independent and impatient of authority, and now that the seigneurs wanted to assume the right to direct the militia and to increase rents they were still more refractory to seigniorial influence. They had also become emancipated in other respects. The English régime, by relieving them of the legal obligation to pay tithes, had encouraged their natural Norman tendency to try to bargain with the curé about the amount to be paid. At the same time, they had ceased to regard military service as an obligation. Altogether, the habitant had achieved a high degree of independence and determination. It must also be remembered, although this fact is not often mentioned, that the Canadian people had not forgotten the shock of defeat, nor certain excesses of the victors.

Thus, when a pro-rebel propagandist arrived with the letter from Congress, and explained to the Canadian of 1775 that every man possesses the natural right to vote for the law by which he is governed and the tax which he will pay, the Canadian was both surprised and flattered. When other messengers added that the Quebec Act merely recognized a right which had always been his, the Canadian was inclined to conclude that his leaders were making too much of any gratitude he might owe the British government. When the pro-rebel agent insinuated that the new charter would confer advantages on the clergy, who would be empowered by the law to collect tithes, on the seigneurs, who would be free to increase rents and charges, and on the government, which would be able to create new taxes, the farmer wondered whether the seigneurs and the clergy were not representing as a benefit a constitution which, in the last analysis, would bring him more charges than advantages. Finally, the Canadian considered that the revolt was a family quarrel. It was not incumbent upon him to take any part in the armed conflict. Nor was it necessary for him to take up arms since the rebel leaders promised that, if they were victorious, they would abolish tithes and seignioral dues. Hence he denied the Church's right to preach the duty of military service and asserted that the pastor who did so was guilty of invading the sphere of the civil authority. Feeling on this point ran so high that the Bishop was accused of "playing the general," and certain curés of being "Englishmen."

All these causes — weakening of the traditional spirit of dis-

cipline, conflict of class interests, emancipation of opinion, skilful propaganda — created or accentuated divisions in all parts
of the province. In the towns — Quebec, Three Rivers, and
Montreal — the majority of the population, living in contact
with the *élite* and the clergy, received their information from
them and reflected their loyalist opinions. On the other hand,
pro-American sentiments predominated in the suburbs of Montreal and Three Rivers, which were also known as gathering
places for dubious and adventurous characters. In the country,
the people fell into three groups according to their respective
opinions. A minority of the habitants accepted the directive of
their clergy to participate in the defence of the province. The
second group, the majority, was resolved to remain neutral, and
their determination to take no part in the military struggle was
strengthened by their knowledge of the inadequacy of the British
defence force. Their neutrality did not prevent them, however,
from feeling a certain satisfaction at seeing their recent conquerors themselves the target of attack. They regarded the invasion
as a passing adventure, and they welcomed the invaders who,
at least in the early stages, paid good prices for their produce.
The quarrel was no concern of theirs, and they had no intention
of risking their skins for recent enemies who, in spite of the
fact that they had recognized French law and religious freedom,
were still foreigners inspiring no feeling of sympathy. The third
group was also largely made up of country people, chiefly
habitants from the Richelieu valley and the Quebec region. Its
members were restless and ambitious individuals, or men who,
having suffered as a result of the war and the conquest, saw in
the invasion an opportunity for revenge as well as for profit
and adventure. The activities of these pro-rebel Canadians were
intensified as the military strength of the invading army increased, and when the occupation extended to a great part of
the province they dominated their parishes. So zealous were
they in providing service and volunteers to the Americans that
they gave the impression of being in the majority, when in fact

they constituted only a fraction of the population, although a hostile, aggressive, and unscrupulous one.

That some Canadians should have become deeply involved in favour of the colonial rebels is not surprising; what is astounding is that Catholics, instead of merely ignoring the exhortations of their pastors, offered open and violent opposition to the Bishop and his clergy. They insulted priests in the pulpit, poured scorn on the Bishop's words, and committed excesses then unheard of: seizing curés, ill-treating them, and handing them over as prisoners to undisciplined American soldiers. The rebellion even reached the point of schism and contempt of the divine service and the sacraments, and a day came when these Canadian pro-rebels opened fire on compatriots and chaplains resisting a foreign invader.

A part of the responsibility for this political and religious crisis, the first since the conquest, in the solidarity of French Canada, must be laid at the Governor's door. Although animated by the best of intentions, Carleton was neither far-sighted nor firm in decision. When trouble first broke out in the British colonies, he accepted the word of the seigneurs that Canadians would build a wall with their bodies to stop the advance of the invaders. He forgot that the loser in battle has never been known to sacrifice himself for the victor. Later, when American agents and British partisans were disseminating propaganda, Carleton did not apply sanctions, nor even interfere with their treasonable activities. After the defeat of Allen and Montgomery, he did not take advantage of the breeze of victory swelling his sails. A show of military force in these cases might have sufficed to rid the country of the invading army, but Carleton took no action. His lack of decision and initiative discouraged the Canadians who, believing that all was lost, took refuge in a neutrality which almost resulted in the loss of the country.

Haldimand's conduct offered a complete contrast to that of Carleton. It was true that he was supported by imposing forces, but he was himself a man of decision and of action. He did not allow the people to doubt for an instant that his will was law. He called the militia to service, and he suppressed propaganda and espionage. Even after the arrival of French forces in the United States, the country was calmer than it had been under Carleton, for the people knew that in the Château Saint-Louis the Governor was on the alert, and that he would not tolerate either insubordination or neutrality.

In 1778, the situation changed once more when the fleur-de-lis of France appeared with French troops on the American horizon, and Canadian hearts swelled with the hope that a French invasion might restore Canada to its former mother country. But this hope proved illusory, for the recapture of Canada had no place in the realistic policy of Versailles. The Seven Years' War had marked a defeat for France, and the Treaty of Paris had confirmed her loss of prestige in the eyes of the world. Under the leadership of the Duc de Choiseul, she had begun to recover, and to build up her military and economic strength in the hope of an eventual revenge, and when the revolt broke out in the American colonies, Vergennes considered the opportunity offered by the situation. It was certainly to the advantage of France to enter into an alliance with the rebels in order to reduce the power of her "natural enemy." This was a political reason for intervention. It was also to her advantage to procure the independence of the Colonies and to assure for herself the benefits of trade with them. This was an economic argument. By taking part in the war, France might recover some part of her former possessions in America, perhaps the Newfoundland fisheries, or Ile Royale, or the West Indies. But when such conjectures were discussed in France "there was no mention of Canada." The silence of French diplomacy on this point was later followed by official renunciation of any attempt to repossess New France.

The rebel colonies were of course ambitious to conquer Canada for themselves, and they were also alarmed at the thought of the re-establishment on their frontiers of that French power which had for so long been a harassing enemy and an obstacle to their expansion. But their leaders had not fathomed all the subtlety of Vergennes' thought. He did not want to restore Canada to France, but neither did he wish it to fall into the hands of the Americans. Instead he wanted it to remain an English province and a constant threat to the American flank. For this threat would force the Americans to seek the favour and protection of France, whose commerce and influence would thereby be enhanced. Vergennes' cool and calculating reasoning directed and dominated French policy throughout the course of the American Revolution. Canada might be a useful pawn in the game of power politics, but France's foreign minister shared Voltaire's conviction that these "few acres of snow" were not worth fighting for.

France's abstention from the Canadian campaign left the problem of Canada's fate still unresolved. In spite of Carleton's temporizing and indecisive policy, the American invasion ended in military defeat. In this case, as when Murray had triumphed, victory was assured by the arrival of a British fleet and British forces in Quebec. But the defeat of the Americans in Canada followed and completed the political failure which had already ruined the invaders' chances of success. Their political failure can be attributed to a number of causes of varying importance. The essential cause was the steadfast opposition of the clergy to the rebel cause. This opposition contained Canadian collaboration which might otherwise have been much more extensive. It contributed immensely to the success of the Montrealers' sortie against Allen and the victorious defence of Quebec by the militia. Evidence that it fostered active loyalty in a considerable proportion of the rural population may be found in the encounter at Saint-Pierre-du-Sud; by helping to keep the others neutral and to prevent them from serving the rebels, it helped to save Canada. For if the majority of Canadians, at the instigation and following the example of certain Anglo-Americans, had taken part in the American revolt, Canada would have been lost to England.

224

Other causes too contributed their cumulative effect to the failure of the invasion. The first and most important of these causes was the inadequacy of the invading force, composed of ill-trained and undisciplined soldiers, without artillery. Another weakness in the army arose from the short-term engagements of the volunteers, resulting almost inevitably in confusion and large-scale desertions. A smallpox epidemic reduced still further the effective fighting force of the enemy. Finally, Carleton led the regulars and militiamen of Quebec in the spirited defence which dealt the death blow to all Montgomery's hopes. When, six months later, reinforcements came in from the south, it was too late; the British fleet and British soldiers had already arrived in Quebec.

While the political and military intervention of the Colonies created internal strife and provoked a two-fold crisis in Canada, it also brought certain benefits. The letters from Congress and the propaganda of the American revolutionaries were instruments of political education for the people of Quebec. They showed them how an elective régime functioned, and explained their rights as British subjects, the principle of popular representation, and the way in which taxes were voted. They introduced to them the notions of personal liberty and political equality. American indoctrination taught Canadians their political alphabet and gave them their first lesson in constitutional law. Both Mgr. Briand and the British officials remarked that after 1775 ordinary Canadians could be heard for the first time discussing public affairs.

The War of American Independence, by creating a political and religious crisis in Canada, marks a crucial period in the country's history. Disaffection among the British element almost made Quebec an American state. If it had done so Canada's French-Catholic personality would gradually have disappeared in the inevitable assimilation of the ethnic group. But, while the American Revolution was the immediate cause of social and religious dissension, it did not make an American state of Quebec. On the contrary, by opening the minds of Canadians to political ideas, it awakened in them a keener consciousness of the condition of the French element in their own country.

APPENDICES

THE QUEBEC ACT[1]
Anno Decimo Quarto
GEORGE III. REGIS.
Cap. LXXXIII.

An Act for making more effectual Provision for the Government of the Province of *Quebec* in *North America*.

Whereas His Majesty, by His Royal Proclamation, bearing Date the Seventh Day of *October*, in the Third Year of His Reign, thought fit to declare the Provisions which had been made in respect to certain Countries, Territories, and Islands in *America*, ceded to His Majesty by the definitive Treaty of Peace, concluded at *Paris* on the Tenth Day of *February*, One thousand seven hundred and sixty-three: And whereas, by the Arrangements made by the said Royal Proclamation, a very large Extent of Country, within which there were several Colonies and Settlements of the Subjects of *France*, who claimed to remain therein under the Faith of the said Treaty, was left, without any Provision being made for the Administration of Civil Government therein; and certain Parts of the Territory of *Canada*, where sedentary Fisheries had been established and carried on by the Subjects of *France*, Inhabitants of the said Province of *Canada*, under Grants and Concessions from the Government thereof, were annexed to the Government of *Newfoundland*, and thereby subjected to Regulations inconsistent with the Nature of such Fisheries: May it therefore please

---

[1]*Const. Docts.*, pp. 570-76. The text of the Act is taken from the original folio black letter form in which it was first issued by the King's Printers. "London: Printed by Charles Eyre and William Strachan, Printers to the King's most Excellent Majesty. MDCCLXXIV."

Your most Excellent Majesty that it may be enacted; and be it enacted by the King's most Excellent Majesty, by and with the Advice and Consent of the Lords Spiritual and Temporal, and Commons, in this present Parliament assembled, and by the Authority of the same, That all the Territories, Islands, and Countries in *North America*, belonging to the Crown of *Great Britain*, bounded on the South by a Line from the Bay of *Chaleurs*, along the High Lands which divide the Rivers that empty themselves into the River *Saint Lawrence* from those which fall into the Sea, to a Point in Forty-five Degrees of Northern Latitude, on the Eastern Bank of the River *Connecticut*, keeping the same Latitude directly West, through the Lake *Champlain*, until, in the same Latitude, it meets the River *Saint Lawrence*; from thence up the Eastern Bank of the said River to the Lake *Ontario*; thence through the Lake *Ontario*, and the River commonly called *Niagara*; and thence along by the Eastern and South-eastern Bank of Lake *Erie*, following the said Bank, until the same shall be intersected by the Northern Boundary, granted by the Charter of the Province of *Pensylvania*, in case the same shall be so intersected; and from thence along the said Northern and Western Boundaries of the said Province, until the said Western Boundary strike the *Ohio*: But in case the said Bank of the said Lake shall not be found to be so intersected, then following the said Bank until it shall arrive at that Point of the said Bank which shall be nearest to the North-western Angle of the said Province of *Pennsylvania*, and thence, by a right Line, to the said North-western Angle of the said Province; and thence along the Western Boundary of the said Province, until it strike the River *Ohio*; and along the Bank of the said River, Westward, to the Banks of the *Mississippi*, and Northward to the Southern Boundary of the Territory granted to the Merchants Adventurers of *England*, trading to *Hudson's Bay*; and also all such Territories, Islands and Countries, which have, since the Tenth of *February*, One thousand seven hundred and sixty-three, been made Part of the Government of *Newfoundland*, be, and they are hereby, during

His Majesty's Pleasure, annexed to, and made Part and Parcel of, the Province of *Quebec,* as created and established by the said Royal Proclamation of the Seventh of *October,* One thousand seven hundred and sixty-three.

Provided always, That nothing herein contained, relative to the Boundary of the Province of *Quebec,* shall in anywise affect the Boundaries of any other Colony.

Provided always, and be it enacted, That nothing in this Act contained shall extend, or be construed to extend, to make void, or to vary or alter any Right, Title, or Possession, derived under any Grant, Conveyance, or otherwise howsoever, of or to any Lands within the said Province, or the Provinces thereto adjoining; but that the same shall remain and be in Force, and have Effect, as if this Act had never been made.

And whereas the Provisions, made by the said Proclamation, in respect to the Civil Government of the said Province of *Quebec,* and the Powers and Authorities given to the Governor and other Civil Officers of the said Province, by the Grants and Commissions issued in consequence thereof, have been found, upon Experience, to be inapplicable to the State and Circumstances of the said Province, the Inhabitants whereof amounted, at the Conquest, to above Sixty-five thousands Persons professing the Religion of the Church of *Rome,* and enjoying an established Form of Constitution and System of Laws, by which their Persons and Property had been protected, governed, and ordered, for a long Series of Years, from the First Establishment of the said Province of *Canada;* be it therefore further enacted by the Authority aforesaid, That the said Proclamation, so far as the same relates to the said Province of *Quebec,* and the Commission under the Authority whereof the Government of the said Province is at present administered, and all and every the Ordinance and Ordinances made by the Governor and Council of *Quebec* for the Time being, relative to the Civil Government and Administration of Justice in the said Province, and all Commissions to Judges and other Officers thereof, be, and the same are hereby revoked, annulled, and made void from and after the First Day of *May*, One thousand seven hundred and seventy-five.

And, for the more perfect Security and Ease of the Minds of the Inhabitants of the said Province, it is hereby declared, That His Majesty's Subjects, professing the Religion of the Church of *Rome* of and in the said Province of *Quebec*, may have, hold, and enjoy, the free Exercise of the Religion of the Church of *Rome*, subject to the King's Supremacy, declared and established by an Act, made in the First Year of the Reign of Queen *Elizabeth*, over all the Dominions and Countries which then did, or thereafter should belong, to the Imperial Crown of this Realm; and that the Clergy of the said Church may hold, receive, and enjoy, their accustomed Dues and Rights, with respect to such Persons only as shall profess the said Religion.

Provided nevertheless, That it shall be lawful for His Majesty, His Heirs or Successors, to make such Provision out of the rest of the said accustomed Dues and Rights, for the Encouragement of the Protestant Religion, and for the Maintenance and Support of a Protestant Clergy within the said Province, as he or they shall, from Time to Time, think necessary and expedient.

Provided always, and be it enacted, That no Person, professing the Religion of the Church of *Rome*, and residing in the said Province, shall be obliged to take the Oath required by the said Statute passed in the First Year of the Reign of Queen *Elizabeth*, or any other Oaths substituted by any other Act in the Place thereof; but that every such Person who, by the said Statute is required to take the Oath therein mentioned, shall be obliged, and is hereby required, to take and subscribe the following Oath before the Governor, or such other Person in such Court of Record as His Majesty shall appoint, who are hereby authorized to administer the same; *videlicet,*

I A. B. *do sincerely promise and swear, That I will be faithful, and bear true Allegiance to His Majesty King* GEORGE, *and him will defend to the utmost of my Power, against all traiterous Conspiracies, and Attempts whatsoever, which shall be made against*

His Person, Crown, and Dignity; and I will do my utmost Endeavour to disclose and make known to His Majesty, His Heirs and Successors, all Treasons, and traiterous Conspiracies, and Attempts, which I shall know to be against Him, or any of Them; and all this I do swear without any Equivocation, mental Evasion, or secret Reservation, and renouncing all Pardons and Dispensations from any Power or Person whomsoever to the Contrary.

So Help Me God.

And every such Person, who shall neglect or refuse to take the said Oath before mentioned, shall incur and be liable to the same Penalties, Forfeitures, Disabilities, and Incapacities, as he would have incurred and been liable to for neglecting or refusing to take the Oath required by the said Statute passed in the First Year of the Reign of Queen *Elizabeth.*

And be it further enacted by the Authority aforesaid, That all His Majesty's *Canadian* Subjects, within the Province of *Quebec,* the religious Orders and Communities only excepted, may also hold and enjoy their Property and Possessions, together with all Customs and Usages relative thereto, and all other their Civil Rights, in as large, ample, and beneficial Manner, as if the said Proclamation, Commissions, Ordinances, and other Acts and Instruments, had not been made, and as may consist with their Allegiance to His Majesty, and Subjection to the Crown and Parliament of *Great Britain*; and that in all Matters of Controversy, relative to Property and Civil Rights, Resort shall be had to the Laws of *Canada,* as the Rule for the Decision of the same; and all Causes that shall hereafter be instituted in any of the Courts of Justice, to be appointed within and for the said Province, by His Majesty, His Heirs and Successors, shall, with respect to such Property and Rights, be determined agreeably to the said Laws and Customs of *Canada,* until they shall be varied or altered by any Ordinances that shall, from Time to Time, be passed in the said Province by the Governor, Lieutenant Governor, or Commander in Chief, for the Time being, by and with the Advice and Consent of the Legislative Council of the same, to be appointed in Manner herein-after mentioned.

Provided always, That nothing in this Act contained shall extend, or be construed to extend, to any Lands that have been granted by His Majesty, or shall hereafter be granted by His Majesty His Heirs and Successors, to be holden in free and common Soccage.

Provided also, That it shall and may be lawful to and for every Person that is Owner of any Lands, Goods, or Credits, in the said Province, and that has a Right to alienate the said Lands, Goods, or Credits, in his or her Life-time, by Deed of Sale, Gift, or otherwise, to devise or bequeath the same at his or her Death, by his or her last Will and Testament; any Law, Usage, or Custom, heretofore or now prevailing in the Province, to the Contrary hereof in any-wise notwithstanding; such Will being executed, either according to the Laws of Canada, or according to the Forms prescribed by the Laws of *England*.

And whereas the Certainty and Lenity of the Criminal Law of *England*, and the Benefits and Advantages resulting from the Use of it, have been sensibly felt by the Inhabitants, from an Experience of more than Nine Years, during which it has been uniformly administered; be it therefore further enacted by the Authority aforesaid, That the same shall continue to be administered, and shall be observed as Law in the Province of *Quebec*, as well in the Description and Quality of the Offence as in the Method of Prosecution and Trial; and the Punishments and Forfeitures thereby inflicted to the Exclusion of every other Rule of Criminal Law, or Mode of Proceeding thereon, which did or might prevail in the said Province before the Year of our Lord One thousand seven hundred and sixty-four; any Thing in this Act to the Contrary thereof in any Respect notwithstanding; subject nevertheless to such Alterations and Amendments as the Governor, Lieutenant-governor, or Commander in Chief for the Time being, by and with the Advice and Consent of the legislative Council of the said Province, hereafter to be appointed, shall, from Time to Time, cause to be made therein, in Manner herein-after directed.

And whereas it may be necessary to ordain many Regulations for the future Welfare and good Government of the Province of *Quebec*, the Occasions of which cannot now be foreseen, nor, without much Delay and Inconvenience, be provided for, without intrusting that Authority, for a certain Time, and under proper Restrictions, to Persons resident there: And whereas it is at present inexpedient to call an Assembly; be it therefore enacted by the Authority aforesaid, That it shall and may be lawful for His Majesty, His Heirs and Successors, by Warrant under His or Their Signet or Sign Manual, and with the Advice of the Privy Council, to constitute and appoint a Council for the Affairs of the Province of *Quebec*, to consist of such Persons resident there, not exceeding Twenty-three, nor less than Seventeen, as His Majesty, His Heirs and Successors, shall be pleased to appoint; and, upon the Death, Removal, or Absence of any of the Members of the said Council, in like Manner to constitute and appoint such and so many other Person or Persons as shall be necessary to supply the Vacancy or Vacancies; which Council, so appointed and nominated, or the major Part thereof, shall have Power and Authority to make Ordinances for the Peace, Welfare, and good Government, of the said Province, with the Consent of His Majesty's Governor, or, in his Absence, of the Lieutenant-governor, or Comander in Chief for the Time being.

Provided always, That nothing in this Act contained shall extend to authorise or impower the said legislative Council to lay any Taxes or Duties within the said Province, such Rates and Taxes only excepted as the Inhabitants of any Town or District within the said Province may be authorised by the said Council to assess, levy, and apply, within the said Town or District, for the Purpose of making Roads, erecting and repairing publick Buildings, or for any other Purpose respecting the local Convenience and Oeconomy of such Town or District.

Provided also, and be it enacted by the Authority aforesaid,

That every Ordinance so to be made, shall, within Six Months, be transmitted by the Governor, or, in his Absence, by the Lieutenant-governor, or Commander in Chief for the Time being, and laid before His Majesty for His Royal Approbation; and if His Majesty shall think fit to disallow thereof, the same shall cease and be void from the Time that His Majesty's Order in Council thereupon shall be promulgated at *Quebec.*

Provided also, That no Ordinance touching Religion, or by which any Punishment may be inflicted greater than Fine or Imprisonment for Three Months, shall be of any Force or Effect, until the same shall have received His Majesty's Approbation.

Provided also, That no Ordinance shall be passed at any Meeting of the Council where less than a Majority of the whole Council is present, or at any Time except between the First Day of *January* and the First Day of *May,* unless upon some urgent Occasion, in which Case every Member thereof resident at *Quebec,* or within Fifty Miles thereof, shall be personally summoned by the Governor, or, in his Absence, by the Lieutenant-governor, or Commander in Chief for the Time being, to attend the same.

And be it further enacted by the Authority aforesaid, That nothing herein contained shall extend, or be construed to extend, to prevent or hinder His Majesty, His Heirs and Successors, by His or Their Letters Patent under the Great Seal of *Great Britain,* from erecting, constituting, and appointing, such Courts of Criminal, Civil, and Ecclesiastical Jurisdiction within and for the said Province of *Quebec,* and appointing, from Time to Time, the Judges and Officers thereof, as His Majesty, His Heirs and Successors, shall think necessary and proper for the circumstances of the said Province.

Provided always, and it is hereby enacted, That nothing in this Act contained shall extend, or be construed to extend, to repeal or make void, within the said Province of *Quebec,* any Act or Acts of the Parliament of *Great Britain* heretofore made, for prohibiting, restraining, or regulating, the Trade or Commerce of His Majesty's Colonies and Plantations in *Ameri-*

ca; but that all and every the said Acts, and also all Acts of Parliament heretofore made concerning or respecting the said Colonies and Plantations, shall be, and are hereby declared to be, in Force, within the said Province of *Quebec*, and every part thereof.

Finis.

To the people of Great Britain, from the delegates appointed by the several English colonies of New-Hampshire, Massachusetts-Bay, Rhode-Island, and Providence Plantations, Connecticut, New-York, New-Jersey, Pennsylvania, the lower counties on Delaware, Maryland, Virginia, North-Carolina, and South-Carolina, to consider of their grievances in general Congress, at Philadelphia, September 5th, 1774.[1]

FRIENDS AND FELLOW SUBJECTS,

WHEN a Nation, led to greatness by the hand of Liberty, and possessed of all the glory that heroism, munificence, and humanity can bestow, descends to the ungrateful task of forging chains for her Friends and Children, and instead of giving support to Freedom, turns advocate for Slavery and Oppression, there is reason to suspect she has either ceased to be virtuous, or been extremely negligent in the appointment of her rulers.

In almost every age, in repeated conflicts, in long and bloody wars, as well civil as foreign, against many and powerful nations, against the open assaults of enemies, and the more dangerous treachery of friends, have the inhabitants of your island, your great and glorious ancestors, maintained their independence and transmitted the rights of men, and the blessings of liberty to you their posterity.

---

[1]*Journals of the Continental Congress*, I, pp. 82-90.

Be not surprized therefore, that we, who are descended from the same common ancestors; that we, whose forefathers partipated in all the rights, the liberties, and the constitution, you so justly boast [of], and who have carefully conveyed the same fair inheritance to us, guarantied by the plighted faith of government and the most solemn compacts with British Sovereigns, should refuse to surrender them to men, who found their claims on no principles of reason, and who prosecute them with a design, that by having our lives and property in their power, they may with the greater facility enslave you.

The cause of America is now the object of universal attention: it has at length become very serious. This unhappy country has not only been oppressed, but abused and misrepresented; and the duty we owe to ourselves and posterity, to your interest, and the general welfare of the British empire, leads us to address you on this very important subject.

Know then, That we consider ourselves, and do insist, that we are and ought to be, as free as our fellow-subjects in Britain, and that no power on earth has a right to take our property from us without our consent.

That we claim all the benefits secured to the subject by the English constitution, and particularly that inestimable one of trial by jury.

That we hold it essential to English Liberty, that no man be condemned unheard, or punished for supposed offences, without having an opportunity of making his defence.

That we think the Legislature of Great-Britain is not authorized by the constitution[2] to establish a religion, fraught with sanguinary and impious tenets, or, to erect an arbitrary form of government, in any quarter of the globe. These rights, we, as well as you, deem sacred. And yet sacred as they are, they have, with many others, been repeatedly and flagrantly violated.

Are not the Proprietors of the soil of Great-Britain Lords of their own property? can it be taken from them without their

---

[2]In the 1774 edition of the Journal, this word is printed *condition.*

consent? will they yield it to the arbitrary disposal of any man, or number of men whatever?—You know they will not.

Why then are the Proprietors of the soil of America less Lords of their property than you are of yours, or why should they submit it to the disposal of your Parliament, or any other Parliament, or Council in the world, not of their election? Can the intervention of the sea that divides us, cause disparity in rights, or can any reason be given, why English subjects, who live three thousand miles from the royal palace, should enjoy less liberty than those who are three hundred miles distant from it?

Reason looks with indignation on such distinctions, and freemen can never perceive their propriety. And yet, however chimerical and unjust such discriminations are, the Parliament assert, that they have a right to bind us in all cases without exception, whether we consent or not; that they may take and use our property when and in what manner they please; that we are pensioners on their bounty for all that we possess, and can hold it no longer than they vouchsafe to permit. Such declarations we consider as heresies in English politics, and which can no more operate to deprive us of our property, than the interdicts of the Pope can divest Kings of sceptres which the laws of the land and the voice of the people have placed in their hands.

At the conclusion of the late war—a war rendered glorious by the abilities and integrity of a Minister, to whose efforts the British empire owes its safety and its fame: At the conclusion of this war, which was succeeded by an inglorious peace, formed under the auspices of a Minister of principles, and of a family unfriendly to the protestant cause, and inimical to liberty.—We say at this period, and under the influence of that man, a plan for enslaving your fellow subjects in America was concerted, and has ever since been pertinaciously carrying into execution.

Prior to this æra you were content with drawing from us the wealth produced by our commerce. You restrained our trade in every way that could conduce to your emolument. You exercised unbounded sovereignty over the sea. You named the ports and nations to which alone our merchandise should be carried, and with whom alone we should trade; and though some of these restrictions were grievous, we nevertheless did not complain; we looked up to you as to our parent state, to which we were bound by the strongest ties: And were happy in being instrumental to your prosperity and your grandeur.

We call upon you yourselves, to witness our loyalty and attachment to the common interest of the whole empire: Did we not, in the last war, add all the strength of this vast continent to the force which repelled our common enemy? Did we not leave our native shores, and meet disease and death, to promote the success of British arms in foreign climates? Did you not thank us for our zeal, and even reimburse us large sums of money, which, you confessed, we had advanced beyond our proportion and far beyond our abilities? You did.

To what causes, then, are we to attribute the sudden change of treatment, and that system of slavery which was prepared for us at the restoration of peace?

Before we had recovered from the distresses which ever attend war, an attempt was made to drain this country of all its money, by the oppressive Stamp-Act. Paint, Glass, and other commodities, which you would not permit us to purchase of other nations, were taxed; nay, although no wine is made in any country, subject to the British state, you prohibited our procuring it of foreigners, without paying a tax, imposed by your parliament, on all we imported. These and many other impositions were laid upon us most unjustly and unconstitutionally, for the express purpose of raising a Revenue.—In order to silence complaint, it was, indeed, provided, that this revenue should be expended in America for its protection and defence.—These exactions, however, can receive no justification from a pretended necessity of protecting and defending us. They are lavishly squandered on court favourites and ministerial dependents, generally avowed enemies to America and employing themselves, by partial representations, to traduce and embroil the

Colonies. For the necessary support of government here, we ever were and ever shall be ready to provide. And whenever the exigencies of the state may require it, we shall, as we have heretofore done, chearfully contribute our full proportion of men and money. To enforce this unconstitutional and unjust scheme of taxation, every fence that the wisdom of our British ancestors had carefully erected against arbitrary power, has been violently thrown down in America, and the inestimable right of trial by jury taken away in cases that touch both life and property.—It was ordained, that whenever offences should be committed in the colonies against particular Acts imposing various duties and restrictions upon trade, the prosecutor might bring his action for the penalties in the Courts of Admiralty; by which means the subject lost the advantage of being tried by an honest uninfluenced jury of the vicinage, and was subjected to the sad necessity of being judged by a single man, a creature of the Crown, and according to the course of a law which exempts the prosecutor from the trouble of proving his accusation, and obliges the defendant either to evince his innocence or to suffer. To give this new judicatory[3] the greater importance, and, as if with design to protect false accusers, it is further provided that the Judge's certificate of there having been probable causes of seizure and prosecution shall protect the prosecutor from actions at common law for recovery of damages.

By the course of our law, offences committed in such of the British dominions in which courts are established and justice duely and regularly administered, shall be there tried by a jury of the vicinage. There the offenders and the witnesses are known, and the degree of credibility to be given to their testimony, can be ascertained.

In all these Colonies, justice is regularly and impartially administered, and yet by the construction of some, and the direction of other Acts of Parliament, offenders are to be taken by force, together with all such persons as may be pointed out

---

[3]In the original pamphlet this word is printed *indicatory*.

as witnesses, and carried to England, there to be tried in a distant land, by a *jury* of strangers, and subject to all the disadvantages that result from want of friends, want of witnesses, and want of money.

When the design of raising a revenue from the duties imposed on the importation of tea into America had in great measure been rendered abortive by our ceasing to import that commodity, a scheme was concerted by the Ministry with the East-India Company, and an Act passed enabling and encouraging them to transport and vend it in the colonies. Aware of the danger of giving success to this insidious manœuvre, and of permitting a precedent of taxation thus to be established among us, various methods were adopted to elude the stroke. The people of Boston, then ruled by a Governor, whom, as well as his predecessor Sir Francis Bernard, all America considers as her enemy, were exceedingly embarrassed. The ships which had arrived with the tea were by his management prevented from returning. —The duties would have been paid; the cargoes landed and exposed to sale; a Governor's influence would have procured and protected many purchasers. While the town was suspended by deliberations on this important subject, the tea was destroyed. Even supposing a trespass was thereby committed, and the Proprietors of the tea entitled to damages.—The Courts of Law were open, and Judges appointed by the Crown presided in them.—The East India Company however did not think proper to commence any suits, nor did they even demand satisfaction, either from individuals or from the community in general. The Ministry, it seems, officiously made the case their own, and the great Council of the nation descended to intermeddle with a dispute about private property.—Divers papers, letters, and other unauthenticated ex parte evidence were laid before them; neither the persons who destroyed the Tea, or the people of Boston, were called upon to answer the complaint. The Ministry, incensed by being disappointed in a favourite scheme, were determined to recur from the little arts of finesse, to open force and unmanly violence. The port of Boston was blocked up by a fleet, and an army placed in the town. Their trade was to be suspended, and thousands reduced to the necessity of gaining subsistance from charity, till they should submit to pass under the yoke, and consent to become slaves, by confessing the omnipotence of Parliament, and acquiescing in whatever disposition they might think proper to make of their lives and property.

Let justice and humanity cease to be the boast of your nation! Consult your history, examine your records of former transactions, nay turn to the annals of the many arbitrary states and kingdoms that surround you, and shew us a single instance of men being condemned to suffer for imputed crimes, unheard, unquestioned, and without even the specious formality of a trial; and that too by laws made expressly for the purpose, and which had no existence at the time of the fact committed. If it be difficult to reconcile these proceedings to the genius and temper of your laws and constitution, the task will become more arduous when we call upon our ministerial enemies to justify, not only condemning men untried and by hearsay, but involving the innocent in one common punishment with the guilty, and for the act of thirty or forty, to bring poverty, distress and calamity on thirty thousand souls, and those not your enemies, but you friends, brethren, and fellow subjects.

It would be some consolation to us, if the catalogue of American oppressions ended here. It gives us pain to be reduced to the necessity of reminding you, that under the confidence reposed in the faith of government, pledged in a royal charter from a British Sovereign, the fore-fathers of the present inhabitants of the Massachusetts-Bay left their former habitations, and established that great, flourishing, and loyal Colony. Without incurring or being charged with a forfeiture of their rights, without being heard, without being tried, without law, and without justice, by an Act of Parliament, their charter is destroyed, their liberties violated, their constitution and form of government changed: And all this upon no better pretence, than because in one of their towns a trespass was committed on some merchandize, said to belong to one of the Companies, and because the Ministry were of opinion, that such high political regulations were necessary to compel due subordination and obedience to their mandates.

Nor are these the only capital grievances under which we labor. We might tell of dissolute, weak and wicked Governors having been set over us; of Legislatures being suspended for asserting the rights of British subjects—of needy and ignorant dependents on great men, advanced to the seats of justice and to other places of trust and importance;—of hard restrictions on commerce, and a great variety of lesser evils, the recollection of which is almost lost under the weight and pressure of greater and more poignant calamities.

Now mark the progression of the ministerial plan for inslaving us.

Well aware that such hardy attempts to take our property from us; to deprive us of that valuable right of trial by jury; to seize our persons, and carry us for trial to Great-Britain; to blockade our ports; to destroy our Charters, and change our forms of government, would occasion, and had already occasioned, great discontent in all the Colonies, which might produce opposition to these measures: An Act was passed to protect, indemnify, and screen from punishment such as might be guilty even of murder, in endeavoring to carry their oppressive edicts into execution; And by another Act the dominion of Canada is to be so extended, modelled, and governed, as that by being disunited from us, detached from our interests, by civil as well as religious prejudices, that by their numbers daily swelling with Catholic emigrants from Europe, and by their devotion to Administration, so friendly to their religion, they might become formidable to us, and on occasion, be fit instruments in the hands of power, to reduce the ancient free Protestant Colonies to the same state of slavery with themselves.

This was evidently the object of the Act:—And in this view, being extremely dangerous to our liberty and quiet, we cannot forebear complaining of it, as hostile to British America.—Superadded to these considerations, we cannot help deploring the unhappy condition to which it has reduced the many English settlers, who, encouraged by the Royal Proclamation, promising the enjoyment of all their rights, have purchased estates in that country.—They are now the subjects of an arbitrary government, deprived of trial by jury, and when imprisoned cannot claim the benefit of the habeas corpus Act, that great bulwark and palladium of English liberty:—Nor can we suppress our astonishment, that a British Parliament should ever consent to establish in that country a religion that has deluged your island in blood, and dispersed impiety, bigotry, persecution, murder and rebellion through every part of the world.

This being a true state of facts, let us beseech you to consider to what end they lead.

Admit that the Ministry, by the powers of Britain, and the aid of our Roman Catholic neighbours, should be able to carry the point of taxation, and reduce us to a state of perfect humiliation and slavery. Such an enterprize would doubtless make some addition to your national debt, which already presses down your liberties, and fills you with Pensioners and Placemen.—We presume, also, that your commerce will somewhat be diminished. However, suppose you should prove victorious—in what condition will you then be? What advantages or what laurels will you reap from such a conquest?

May not a Ministry with the same armies inslave you—It may be said, you will cease to pay them—but remember the taxes from America, the wealth, and we may add, the men, and particularly the Roman Catholics of this vast continent will then be in the power of your enemies—nor will you have any reason to expect, that after making slaves of us, many among us should refuse to assist in reducing you to the same abject state.

Do not treat this as chimerical—Know that in less than half a century, the quit-rents reserved to the Crown, from the numberless grants of this vast continent, will pour large streams of wealth into the royal coffers, and if to this be added the power of taxing America at pleasure, the Crown will be rendered independent on [of] you for supplies, and will possess more treasure than may be necessary to purchase the *remains of* Liberty in your Island.—In a word, take care that you do not fall into the pit that is preparing for us.

We believe there is yet much virtue, much justice, and much public spirit in the English nation—To that justice we now appeal. You have been told that we are seditious, impatient of government and desirous of independency. Be assured that these are not facts, but calumnies.—Permit us to be as free as yourselves, and we shall ever esteem a union with you to be our greatest glory and our greatest happiness, we shall ever be ready to contribute all in our power to the welfare of the Empire—we shall consider your enemies as our enemies, and your interest as our own.

But if you are determined that your Ministers shall wantonly sport with the rights of Mankind—If neither the voice of justice, the dictates of the law, the principles of the constitution, or the suggestions of humanity can restrain your hands from shedding human blood in such an impious cause, we must then tell you, that we will never submit to be hewers of wood or drawers of water for any ministry or nation in the world.

Place us in the same situation that we were at the close of the last war, and our former harmony will be restored.

But lest the same supineness and the same inattention to our common interest, which you have for several years shewn, should continue, we think it prudent to anticipate the consequences.

By the destruction of the trade of Boston, the Ministry have endeavoured to induce submission to their measures.—The like fate may befal us all, we will endeavour therefore to live without trade, and recur for subsistence to the fertility and bounty of our native soil, which will afford us all the necessaries and some of the conveniences of life.—We have supended our importation from Great Britain and Ireland; and in less than a year's time, unless our grievances should be redressed, shall discontinue our exports to those kingdoms and the West-Indies.

It it with the utmost regret however that we find ourselves

compelled by the overruling principles of self-preservation, to adopt measures detrimental in their consequences to numbers of our fellow subjects in Great Britain and Ireland. But we hope, that the magnanimity and justice of the British Nation will furnish a Parliament of such wisdom, independance and public spirit, as may save the violated rights of the whole empire from the devices of wicked Ministers and evil Counsellors whether in or out of office, and thereby restore that harmony, friendship and fraternal affection between all the Inhabitants of his Majesty's kingdoms and territories, so ardently wished for by every true and honest American.

TO THE INHABITANTS OF THE
PROVINCE OF QUEBEC[1]

Friends and fellow-subjects,

WE, the Delegates of the Colonies of New-Hampshire, Massachusetts-Bay, Rhode-Island and Providence Plantations, Connecticut, New-York, New-Jersey, Pennsylvania, the Counties of Newcastle Kent and Sussex on Delaware, Maryland, Virginia, North-Carolina and South-Carolina, deputed by the inhabitants of the said Colonies, to represent them in a General Congress at Philadelphia, in the province of Pennsylvania, to consult together concerning the best methods to obtain redress of our afflicting grievances, having accordingly assembled, and taken into our most serious consideration the state of public affairs on this continent, have thought proper to address your province, as a member therein deeply interested.

When the fortune of war, after a gallant and glorious resistance, had incorporated you with the body of English subjects,

---

[1]*Journals of the Continental Congress,* I, pp. 105-113.

we rejoiced in the truly valuable addition, both on our own and your account; expecting, as courage and generosity are naturally united, our brave enemies would become our hearty friends, and that the Divine Being would bless to you the dispensations of his over-ruling providence, by securing to you and your latest posterity the inestimable advantages of a free English constitution of government, which it is the privilege of all English subjects to enjoy.

These hopes were confirmed by the King's proclamation, issued in the year 1763, plighting the public faith for your full enjoyment of those advantages.

Little did we imagine that any succeeding Ministers would so audaciously and cruelly abuse the royal authority, as to withhold from you the fruition of the irrevocable rights, to which you were thus justly entitled.

But since we have lived to see the unexpected time, when Ministers of this flagitious temper, have dared to violate the most sacred compacts and obligations, and as you, educated under another form of government, have artfully been kept from discovering the unspeakable worth of *that* form you are now undoubtedly entitled to, we esteem it our duty, for the weighty reasons herein after mentioned, to explain to you some of its most important branches.

"In every human society," says the celebrated Marquis *Beccaria*, "there is an *effort, continually tending* to confer on one part the heighth of power and happiness, and to reduce the other to the extreme of weakness and misery. The intent of good laws is to *oppose this effort*, and to diffuse their influence *universally* and *equally*."

Rulers stimulated by this pernicious "effort," and subjects animated by the just "intent of opposing good laws against it," have occasioned that vast variety of events, that fill the histories of so many nations. All these histories demonstrate the truth of this simple position, that to live by the will of one man, or set of men, is the production of misery to all men.

On the solid foundation of this principle, Englishmen reared

248

up the fabrick of their constitution with such a strength, as for ages to defy time, tyranny, treachery, internal and foreign wars: And, as an illustrious author[2] of your nation, hereafter mentioned, observes,—"They gave the people of their Colonies, the form of their own government, and this government carrying prosperity along with it, they have grown great nations in the forests they were sent to inhabit."

In this form, the first grand right, is that of the people having a share in their own government by their representatives chosen by themselves, and, in consequence, of being ruled by *laws*, which they themselves approve, not by *edicts* of *men* over whom they have no controul. This is a bulwark surrounding and defending their property, which by their honest cares and labours they have acquired, so that no portions of it can legally be taken from them, but with their own full and free consent, when they in their judgment deem it just and necessary to give them for public service, and precisely direct the easiest, cheapest, and most equal methods, in which they shall be collected.

The influence of this right extends still farther. If money is wanted by Rulers, who have in any manner oppressed the people, they may retain it, until their grievances are redressed; and thus peaceably procure relief, without trusting to despised petitions, or disturbing the public tranquillity.

The next great right is that of trial by jury. This provides, that neither life, liberty nor property, can be taken from the possessor, until twelve of his unexceptionable countrymen and peers of his vicinage, who from that neighbourhood may reasonably be supposed to be acquainted with his character, and the characters of the witnesses, upon a fair trial, and full enquiry, face to face, in open Court, before as many of the people as chuse to attend, shall pass their sentence upon oath against him; a sentence that cannot injure him, without injuring their own reputation, and probably their interest also; as the question may turn on points, that, in some degree, concern the general welfare; and if it does not, their verdict may form a precedent, that,

---

[2]Montesquieu, *L'Esprit des Loix*, XIX, Chap. 27.

on a similar trial of their own, may militate against themselves.

Another right relates merely to the liberty of the person. If a subject is seized and imprisoned, tho' by order of Government, he may, by virtue of this right, immediately obtain a writ, termed a Habeas Corpus, from a Judge, whose sworn duty it is to grant it, and thereupon procure any illegal restraint to be quickly enquired into and redressed.

A fourth right, is that of holding lands by the tenure of easy rents, and not by rigorous and oppressive services, frequently forcing the possessors from their families and their business, to perform what ought to be done, in all well regulated states, by men hired for the purpose.

The last right we shall mention, regards the freedom of the press. The importance of this consists, besides the advancement of truth, science, morality, and arts in general, in its diffusion of liberal sentiments on the administration of Government, its ready communication of thoughts between subjects, and its consequential promotion of union among them, whereby oppressive officers are shamed or intimidated, into more honourable and just modes of conducting affairs.

These are the invaluable rights, that form a considerable part of our mild system of government; that, sending its equitable energy through all ranks and classes of men, defends the poor from the rich, the weak from the powerful, the industrious from the rapacious, the peaceable from the violent, the tenants from the lords, and all from their superiors.

These are the rights, without which a people cannot be free and happy, and under the protecting and encouraging influence of which, these colonies have hitherto so amazingly flourished and increased. These are the rights, a profligate Ministry are now striving, by force of arms, to ravish from us, and which we are, with one mind, resolved never to resign but with our lives.

These are the rights *you* are entitled to and ought at this moment in perfection, to exercise. And what is offered to you by the late Act of Parliament in their place? Liberty of conscience in your religion? No. God gave it to you; and the temporal powers with which you have been and are connected, firmly stipulated for your enjoyment of it. If laws, divine and human, could secure it against the despotic caprices of wicked men, it was secured before. Are the French laws in *civil* cases restored? *It seems so.* But observe the cautious kindness of the Ministers, who pretend to be your benefactors. The words of the statute are—that those "laws shall be the rule, until they shall be *varied* or *altered* by any ordinances of the Governor and Council." Is the "certainty and lenity of the *criminal* law of England, and its benefits and advantages," commended in the said statute, and said to "have been sensibly felt by you," secured to you and your descendants? No. They too are subjected to arbitrary *"alterations"* by the Governor and Council; and a power is expressly reserved of appointing "such courts of *criminal, civil, and ecclesiastical* jurisdiction, as shall be thought proper." Such is the precarious tenure of mere *will,* by which you hold your lives and religion. The Crown and its Ministers are impowered, as far as they could be by Parliament, to establish even the *Inquisition* itself among you. Have you an Assembly composed of worthy men, elected by yourselves, and in whom you can confide, to make laws for you, to watch over your welfare, and to direct in what quantity, and in what manner, your money shall be taken from you? No. The power of making laws for you is lodged in the governor and council, all of them dependent upon, and removeable at, the *pleasure* of a Minister. Besides, another late statute, made without your consent, has subjected you to the impositions of *Excise,* the horror of all free states; thus wresting your property from you by the most odious of taxes, and laying open to insolent tax-gatherers, houses, the scenes of domestic peace and comfort, and called the castles of English subjects in the books of their law. And in the very act for altering your government, and intended to flatter you, you are not authorized to "assess, levy, or apply any *rates* and *taxes,* but for the inferior purposes of *making roads,* and erecting and repairing *public buildings,* or for other *local* conveniences, within your respective towns and districts." Why this degrading distinction? Ought not the property, honestly acquired by *Canadians*, to be held as sacred as that of *Englishmen?* Have not Canadians sense enough to attend to any other public affairs, than gathering stones from one place, and piling them up in another? Unhappy people! who are not only injured, but insulted. Nay more!—With such a superlative contempt of your understanding and spirit, has an insolent Ministry presumed to think of you, our respectable fellow-subjects, according to the information we have received, as firmly to perswade themselves that your gratitude, for the injuries and insults they have recently offered to you, will engage you to take up arms, and render yourselves the ridicule detestation of the world, by becoming tools, in their hands, to assist them in taking that freedom from *us*, which they have treacherously denied to *you*; the unavoidable consequence of which attempt, if successful, would be the extinction of all hopes of you or your posterity being ever restored to freedom: For idiocy itself cannot believe, that, when their drudgery is performed, they will treat you with less cruelty than they have us, who are of the same blood with themselves.

What would your countryman, the immortal *Montesquieu*, have said to such a plan of domination, as has been framed for you? Hear his words,[3] with an intenseness of thought suited to the importance of the subject.—"In a free state, every man, who is supposed a free agent, *ought to be concerned in his own government*: Therefore the *legislative* should reside in the whole body of the *people*, or their *representatives*."—"The political liberty of the subject is a *tranquillity of mind*, arising from the opinion each person has of his *safety*. In order to have this liberty, it is requisite the government be so constituted, as that one man need not be *afraid* of another. When the power of *making* laws, and the power of *executing* them, are *united* in the same person, or in the same body of Magistrates, *there can be no liberty*; because apprehensions may arise, lest the same *Monarch* or *Senate*, should *enact* tyrannical laws, to *execute* them in a tyrannical manner."

---

[3]Montesquieu, *L'Esprit des Loix*, XI, Chap. 6.

"The power of *judging* should be exercised by persons taken from the *body of the people*, at certain times of the year, and pursuant to a form and manner prescribed by law. *There is no liberty*, if the power of *judging* be not *separated* from the *legislative* and *executive* powers."

"Military men belong to a profession, which *may be* useful, but *is often* dangerous."—"The enjoyment of liberty, and even its support and preservation, consists in every man's being allowed to speak his thoughts, and lay open his sentiments."

Apply these decisive maxims, sanctified by the authority of a name which all Europe reveres, to your own state. You have a Governor, it may be urged, vested with the *executive* powers, or the powers of *administration*: In him, and in your Council, is lodged the power of *making laws*. You have *Judges*, who are to *decide* every cause affecting your lives, liberty or property. Here is, indeed, an appearance of the several powers being *separated* and *distributed* into *different* hands, for checks one upon another, the only effectual mode ever invented by the wit of men, to promote their freedom and prosperity. But scorning to be illuded by a tinsel'd outside, and exerting the natural sagacity of Frenchmen, *examine* the specious device, and you will find it, to use an expression of holy writ, "a whited sepulchre," for burying your lives, liberty and property.

Your *Judges*, and your *Legislative Council*, as it is called, are *dependant* on your *Governor*, and *he* is *dependant on the servant* of the Crown, in Great-Britain. The *legislative, executive* and *judging* powers are *all* moved by the nods of a Minister. Privileges and immunities last no longer than his smiles. When he frowns, their feeble forms dissolve. Such a treacherous ingenuity has been exerted in drawing up the code lately offered you, that every sentence, beginning with a benevolent pretension, concludes with a destructive power; and the substance of the whole, divested of its smooth words, is—that the Crown and its Ministers shall be as absolute throughout your extended province, as the despots of Asia or Africa. What can protect your property from taxing edicts, and the rapacity of necessitous and

cruel masters? your persons from Letters de Cachet, goals, dun-
geons, and oppressive services? your lives and general liberty
from arbitrary and unfeeling rulers? We defy you, casting your
view upon every side, to discover a single circumstance, promising from any quarter the faintest hope of liberty to you or your
posterity, but from an entire adoption into the union of these
Colonies.

What advice would the truly great man before-mentioned,
that advocate of freedom and humanity, give you, was he now
living, and knew that we, your numerous and powerful neighbours, animated by a just love of our invaded rights, and united
by the indissoluble bands of affection and interest, called upon
you, by every obligation of regard for yourselves and your
children, as we now do, to join us in our righteous contest, to
make common cause with us therein, and take a noble chance
for emerging from a humiliating subjection under Governors,
Intendants, and Military Tyrants, into the firm rank and condition of English freemen, whose custom it is, derived from
their ancestors, to make those tremble, who dare to think of
making them miserable?

Would not this be the purport of his address? "Seize the
opportunity presented to you by Providence itself. You have
been conquered into liberty, if you act as you ought. This work
is not of man. You are a small people, compared to those who
with open arms invite you into a fellowship. A moment's re-
flection should convince you which will be most for your interest
and happiness, to have all the rest of North-America your un-
alterable friends, or your inveterate enemies. The injuries of
Boston have roused and associated every colony, from Nova-
Scotia to Georgia. Your province is the only link wanting, to
compleat the bright and strong chain of union. Nature has
joined your country to theirs. Do you join your political interests. For their own sakes, they never will desert or betray
you. Be assured, that the happiness of a people inevitably depends on their liberty, and their spirit to assert it. The value
and extent of the advantages tendered to you are immense.

Heaven grant you may not discover them to be blessings after they have bid you an eternal adieu."

We are too well acquainted with the liberality of sentiment distinguishing your nation, to imagine, that difference of religion will prejudice you against a hearty amity with us. You know, that the transcendant nature of freedom elevates those, who unite in her cause, above all such low-minded infirmities. The Swiss Cantons furnish a memorable proof of this truth. Their union is composed of Roman Catholic and Protestant States, living in the utmost concord and peace with one another, and thereby enabled, ever since they bravely vindicated their freedom, to defy and defeat every tyrant that has invaded them.

Should there be any among you, as there generally are in all societies, who prefer the favours of Ministers, and their own private interests, to the welfare of their country, the temper of such selfish persons will render them incredibly active in opposing all public-spirited measures, from an expectation of being well rewarded for their sordid industry, by their superiors; but we doubt not you will be upon your guard against such men, and not sacrifice the liberty and happiness of the whole Canadian people and their posterity, to gratify the avarice and ambition of individuals.

We do not ask you, by this address, to commence acts of hostility against the government of our common Sovereign. We only invite you to consult your own glory and welfare, and not to suffer yourselves to be inveigled or intimidated by infamous ministers so far, as to become the instruments of their cruelty and despotism, but to unite with us in one social compact, formed on the generous principles of equal liberty, and cemented by such an exchange of beneficial and endearing offices as to render it perpetual. In order to complete this highly desirable union, we submit it to your consideration, whether it may not be expedient for you to meet together in your several towns and districts, and elect Deputies, who afterwards meeting in a provincial Congress, may chuse Delegates, to represent your province in the continental Congress to be held at Philadelphia on the tenth day of May, 1775.

In this present Congress, beginning on the fifth of the last month, and continued to this day, it has been, with universal pleasure and an unanimous vote, resolved, That we should consider the violation of your rights, by the act for altering the government of your province, as a violation of our own, and that you should be invited to accede to our confederation, which has no other objects than the perfect security of the natural civil rights of all the constituent members, according to their respective circumstances, and the preservation of a happy and lasting connection with Great-Britain, on the salutary and constitutional principles herein before mentioned. For effecting these purposes, we have addressed an humble and loyal petition to his Majesty, praying relief of our and your grievances; and have associated to stop all importations from Great-Britain and Ireland, after the first day of December, and all exportations to those Kingdoms and the West-Indies, after the tenth day of next September, unless the said grievances are redressed.

That Almighty God may incline your minds to approve our equitable and necessary measures, to add yourselves to us, to put your fate, whenever you suffer injuries which you are determined to oppose, not on the small influence of your single province, but on the consolidated powers of North-America, and may grant to our joint exertions an event as happy as our cause is just, is the fervent prayer of us, your sincere and affectionate friends and fellow-subjects.

By order of the Congress,

HENRY MIDDLETON, *President.*

MANDATE CONCERNING THE INVASION OF CANADA BY AMERICAN FORCES[1]

Jean-Olivier Briand, by the mercy of God and the grace of the Holy See, Bishop of Quebec, etc., etc., etc.,

To all the peoples of this colony, greeting and benediction. A troop of subjects in revolt against their lawful Sovereign, who is also yours, has invaded this Province, less in the hope of being able to maintain a position there than with a view to involving you in their revolt, or at least engaging you not to oppose their pernicious design. The singular kindness and leniency with which we have been governed by His Very Gracious Majesty King George III since the arbitrament of war has made us his subjects, and the recent benefits with which he has favoured us, in restoring the use of our laws and the free practise of our religion and in allowing us to enjoy all the privileges and advantages of British subjects, these are favours great enough in themselves to inspire your gratitude and your zeal to promote the interests of the British Crown. But at this moment your hearts should be stirred by still more urgent motives. Your religion and the oaths which you have taken impose upon you an indispensable obligation to defend to the utmost your country and your King. Close your ears, therefore, dear Canadians, to the voices of sedition which seek to destroy your happiness by stifling the sense of submission to your lawful superiors graven in your hearts by your education and your religion. Be joyful in the execution of orders from a beneficent government which seeks no other goal than your interest and your happiness. There is no question of carrying the war into distant provinces; you are being asked merely to help repulse the enemy and turn back the invasion which threatens this province. Your religion and your interests unite to guarantee your zeal in the defence of our frontiers and our property.

---

[1]*Mandements des Evêques de Québec*, II, pp. 264-65.

Given in Quebec, under our hand, the seal of our arms, and the signature of our secretary, May 22, 1775.

J. Ol., Bishop of Quebec
by Monseigneur
F. Perrault, Priest, Secretary.

CIRCULAR LETTER CONCERNING THE RE-ESTABLISHMENT OF THE MILITIA[1]

Sir

Always attentive to the honour and good of the province entrusted to his care, His Excellency General Carleton has today added another to the list of favours already granted by re-establishing the militia companies in this province. This means of maintaining public order in our parishes and policing our rural population is at the same time a mark of esteem and confidence honouring all citizens of the province, and especially those who will hold military commissions. It is the intention of the Governor to choose as officers only candidates who are acceptable to the public. I do not doubt that this benefit will inspire in all hearts a gratitude proportionate to its importance and . . . worthy of the reputation of Canadians. These are the sentiments which you must seek to inspire in your parishioners when, after mass on the first feast day, the proclamation and the letter addressed to you by His Excellency are read and posted at the church door in the usual fashion.

I am respectfully,

sir,

your very humble and obedient servant,
Montgolfier.

Montreal, 13 June, 1775.

---

[1]*Mandements des Evêques de Québec*, II, pp. 265-66.

ARTICLES OF CAPITULATION[1]

Made and entered into between RICHARD MONTGOMERY, *Esquire, Brigadier-General of the Continental Army, and the Citizens and Inhabitants of Montreal, represented by the Suscribers,* John Porteous, Pierre Panet, John Blake, Pierre Meziere, James Finlay, Saint George Dupree, James McGill, Louis Carrignant, Richard Huntly, Francois Mathiot, Edward William Grey, *and* Pierre Guy, *duly elected for that purpose.*

Article I

That the citizens and inhabitants of Montreal, as well individuals as religious orders and communities without any exceptions shall be maintained in the free possession and enjoyment of their rights, goods and effects moveable and immoveable of what nature soever they may be.

Article II

That the inhabitants French and English shall be maintained in the free exercise of their religion.

Article III

That trade in general, as well within the province as in the upper countries and parts beyond the seas, shall be carried on freely as heretofore, and passports shall be granted for that purpose.

Article IV

That passports shall also be granted to those who may want them, for the different parts of this province, or elsewhere, on their lawful affairs.

---

[1]*Articles of Capitulation made and entered into between Richard Montgomery, Esquire, Brigadier-General of the Continental Army, and the citizens and inhabitants of Montreal,* Broadsheet, Philadelphia, 1775.

Article V

That the citizens and inhabitants of the town and suburbs of Montreal shall not be compelled, on any pretence whatsoever, to take up arms against the Mother Country, nor to contribute in any manner towards carrying on war against her.

Article VI

That the citizens and inhabitants of the town and suburbs, or any other part of the country, who have taken up arms for the defence of this province, and are taken prisoners, shall be set at liberty.

Article VII

That Courts of Justice shall be established for the determination of property, and that the Judges of the said Courts shall be elected by the people.

Article VIII

That the inhabitants of the town shall not be subjected to lodge troops.

Article IX

That no inhabitants of the country, or Savages, shall be permitted to enter the town until the Commandant shall have taken possession and provided for the security thereof.
Montreal, 12th November, 1775.

John Porteous,	*P. Panet,*
R. Huntly,	*Mathiot,*
John Blake,	*Carrignant,*
Edward Wm. Gray,	*Meziere,*
James Finlay,	*St. George Dupree,*
James McGill,	*Guy.*

LETTER TO MONTGOMERY FROM THE INHABITANTS OF THREE SUBURBS OF MONTREAL[1]

To Mr. Richard Montgomery, Brigadier-General of the Continental Army—the inhabitants of three suburbs of Montreal.

Sir,

The shadows in which we were enveloped are at last dispersed—the day has dawned, our chains are broken, and a happy freedom restores us to ourselves—a freedom which we have long desired, and which today makes it possible for us to bear witness to our satisfaction at being united with our colonial brothers of whom you are worthy representatives.

Although the citizens of the city of Montreal have heaped scorn upon us and continue to do so every day, we declare that we abhor their conduct towards our brothers and friends. We declare that the capitulation proposed by them is a treaty between enemies, and not a pact of association and fraternal union.

These same citizens have always regarded us, and still regard us, as rebels. We are not offended by this designation since we share it with our brothers in the Colonies, but in spite of them and in accordance with our own desire, we accept the union as we accepted it in our hearts as soon as the address of October 26, 1774 reached us. We could have given our answer then if we had dared. You certainly know, sir, that since that date even silence has been suspect, and that the man who dared to think and say what he thought was rewarded with prison, irons, or at least with the scorn and indignation of his fellow citizens.

We now consider those same citizens as a conquered people, and not a people entering into a union. They call us ignorant, and it is true that we appeared to be so, lost as we were in a despotic state. We are ignorant—so they say—but how can they know us and judge what we are, since true merit, the man of

---

[1]Verreau, *Invasion du Canada*, pp. 85-6.

talent, was not even admitted to the anteroom. We do not consider the moment opportune to give Your Excellency details of the oppression we have suffered and to name its authors. The time will come for these revelations.

All ignorant and rebellious as they say we are, we delcare—and we beg Your Excellency to convey our declaration to the Colonial Congress—we declare that our hearts have always desired the Union, that we regarded and received the troops of the Union as our own, that we accept the association offered to us by our brothers of the Colonies, and that we have never expected to be admitted into an association and to profit from its advantages without contributing our share. Even though we are ignorant, we are men of reason; the same laws, the same prerogatives, proportionate taxes, sincere union, permanent association, these are our resolutions, which conform in spirit with the address from our brothers.

MANDATE TO REBELLIOUS SUBJECTS DURING THE AMERICAN WAR[1]

Jean-Olivier Briand, by the mercy of God and the authority of the Holy See, Bishop of Quebec.

To the people of this diocese, greeting and benediction in the name of our Lord.

When God sought to lead the Jews who had turned away from Him and abandoned His law to repent of their monstrous faithlessness and apostasy, he spoke to Jeremiah and ordered him to speak to these stubborn and stiff-necked miscreants in words expressing both the goodness of God and the heinousness

---

[1]*Mandements des Evêques de Québec*, II, pp. 269-79.

of their sin: "Thus saith the Lord; Shall they fall and not arise? Shall he turn away and not return? Why then is this people of Jerusalem slidden back by a perpetual backsliding? They hold fast deceit and they refuse to return." (Jeremiah 8:4, 5) Is not that, brethren, a true picture of what is taking place in a great number of the people of this colony? You are too intelligent not to have recognized the gross trickery and iniquitous deceit which prepared the trap into which you walked with deplorable blindness and with a sort of fanatical frenzy. Why then, now that you have recognized the fraud, do you not turn away from it? Why do you still suffer its influence? Is not this strange folly? What is it which prevents you from repenting of it? Is it despair, fear of being denied pardon? In that case you would be guilty of a second, and more serious, error. Is it not said that the shorter the life of folly the better, and that it is better to repent late than not at all? It is true that you have irritated your Sovereign; but he is kind, and all are agreed that we live under a gentle and peace-loving government, one which sets a high value on human life and which is distinguished by clemency and leniency. You cannot fail to have been convinced of this in the seventeen years during which you have lived under its rule. Here a man may be accused without being considered guilty; he may even be proved guilty without being condemned. The circumstances of the case are examined, and often the slightest excuse suffices to exempt the culprit from the full rigour of the law. Now, dear brethren, His Gracious Majesty, Parliament, and His Excellency Lord Carleton all know that you have been misled, cheated, deceived, that you have been frightened by prophecies of calamity with no shadow of foundation, and that you have been promised favours offensive to religion, justice, and reason. You may rest assured that these considerations have already had their effect on the minds and hearts of those whose power you fear. They would result in your being forgiven at least your most serious offences, if you hasten to give evidence of repentance and loyalty. But if you persist in your rebellion, you will suffer the most rigorous punishment. What could save you from such sanctions? Do you suppose that an empire as powerful as the British Empire, whose navy can resist the united navies of Europe, will be denied, and that it will not accomplish the task which it has set itself? Only stubborn stupidity or great ignorance could harbour such an idea.

Your own interest then commands you to return forthwith to the path of duty. We exhort you, dear brethren, we beseech you, on the body of Jesus Christ, to do so. In this we propose no other goal than your own good, both spiritual and temporal. First, your temporal good; for, dear brethren, you cannot be unaware of the fatal effects of stubborn resistance. Your rebellion, which defied religion, good sense, and reason, deserved exemplary and rigorous punishment from a prince from whom until now you have received only signal marks of kindness. Kindness such as his is extremely rare in a powerful conqueror, and was quite unexpected; for you it has meant that a change of sovereignty resulted in greater well-being. Remember that when you joined the revolt no one was suffering from the effects of the late war. Not only had the losses which you had suffered been repaired, but your fortunes had greatly increased, and your property had become much more valuable. You should have praised and thanked Providence for your good fortune; duty and gratitude should have been ties binding you inseparably to the person, the authority, and the glory of your Sovereign. He had a right to expect such loyalty, and he was secure in the conviction that he could count upon it. Had you followed the rules of gratitude and the precepts of your religion, his hopes would not have been deceived.

Relying on this conviction, the King, faced with the necessity of using force in order to recall his rebellious provinces to their duty and obedience, did not fear to withdraw from ours troops no longer required here to ensure the submission which he was sure you felt in your minds and hearts. You should have been expected, and you were expected, to be ardent in support of the interests of a beneficent King, and of a court and Parliament devoted to you and busy with plans to make you a happy, rich, and flourishing people. With what surprise must England have learned of your defection, your disobedience, your revolt, and your union with rebels! How great must have been her anger and indignation! Have you not reason to fear that her kindness thus betrayed may change to fury, that she may mete out just punishment instead of the favours already lavished upon you, and of other very special favours which she had in store for you? If by a show of some part of her formidable strength your eyes had been opened to your duty, she would perhaps also have pardoned you in consideration of your ignorance and simplicity and of the tricks, ruses, lies, deceit, the threats, and false, unreasonable and unfounded promises with which your insidious enemies seduced and perverted you, involving you in their iniquitous designs, not for love of you or thought for your good, but out of envy and jealousy of the preference accorded to you.

No, no, dear bretheren, the colonists did not seek your welfare; it was not brotherly love which brought them into this colony; it was not in order to procure for you the liberty which you already enjoyed and from which you were about to derive still greater advantages, that a handful of men, unskilled in military art, descended on the countryside and seized the defenceless towns of Montreal and Three Rivers. It was with a very different motive, a motive which, did you but comprehend it, would cover you with shame and disgrace, and which, if you plumbed all its depths of malice and treason, would fill you with rage and fury against the perfidious enemies whom you have been foolish enough to call brothers and friends of our people.

Suffer your father in God, whom you hate although he has never done you any harm, although he has desired only your good and has constantly striven to procure it, dedicating to that purpose all his frail physical and mental powers; suffer him, I say, to teach you that of which you are, by your own choice, ignorant, closing your ears to the advice of those who are attached to you by the bonds of religious and patriotic duty,

265

and opening them wide to the poisonously wicked and self-seeking lies of your cruelest enemies. Suffer, once more, that I open your eyes and reveal to you the criminal motives which, to your shame, they have called into play in their effort to pervert you and to make you unworthy of the favour of our Sovereign. I cannot think of these motives without shedding bitter tears, because I love you; without blushing in confusion, because I am truly attached to you and your shame is mine; and because I hate deceit as Our Lord himself holds in horror the man of faithless heart, as He curses him who sets a trap for a blind man. *Maledictus qui ponit offendiculum ante pedes caeci.* These, dear brethren, are the crimes by which the southern colonies have betrayed you. Jealous, mad with jealousy, at the favours granted to you by the government, and which you did not sufficiently recognize, they went to London and bent all their efforts to prevent the granting of these favours. They have not yet relinquished those efforts; but, as their manœuvres proved fruitless, they turned their attack against you. They knew that you had little instruction, and no knowledge of politics or your own interest; they considered you stupid and ignorant, and they concluded that they could not prevent the Court from being disposed in your favour nor shake its conviction of your loyalty and bravery and your sincere devotion to your religion. Your enemies, who understand the teachings and spirit of your religion better than you did yourselves, undertook to make you unworthy of the favours which had been granted to you. For your misfortune, as we shall point out to you, they succeeded, and you became guilty of revolt, cowardice, and a form of denial of the religion of your fathers. They represented the Bill as an attack on your liberty, as tending to enslave you and place you at the mercy of your seigneurs and the nobility, they promised you exemption from seignorial dues, and you loved this injustice; they promised that you would pay no more tithes, and you were not moved with horror at such sacrilegious ingratitude towards the God without whose blessing your fields would remain infertile and your labour would be fruitless.

These are the reasons with which they persuaded you. But consider what they must have thought of you, to propose to you motives which shock reason, justice, equity, the order established in all nations, and a law observed in all Catholic countries, a law founded in natural law, and more expressly in the divine law of the Old and New Testaments, in civil and ecclesiastical law as to its essential principle and operation; and in all laws, natural, divine, ecclesiastical, and civil; there is no nation in the world whose religion is not the charge of special persons, and which does not provide for the subsistence of its priests. Must they not have regarded you as an impious people devoid of religion, reason, and principles, with no sense of justice or equity, in a word, must they not have thought you worse than the most barbarous savages? They succeeded in the task they had undertaken, not by their direct addresses to the Court, which failed; but by degrading you; so that it was you who plunged the sword into your own hearts. Not only did you deprive yourselves of the favours already granted to you, but you destroyed and nullified the terms of capitulation, the peace treaty, and the other declarations by which the King had annexed you to the English nation, placed you on the same footing with his ancient subjects, and granted you the same rights and prerogatives. By your own act, you are now no more than a twice-conquered people, subject to the will of a conquering sovereign. All your possessions are justly liable to confiscation by the Crown and you yourselves are threatened with the harrowing prospect of exile, if the government should consider such a penalty necessary or useful for the conservation of its conquest.

This is the abyss, these are the misfortunes into which you have been cast by these false friends, these unnatural traitors, and barbarous brothers. So much for your temporal condition. Let us now consider your spiritual good, I mean your religion and your salvation.

To what dangers have you exposed that religion! What obstacles you have placed in the path of your salvation!

267

First of all, dear brethren, you have committed the high crime of perjury; you have been accessories to every manifestation of sedition; you have been guilty of all those deaths which could truly be qualified as murder, you bear the responsibility for all the harm done to your neighbour, for all the losses he has suffered, as well as for the expense which your disobedience, and in some cases your rebellion, has imposed upon the Government. Consider next the abyss of sin into which you have plunged. . . . How is it possible for you to escape from it? How can you repair the damage, which cannot be forgiven until reparation has been made. In the words of Saint Augustine: *non dimittitur peccatum, nisi restituatur ablatum.* Brethren, my heart has been torn by this thought for more than ten months. I did not fear that the colony would be conquered, and for two reasons: because I had faith in God and in our Holy Protectress, and because I was informed as to the strength of the enemy and the state of our forces. But I was preoccupied by the thought of your salvation, and the means by which I might touch your consciences, especially in the matter of restitution. That was the consideration which forced me to withhold the sacraments until the affair was over and His Majesty had granted an amnesty. See, brethren, and judge for yourselves, the nature of the obstacles which you have placed in the way of your salvation, how difficult a task it is to bring you to that condition of repentance which is absolutely essential in order that you may obtain pardon for your sins before God.

In the second place, how great are the dangers to which you have exposed your religion! It is true that you were unaware of these dangers, and that you did not understand them. I believe, brethren, that you are, for the most part, too deeply attached to the religion of your fathers to want to change it or to deny it. And yet, it is only too true that you would have taken that course had God not been merciful, and once Quebec had been taken, you would have become apostates, schismatics, and pure heretics, sharing the error of the most cruel enemies of the Roman religion, the Protestant sect most widely separated from it. For no other sect has persecuted Roman Catholics as the Boston Protestant sect has; no other has outraged priests, and profaned churches and relics of the saints as it has done; no other has launched such blasphemous attacks against the faith of Catholics in the protection of the saints and of the Holy Mother of God. Would you have persisted in resisting temptation, you who can fairly be said to have little knowledge of your religion, who are steeped in ignorance on almost all the points of your faith and the proofs of its infallibility, you who, like poor blind mad fanatics had made it a principle not to listen to those who were given to you by God to serve as your leaders and guides, to be your light and the defenders of your faith. There can be no doubt, brethren, that their calumny and trickery, their lies concerning your religion would soon have seduced you from your faith. I do not doubt that they would even have succeeded in making you deplore the fate of your fathers and the experience of your early years. You would soon have been heard singing hymns of thanksgiving for your deliverance from the alleged superstition of papism and your discovery of the truth.

If you have retained even a little of your faith, brethren, you must indeed be seized with terror when you consider seriously the extent and the imminence of the danger to which you have been exposed. For, apart from those who have declared publicly that the Colonists' religion was a good religion and who have boasted of being Protestants, it is evident that all, or almost all, of those who did not follow the teaching of their priests, who refused to listen as they spoke from the pulpit or in the confessional, are guilty of schism and have separated themselves from the Church; since by separating themselves from their own pastors they have separated themselves from their Bishop to whom they are united by their faith, as the Bishop himself is united with the Holy See, the centre of the Catholic Church. Jesus Christ declared that whosoever did not listen to the ministers whom He had sent to teach the world and to govern His Church, did not listen to Him; and that he who resisted and despised his priests, resisted and despised Him: *Qui vos audit, me audit . . . qui vos spernit, me spernit . . . qui vos recipit, me recipit.* In like manner your conduct is proof of your leaning towards heresy.

I know that, ignorant as many of you are, you have not consciously entertained heretical doctrines, you have not professed the heresy of the Puritans and the Independents who reject the idea of a minister established by God to teach and convince, but you have acted as if you had embraced this heretical opinion, specifically condemned by the Sacred Council of Trent. In its twenty-third session, the Council anathematized those who maintain that all are priests, that the only sacred office is that of preaching the gospel, an office to which the people and the secular power appoint a person whom they deem fit for it, who may be removed at will and reduced to the status of layman. (See the first and fourth canons of the twenty-third session.)

You will perhaps say, and indeed you have said, that it is not the business of priests to make war or to concern themselves with it, and it is quite true that their ministry debars them from shouldering a musket or shedding blood; but is it not their duty to judge whether a war is just or unjust, as it is to give judgment on the obedience and the service which subjects owe to their sovereign? You must surely know that since swearing an oath is a religious act it concerns the Church. And when you have unwisely sworn oaths which you are unable to honour, do you not come to us to ask to be relieved of them, as you ask to be relieved of vows? You fall into gross error when you say that it is not for priests to meddle with war. Or alternatively, if, knowing that you were obliged to consult them, you did not do so, you have sinned with malice aforethought against the Holy Spirit and your own conscience.

The list of sins against God of which you have been guilty is a long one! First, the sin of disobedience to the lawful Sovereign; the sinner guilty of such resistance is damned. Secondly, the sin of perjury. You have also on your consciences the consequences of your forswearing: enormous expense to the

Crown, and damage to private property. Thirdly, you are guilty of the thefts and murders which have been committed, of the fires which have been set. And what of the persecution of priests of Jesus Christ, your fathers in the faith? Did it not stem from you? Did you not have some part in it even though you were not yourselves informers or accusers? Would these crimes have been committed if you had done your duty? And what of the sacrilegious informers, the would-be assassins of priests of Our Lord? Could they not be compared to a Nero or a Domitian? Nay, their crimes were even more odious; for the emperors were not Christians. What can I say of those who insulted and imposed silence upon priests as they were expounding the word of God, of men who, if they had had a rifle in their hands, would have killed the preacher in the pulpit with less compunction than they would have killed a dog? What of those impious and sacrilegious individuals who had so little respect for the sacrament and the mercy of Our Lord that they dared reveal to heretics, enemies of our religion, the salutary counsel given by charitable pastors in the secret of the confessional? What of those who tried to force their pastors to ignore or infringe our orders? Is the state of mind of these persons such as to make them worthy to receive absolution? Is the man who holds a pistol at the priest's throat and demands absolution worthy to receive it? Obviously not; and the priest who granted it would be guilty of an offence.

What can one think of these persons? They are all liable to excommunication, and especially those who committed acts of violence, or spoke insolently in churches, or advised or applauded such offences, as well as almost all of those who were involved in the expedition during which Monsieur Bailly was wounded. The memory of that action, an everlasting shame to Canadians, will evoke the image of a more than barbarously cruel nation. The Americans themselves, deeply shocked, remarked that if ever they had a Canadian to roast, they would find a hundred others to turn the spit. And it is a fact that loyal subjects who have fallen into the enemy's hands have in all cases had more reason to complain of Canadians, their compatriots and brothers in the faith, than of foreigners. It was Canadians who robbed, looted, murdered, burned, kidnapped brother Canadians; it was Canadians who incited and spurred on the invaders to violence and depredation. If their urgings had always been followed, the toll of destruction would have been still greater than it was. Poor Canadians! Your name was covered with glory throughout Europe, and kingdoms rang with your praise! And now you will be known as the most traitorous, barbarous, and unworthy of peoples. I blush to think of it; I am deeply grieved; for I have not ceased to have for you the heart of a father. And I evoke the image of your crimes, not merely in a spirit of reproach or insult, but in order that you may see them with the eyes of religion, that you may comprehend their enormity, and that, weeping bitterly for them, you may achieve the true and proper condition of repentance which will make you worthy to be freely and completely forgiven by Our Lord. That is the one goal of my prayers and sacrifices. My hope is that you will give me consolation and proof that my prayers have been granted, before my Creator and Judge calls me to Him. The spell will be broken, your eyes will be opened, you will blush for your past errors, and, turning your eyes towards the cross upon which Jesus prayed for those who crucified Him, confident in His infinite mercy, you will not despair of moving Him to compassion; kneeling, in tears and with a contrite and humble heart, before those same ministers whom you have persecuted, scorned, insulted, you will confess your sins; cured of your unjust prejudice against them, you will thank them for the firmness which saved you from the sacrilegious absolution and communion which would have increased the number of your sins, kept you in a state of spiritual blindness, and perhaps led you to harden your heart in final impenitence. I promise you that you will find in them the same Christian charity and compassion which you have always known. You will see for yourselves that they are filled with the spirit of Our Lord who pardoned the good thief who had just reviled him. It is of course true that although they can reconcile you with God, they cannot exempt you from satisfying God's justice by doing penance. But the penalty will be proportionate to your powers, and its bitterness and severity will be mitigated by the sincerity of your repentance.

Finally, I hope, dear children, that your fault may have happy results for your salvation and your religion, and that God, who can derive good from evil, may make use of it to attach you more closely to your pastors, to make you more docile, more respectful, and more obedient. The origin of all your misfortunes lies in your failure to be guided by these virtues. If you had consulted your pastors as you should have done, if you had had that confidence in them which God orders you to have, you would have been untouched by the disorders which have troubled the other colonies. *Labia sacerdotis custodient scientiam, et legem requirent ex ore ejus*; "Knowledge is entrusted to the lips of the priest, and the people will come to receive from his mouth knowledge of the law."

D'ESTAING'S PROCLAMATION[1]

Declaration addressed in the name of the King to all former French subjects in North America.

The undersigned, with the authorization of His Majesty, and clothed thereby with the truest of titles and one which effaces all others; charged in the name of the Father of his country and the beneficent protector of his subjects to offer support to those born to enjoy the benefits of his government, to all his compatriots in North America.

[1]Doniol, H., *Histoire de la participation de la France à l'établissement des Etats-Unis d'Amérique*, III, pp. 464-66.

You were born French, you could not have ceased to be French. A war, which had been declared only by the capture of almost all our seamen, and in which our common enemies owed their principal victories to the courage, talent, and number of the brave Americans who are at war with them today, took from you what is dearest to all men, the very name of your country. You are threatened with this greatest of all misfortunes, being forced to raise a parricidal hand against your motherland. A new war must now make you fear that you may be obliged to submit to this law, more revolting than slavery. The present war began, as the last one did, with acts of piracy against the most valuable part of our trade. The prisons of America have too long been filled with the groans of unhappy French prisoners. War was declared in the month of March last by an authentic act of English sovereignty declaring to all orders of the state that to carry on trade and to allow others to do so was an offence against England, that to state frankly that it was being done was to defy her, that she would be avenged, that she reserved the right to do so when it was to her advantage, and to attack by surprise even more legally than during the last war; she declared that she had the right and the will, and she demanded the means, to do so.

After the proclamation of the present war, the scourge was delayed and its scope limited as far as possible by a Monarch whose peaceful and disinterested views demanded no other mark of your former allegiance than your own happiness, but he was finally obliged to answer force with force and to take reprisals for repeated acts of hostility. If necessity carries his arms or those of his allies into a country which is still dear to him, you need not fear fire or devastation. If gratitude and the sight of a flag which has always been revered by those who followed it should attract to the forces of France or the United States Indians who loved us and upon whom presents were lavished by the king they called their father, those Indians will never use against you their cruel methods of waging war. They will renounce such methods or cease to be our friends.

It is not by threatening our compatriots that we shall try to avoid fighting them, nor will this declaration be weakened by insults to a great and brave nation whom we can respect and whom we hope to defeat.

I need not say to those of you who were born noblemen of France, as I was, that there is only one royal house under which Frenchmen could be happy and serve with joy; because its head, and those who are closely bound to him by ties of blood, have in all ages and through a long line of monarchs been pleased to bear, as they are still pleased to bear, the title which Henry IV regarded as his proudest title. I will not try to awake regrets for those distinctions, special marks and decorations, treasures precious to all of us who think in common, and of which, for our common misfortune, French Americans who had shown themselves so worthy of them are now deprived. I hope and promise that Canadians will soon again be wearing these rewards of zeal. They will earn them by becoming the friends of our allies.

I need not ask the companions in arms of Monsieur le Marquis de Levi, who have shared in his glory, admired his talent and military skill, been charmed by his cordiality and frankness, so characteristic of our noble families, whether other peoples can boast other names with which they would prefer to see their own associated. Could Canadians who saw the hero Montcalm fall in their defence be the enemies of his descendants? At the name of Montcalm, their arms would fall from their hands!

I need not point out to ministers of the Church that their work of evangelization will require the special protection of Providence in order that belief may not be weakened by example, that temporal interest may not triumph over spiritual good, that unscrupulous sovereigns from whom political concessions have been wrested by force, may not gradually withdraw those concessions as they have less to fear. Nor need I point out that the ministers of religion must form one body in the state, and that no body could be more highly respected or have more power than that of the Canadian clergy taking part in the government; for their conduct has inspired the respect and the confidence of the people.

I need not point out to this people, to my compatriots in general, that a great monarchy, with the same religion, the same customs, the same language as they, a country where they have relations, old friends and brothers, is an inexhaustible source of commerce and of wealth, nor that these benefits can more surely and easily be acquired by reunion with powerful neighbours than by association with strangers from another hemisphere, in whom everything is different and who sooner or later would reveal themselves as jealous and despotic sovereigns and treat them as a defeated people, worse probably than their former compatriots who had caused them to be conquered. I need not point these things out to a whole people, for a people, when it acquires the right to think and to act, knows its own interest; it knows that to ally itself with the United States is to ensure its own happiness; but I shall declare, and I do formally declare in the name of His Majesty who authorized and commanded me to do so, that all his former subjects in North America who cease to recognize the sovereignty of England can count on his protection and support.

Done on board His Majesty's vessel, *Le Languedoc*, in Boston Harbour, this twenty-eighth day of October, one thousand seven hundred and seventy-eight.

Estaing

Bigrel de Grand-Clos,
Secretary appointed by the King, attached to the squadron commanded by M. Le Comte d'Estaing

On board *Le Languedoc*, from the press of F. P. Demange, printer to the King and to the Squadron.

Archives de la Marine, B⁴ 141, folios 248-249 *(Imprimé)*.

PROCLAMATION OF LA FAYETTE TO THE CANADIANS[1]

The persuasive love which has always animated the Heart of the King for the Inhabitants of Canada, and the desire of withdrawing them from the Dominion of the English, have determined His Majesty to send into one of the American Ports Land and Sea Forces capable of effecting this grand object.

The moment of their arrival *(ou point)* at the spot where they should join the troops of the United States; the General of the two Allied Nations will take care to concert the most speedy measures to fulfil the vision of Congress and the King in effecting *(travaillant)* the Independency of Canada, and if the French will fly with joy, to succour their distressed Brethren, doubt not they will hasten to shake off the yoke of the Common Enemy — The time is at last arrived when Canada will be set free *(rendue à lui même)* and in joining itself to the Thirteen Independent States, will bind again *(va reserrer)* the Cord of that strict Friendship which unites them for ever to France — By how many motives ought such an Alliance to be dear to the Inhabitants of Canada, to those who feel the Blood of France run in their Veins, and who under the Tyranny of a foreign Government have not ceased to glory in the Name: Admitted to the Confederacy, to which Congress has not ceased to call them, and the affection of the King to invite them, they will partake all its advantages and begin by choosing a Constitution that will suit themselves — The Clergy, *Noblesse* and People — All the orders of the State too long forgotten and neglected, will see their Religion, Privileges and Manners flourish again — They will find again in their Ally dear Brethren to whom they are attached from a Community of Birth, Sentiment and Customs, and will have no more to fear the Profanation, Scorn and Insult of a foreign Master. After too many Proofs of Patriotism & Honour which has always distinguished the Canadians,

---

[1]C.O. mg. 11. Q series, XVII, pt 1, pp. 175-80. The French text has not been discovered.

His Majesty, as well as the Congress of the United States, cannot believe they would do them sufficient Justice, if they employed any other Motives to recall them to what they owe to their Countrymen of France, to the Americans and themselves, than the Reasons they will find in their own Hearts, to animate them to Vengeance, to the love of Liberty, to make them fly under our Colours in completing by their Co-operation the first condition of the Alliance between France and the United States.

It is with particular satisfaction that the Marquis de La Fayette, Major-General in the Service of the said States of America, commanding the King's Regiment of Dragoons and Commander-in-Chief of the American Troops designed to co-operate in Canada, with the French Army etc. etc. etc. According to the Power & Instructions which we have to this Effect, declared in the name of the King, and in the name of the Congress of the United States, to whomever it may concern, that in the just war in which His Majesty finds himself engaged, and in consequence of the Reprisals to which he has been forced, by the Hostilities of Great Britain, he hath been pleased to order an Army by Land and by Sea to co-operate with those of the United States, for the Deliverance of Canada — that in joining with the United States to Engage Canada in the Confederacy, and by Consequence in the Alliance, which binds them to France, His Majesty invites the *Noblesse* and all the Inhabitants to join the combined Army for this happy Revolution — that His Majesty judging of the affectation of the Canadians by the feelings of his own Heart, is intimately persuaded, as well as the Congress of the United States, that the Allied Troops will find in the Country all the Resources and Succours of which (without doing the least wrong to the Interest of the Inhabitants) it is susceptible — that the Canadians will endeavour to bring back the ancient Dispostion of the Savages & to procure from them all the Intelligence which can contribute to our Success.

Though very far from thinking that any French in Canada, are capable of joining to spill the Blood of his own Brethren, the Wisdom of His Majesty and the Congress engage them to forewarn *(prévenir)* the Canadians, that the least Succour given the British Troops in their Preparation of Defence, in augmenting the Difficulties and Dangers of the Allies, should be considered by them as an Act of Hostility.

Mon^sor. the Count de *Rochambeau*, Lieut. General of the King's Army, Grand Cross of the Royal and Military Orders of St. Louis, and Commander-in-Chief of His Majesty's Army *(doit)* will publish after his arrival, a more particular Invitation to join Canada to the Confederacy of the United States, and we shall be charged to renew with the Canadians the fraternal Disposition of said States in the Assembly to be called for that Purpose.

The Instructions at present made public, communicate to the Canadians the Design of His Majesty and the Congress of the United States for their Deliverance, and to invite them to second our Efforts in breaking themselves the Fetters under which they groan.

Dated Head Quarters on Connecticut River
    (Signed)
                La Fayette
                By the General's Order
                    Captain's Secretary
Indorsed —
    Copy.
        Real inclosed in Sir H. Clinton's
        Letters the 18th Oct., 1780.
            No. 2
       In Govr. Haldimand's (Private)
         of 25th Oct., 1780 (2)

ABBREVIATIONS USED

Blockade   *Blockade of Quebec in 1775-1776 by the American Revolutionists (Les Bastonnais).* Ed. by F. C. Würtele (Literary and Historical Society of Quebec, DIO, Historical Documents: Quebec, 1905-1906), Seventh and Eighth series. Ainslie's Journal is designated by his initial (A).

Const. Docts.   *Documents Relating to the Constitutional History of Canada.*

Invasion   *Invasion du Canada.* Memoirs most frequently quoted are designated by the initial of the author: (S) Sanguinet, (B) Badeaux, (L) de Lorimier.

J. C. C.   *Journals of the Continental Congress.*

R. A. Q.   *Rapport de l'archiviste de la province de Québec.* The journal of the Baby-Taschereau-Williams commission is designated by the initials of the commissioners: (BTW).

280

BIBLIOGRAPHY

MANUSCRIPT SOURCES

Public Archives of Canada:

B. Series. Correspondence and papers of Governors Carleton and Haldimand.

Berthelot, Amable, Introduction à l'année 1775.

Bibliothèque Sainte-Geneviève No. 2088, Abbé de la Valinière, Mémoires sur l'état actuel du Canada.

British Museum Additional Manuscripts, Hardwick Papers, Civil Government of Quebec, etc.

C¹¹A, Canada et Dépendances. Official correspondence, Canada and France.

C¹¹E. Cebet and Cazeau documents.

Cazeau, François, Letters of, 1782-91, MSS Group 23, B.19.

Colonial Office, America and West Indies, 1789-93, I.

Colonial Office, 42, Canada, Original Correspondence, 1771-86.

Dartmouth Papers, 1788-98. Correspondence and papers of Lord Dartmouth, Secretary of State for the Colonies.

E Series, State Book, Quebec. Minute Books of Legislative and Executive Councils from 1764.

Foreign Office, 4, America, United States of, 1780-92, Series one.

France, Ministère des Affaires étrangères, Etats-Unis. Correspondence between French ministers and Versailles.

M Series, Miscellaneous. Documents formerly classified under serial and accession numbers, and now catalogued under separate titles.

Memorial of Peter Livius. Formerly catalogued under M. 689.

Murray Papers, 1759-86. Correspondence and papers of General James Murray.

Q., Quebec Series. Correspondence of the Governors of Canada, transcripts from C.O. 42, and official copies, 1771-1840.

S. Series, Sundries. Correspondence and papers from the Governor's office.

Saint-Sulpice, Documents du Séminaire de. Copies of documents, 1636-1830.

Shelburne Collection, 1763-83. Documents concerning Canada.

Private Archives:

Archevêché de Montréal, Correspondance.

Archevêché de Québec, Lettres et documents.

Evêché de Joliette, Correspondance.

Séminaire de Québec, Fonds Verreau, Boîte 9.

Université de Montréal, Baby Papers.

PRINTED SOURCES

Adams, Samuel. *The Writings of Samuel Adams.* Collected and ed. by H. A. Cushing (New York, 1904-07), 4 vols.

Canada and the American Revolution

Ainslie, Charles. See *Blockade*.

Allaire, Abbé J.B.A. *Dictionnaire biographique du clergé canadien-français* (Montréal, 1910-11) , 2 vols.

Allen, Ethan. *Ethen Allen's Narrative of the Capture of Saratoga and of his Captivity* (Burlington, 1849).

American Archives, consisting of a collection of authentic records, state papers, debates, and other notices of public affairs, the whole forming a documentary history of the origin and progress of the North American Colonies, of the causes and accomplishment of the American Revolution, and of the Constitution of government for the United States to the final ratification thereof. . . . In six series . . . by Peter Force, prepared and published under authority of an Act of Congress (Washington, 1837-53). Nine volumes were published: Fourth series, I-VI, and Fifth series, I-III.

Anburey, Thomas. *With Burgoyne from Quebec. An Account of the life at Quebec and of the famous battle of Saratoga*. First published in 1789 as volume one of *Travels through the Interior parts of North America*, by Thomas Anburey. Ed., with introduction and notes by Sydney Jackman (Toronto, 1963).

Arnold, Benedict. "Arnold's Letters on his expedition to Canada in 1775," *Collection of the Maine Historical Society* (Portland, 1861).

Articles of Capitulation, made and entered into between Richard Montgomery, Esquire, Brigadier-General of the Continental Army and the Citizens and Inhabitants of Montreal (Philadelphia, 1775), Broadsheet. See appendices.

Audet, F. J. "Sir Frederick Haldimand," *Proceedings and Transactions of the Royal Society of Canada* (1923), Section I.   "Simon Sanguinet et le projet d'université de 1790," *Proceedings and Transactions of the Royal Society of Canada*, 1936.

Baby, L. F. G. *L'Exode des classes dirigeantes à la cession du Canada* (Montreal, 1899).

Badeaux, J. B. See Verreau.

Beaujeu, Monongahela de. *Documents inédits sur le Colonel de Longueuil* (Montréal, 1891).

Berthelot, A. See Verreau.

Blockade of Quebec by the American Revolutionists (Les Bastonnais). Ed. by Fred C. Würtele (Literary and Historical Society of Quebec, Historical Documents: Quebec, 1905-06) , Seventh and Eighth series. The collection includes the following documents: "Journal of the most remarkable occurrences in the Province of Quebec from the appearance of the Rebels in September 1775 until their retreat on the sixth of May," by Charles Ainslie; "Journal of the most remarkable occurrences in Quebec since Arnold appeared before the town on the 14th November, 1775"; "Orderly Book begun by Captain Anthony Vialar of the British Militia, the 17th of September 1775 and kept by him till November 16th when continued by Captain Robert Lester"; "Rôle général de la milice canadienne. . . ." And, "Nouveau rôle de la milice canadienne qui a fait le service pendant le blocus de Québec. . . ."

Boissonnault, Charles-Marie. "Révolte en Amérique," *Revue de l'Université Laval* (1948).

Bradley, Arthur Grenville. *Lord Dorchester* (Toronto, 1907).

Burt, Alfred Le Roy. *The Old Province of Quebec* (Toronto and Minneapolis, 1933). "Sir Guy Carleton and his first Council," *Canadian Historical Review* (Dec. 1953), IV.   *Guy Carleton, Lord Dorchester*, revised version, Canadian Historical Association booklets, No. 5 (Ottawa, 1905).

Buxton, Georges. *L'Influence de la Révolution américaine sur le developpement constitutionel du Canada* (Paris, 1929).

Caldwell, Henry. "The Invasion of Canada, Letter attributed to Major Henry Caldwell." Literary and Historical Society of Quebec, Historical Documents, Second series.

Cambridge History of the British Empire, VI, Canada and Newfoundland (Cambridge, 1930).

Canada and its Provinces, III, Canada and the American Revolution (Toronto, 1913).

Carayon, Auguste. *Première Mission des Jésuites au Canada. Lettres et documents inédits* (Paris, 1864).

Caron, Ivanhoe. "Les Canadiens au lendemain de la capitulation de Montréal," *Proceedings and Transactions of the Royal Society of Canada* (1921).
"Les Canadiens-français et l'invasion américaine de 1774-1775," *Proceedings and Transactions of the Royal Society of Canada* (1929).

Carroll, Charles. *Journal of Charles Carroll of Carrollton during his visit to Canada in 1776, as one of the commissioners from Congress, with a memoir and notes by Brantz Mayer* (Phil., 1845).

Catalogne, Gédéon. "Mémoire de Gédéon de Catalogne," *Bulletin des recherches historiques* (1915).

Cavendish, Sir Henry. *Debates in the House of Commons in the year 1774 for making more effectual provision for the Government of the Province of Quebec* (London, 1839).

Charland, Thomas Marie. "La Mission de John Carroll au Canada en 1776 et l'interdit du P. Floquet," *Société canadienne de l'histoire de l'Eglise catholique, Rapport*, 1933-34.

Chastellux, François Jean, marquis de. *Voyages dans l'Amérique septentrionale dans les années 1780, 1781, et 1782* (Paris, 1786).

Chittenden, Lucius Eugène. *The Capture of Ticonderoga* (Montpelier, 1879).

Choiseul, duc de. *Mémoires du duc de Choiseul, 1749-1795* (Paris, 1904).

Clinton, George. *Public Papers of George Clinton, first Governor of New York* (New York and Albany, 1899-1914), 10 vols.

Codman, J. *Arnold's Expedition to Quebec* (New York, 1901). Appendix A, 313-21, contains a list of journals, American, English, French, and Canadian, describing Arnold's march through the wilderness and the siege of Quebec.

Coffin, V. *The Province of Quebec and the Early American Revolution* (Madison, 1896).

Collections of the Massachusetts Historical Society (Boston, 1852-71), Fourth series.

Collections of the New York Historical Society for the Year 1880, "Journal of the most remarkable occurrences in Quebec, 1775-1776" (New York, 1881).

Corwin, Edward Samuel. *French Policy and the American Alliance of 1778* (Princeton, 1916).

Coupland, R. *The Quebec Act* (Oxford, 1925).

De Lorimier. See Verreau.

Digby, William. *The British Invasion from the North. The Campaigns of Generals Carleton and Burgoyne from Canada, 1775-1777, with the Journal of Lieutenant William Digby*. Ed. by J. P. Baxter (Albany, 1887).

"Documents relatifs à la reddition du fort Saint-Jean et du fort Chambly (1775)," *Rapport des Archives canadiennes pour 1914 et 1915*. Appendice B.

"Documents relatifs à la révolution américaine de 1775," *Revue de l'Université Laval*. I, septembre à décembre, 1946; II, novembre, 1947 à juin, 1948.

Documents relating to Canadian Currency, Exchange and Finance during the French Period. Ed. by Adam Shortt (Ottawa, 1925), 2 vols.

Documents relating to the Constitutional History of Canada. Ed. by Adam Shortt and Arthur Doughty (Ottawa, 1918), 2 vols.

"Documents relating to the War of 1775," *Canadian Archives, Report for 1904*. Appendix I.

Doniol, Henri. *Histoire de la participation de la France à l'établissement des Etats-Unis d'Amérique* (Paris, 1886-92), 5 vols. Diplomatic correspondence and documents.

Donoughue, Bernard. *British Politics and the American Revolution; The Path to War, 1773-1775*, (London and New York, 1965).

Du Calvet, Pierre. *Appel à la justice de l'Etat* (London, 1784).

Canada and the American Revolution

Duane, William. *Canada and the Continental Congress* (Phil., 1850).

Ferland, J. B. A. Mgr. *J. O. Plessis* (Quebec, 1878).

Fobes, Simon. "Simon Fobes' Narrative," *Historical Collection of the Mahoning Valley*, I.

Franklin, Benjamin. *The Interest of Great Britain considered with regard to her colonies and the Acquisition of Canada and Guadeloupe* (London, 1760). *Letters and Papers of Benjamin Franklin and Richard Jackson, 1753-1785.* Ed. and annotated with an introduction by Carl Van Doren (Phil., 1938).

Frishes, Sydney G. *The True History of the American Revolution* (Phil. and London, 1902).

Gaspé, Philippe Aubert de. *Les Anciens Canadiens* (1934 edition).

Quebec Gazette (1774-83).

Germain, Albert Henry. *Catholic Military and Naval Chaplains, 1776-1917* (Washington, 1929).

Gosselin, Auguste. *L'Eglise du Canada depuis Mgr. de Laval jusqu'à la conquête* (Québec, 1914). *L'Eglise au Canada après la conquête* (Québec, 1916), 2 vols.

Griffin, M. I. J. *Catholics and the American Revolution* (Ridley Park, Pa., 1907-11).

Groulx, Lionel. *Lendemains de Conquête* (Montréal, 1920).

Guedalla, Philip. *Fathers of the Revolution* (New York and London, 1926).

Hadden, James Murray. *Hadden's Journal and Orderly Books; a journal kept in Canada upon Burgoyne's Campaign in 1776 and 1777. Also orders kept by him and issued by Sir Guy Carleton, Lieut. General John Burgoyne, and Major William Phillips in 1776, 1777, and 1778.* Ed. by Horatio Rogers (Albany, 1884).

Hamon, Joseph. *Le Chevalier de Bonvouloir, Premier Emissaire secret de la France auprès du Congrès de Philadelphie avant l'Indépendence américaine* (Paris, 1953).

Henry, John Joseph. *An Accurate and Interesting Account of the Hardships and Sufferings of the Band of Heroes who traversed the Wilderness in the Campaign against Quebec in 1775* (Lancaster, 1812).

Howe, Archibald M. *Colonel John Brown of Pittsfield, the brave accuser of Benedict Arnold* (New York, 1908).

Hudleston, Francis J. *Gentleman Johnny Burgoyne. Misadventure of an English general in the Revolution* (Indianapolis, 1927).

Hunt, Louise L. *Biographical notes concerning General Richard Montgomery, together with hitherto unpublished letters* (Poughkeepsie, 1876).

"Journal of the most remarkable events which happened in Quebec between the months of July 1775 and June 1776." Private collection of Dr. Doughty.

"Journal of the most remarkable occurrences in Quebec since Arnold appeared before the town on the 14th November, 1775." See *Blockade*.

"Journal par Messrs. Franç. Baby, Gab. Taschereau et Jenkins William dans la tournée qu'ils ont faite dans le district de Québec par ordre du Général Carleton tant pour l'établissement des milices dans chaque paroisse que pour l'examen des personnes qui ont assisté ou aidé les rebels dont nous avons pris des notes (1776)," *R.A.Q.* (1927-28, 435-99; 1929-30, 138-40).

Journals (secret) of the Acts and Proceedings of Congress from the first meeting thereof to the dissolution of the Confederation by the adoption of the Constitution of the United States (Boston, 1820), 4 vols.

Journals of the Continental Congress, 1774-1789. Ed. from the original records in the Library of Congress by Worthington Chauncey Ford (Washington, 1904-37), 34 vols.

Journals of Each Provincial Congress of Massachusetts in 1774 and 1775, and of the Committee of Safety, with an appendix containing the proceedings of the County Conventions. Ed. by William Lincoln (Boston, 1838).

Journals of the Provincial Congress, Provincial Convention, Committee of Safety

and *Council of Safety of the State of New York, 1775-1778* (Albany, 1842), 2 vols.
Kalm, Per. *Le Voyage de Kalm en Amérique* (Montréal, 1880). French translation and summary. *The America of 1750; Per Kalm's Travels in North America.* Ed. by Benson (New York, 1957).
Kerr, W. B. "The American Invasion of N.S.," *Canadian Defense Quarterly.* XIII.
Kingsford, William. *The History of Canada* (Toronto, 1892), V, VI, VII.
Knox, William. *The Justice and Policy of the Late Act of Parliament for making more Effectual Provision for the Government of the Province of Quebec* (London, 1774).
La Fayette, Marie Joseph Motier, marquis de. *The Letters of La Fayette to Washington.* Ed. by Louis Gottschalk (New York, 1944). *Mémoires, correspondance et manuscrits du général La Fayette, publiés par sa famille* (Paris, 1837-38) , 6 vols. "Letters from La Fayette to Luzerne, 1780-1782," *American Historical Review* (1914-15), XX, 341-67, 576-612.
La Valinière, Huet de. *Curious and interesting dialogue, French and English; in which everyone is furnished with arguments to defend his religion against all false assertions whatever* (New York: printed by Thomas Greenleaf for the author, 1790).
La Valinière, Huet de. *Vraie histoire; ou simple précis des infortunes, pour ne pas dire des persécutions qu'a souffert et que souffre encore le Rev. P. H. de La V., mis en vers par lui-même en juillet, 1792* (Albany, 1792) .
Labaree, Benjamin J. *The Boston Tea Party.*
Lanctot, G. et al. *Les Canadiens français et leurs voisins du Sud* (Montréal, 1941).
Laurent, Laval. *Québec et l'Eglise aux Etats-Unis sous Mgr. Briand et Mgr. Plessis* (Montréal, 1945).
Laws of the State of New York (New York, 1789), 2 vols.
Le Febvre, Jean J. *Les Franco-Américains et l'invasion américaine* (Boston, 1949).
Le Febvre, L. *Les Canadiens Français et la révolution américaine* (Boston, 1949). "Lettres écrites pendant l'invasion américaine en 1776 et 1777." See Verreau.
Lichtenberger, André. *Montcalm et la tragédie canadienne* (Paris, 1934).
Lossing, Benson J. *The Life and Times of General Philip Schuyler* (1883), 2 vols.
Mandements, lettres pastorales et circulaires des Evêques de Québec (Québec, 1888), II.
Marion, Séraphin. "L'Acte de Québec," *Les Cahiers des dix* (Montréal, 1963).
Masères, Francis. *An Account of the Proceedings of the British and other Protestant Inhabitants of the Province of Quebeck in North America, in order to obtain an House of Assembly in that Province* (London, 1775). *Additional papers concerning the Province of Quebeck* (London, 1776). *The Canadian Freeholder in Two Dialogues between an Englishman and a Frenchman settled in Canada* (London, 1777-79), 3 vols. *A collection of Several Commissions and other Public Instruments, Proceeding from His Majesty's Royal Authority relating to the Province of Quebeck in North America* (London, 1772). *Mémoire à la défense d'un Plan d'Acte de Parlement pour l'établissement des Lois de la Province de Québec.* Dressé par Mr. François Masères, etc., etc. . . (Londres, 1772).
McCoy, William. *Journal of a March of a Company of Provincials from Carlisle to Boston and thence to Quebec* (Glasgow, 1776), IV. Reprinted in *Pennsylvania Archives.*
McIlwraith, Jean. *Sir Frederick Haldimand* (London and Toronto, 1926).
Meigs, R. J. "Journal of the Expedition against Quebec." See Roberts, K.
Melvin, James. *Journal of the expedition to Quebec in the year 1775 under the command of Colonel Benedict Arnold* (Phil., 1864).
Meng, John J. "The Place of Canada in French diplomacy of the American Revolution," *Bulletin des recherches historiques* (1933), XXXIX. *Despatches and Instructions of Conrad Alexandre Gérard, 1778-1780,* with an historical introduction and notes by John J. Meng (Paris, 1939).

Canada and the American Revolution

Metzger, Charles H. *The Quebec Act. A primary cause of the American Revolution* (New York, 1936).

Mondésir, Edouard de. *Souvenirs,* with an introduction by Gilbert Chinard (Baltimore, 1942).

Monson, George. "Journal of the Expedition to Quebec." See Roberts, K.

Montcalm, Louis Joseph de. *Journal du marquis de Montcalm durant ses campagnes au Canada, 1756-1759* (Québec, 1895). *Lettres du marquis de Montcalm au chevalier de Lévis* (Québec, 1894).

Monty, Ernest. "Major Clément Gosselin," *Mémoires de la Société Généalogique* (janvier, 1948).

Neatby, Hilda. "Jean Olivier Briand. A 'Minor Canadian'," Presidential Address, *Canadian Historical Association, Report,* 1963.

New York Gazette and Weekly Mercury (1775).

"Orderly Book begun by Captain Anthony Vialar of the British Militia, the 17th of September 1775 and kept by him till November 16th when continued by Captain Robert Lester." See *Blockade.*

"Ordinances made for the Province of Quebec by the Governor and Council of the said Province since the Establishment of the Civil Government," *Reports of the Public Archives of Canada* (1913, 1914-15).

"Ordonnances et proclamations du règne militaire, 1760-1764," *Rapport des Archives canadiennes pour 1918.* Appendice B.

Ormesson, Wladimir d'. *La première mission officielle de la France aux Etats-Unis* (Paris, 1924).

Pennsylvania Archives, Selected and arranged from original Documents in the Office of the Secretary of the Commonwealth (Phil., 1853).

Porlier. "Mémoire de M. Porlier," *Bulletin des recherches historiques.* VI.

The Public Records of the State of Connecticut, from October 1776 to February 1777 inclusive, with the Journal of the Council of Safety from October 11, 1776 to May 6, 1778 inclusive, and an appendix (Hartford, 1894-1943), 5 vols.

R.A.Q., "Guerre de 1775-76. Sentiments des Sauvages" (1924), Appendice I.

Viger, J. "Règne militaire en Canada," *Mémoires de la Société historique de Montréal* (Montréal, 1870).

Relation par lettres de l'Amérique Septentrionale, 1709-1710. Ed. by C. de Rochemonteix. This narrative, based upon contemporary memoirs, and attributed to Father Silvy, was written by Denis Radot.

The Remembrancer, or Impartial Repository of public events (London, 1775).

Reports on the laws of Quebec, 1776-1770. Ed. with introduction and notes by W. P. M. Kennedy and Gustave Lanctot (Ottawa, 1931).

The Revolutionary Diplomatic Correspondence of the United States. Ed. by Francis Wharton (Washington, 1889).

Riedesel. *Memoirs and letters and Journals of Major General Riedesel.* Trans. by W. L. Stone (Albany, 1868), 2 vols.

Roberts, Kenneth L. *March to Quebec, Journals of the members of Arnold's expedition.* Compiled and annotated by Kenneth L. Roberts (New York, 1938). The collection includes the journals of: Col. Arnold, Capt. Henry Dearborn, Simon Fobes, Caleb Haskell, John Joseph Henry, Major R. Meigs, James Melvin, George Monson, John Montresor, George Morrison, Dr. Isaac Senter, Ephraim Squier, Abner Stockton, and Capt. Simeon Thayer.

"Rôle général de la milice canadienne. . . ." And, "Nouveau rôle de la milice canadienne qui a fait le service pendant le blocus de Québec. . . ." See *Blockade.*

Roy, Joseph E. *Histoire de la Seigneurie de Lauzon* (Lévis, 1897-1904), 3 vols.

Roy, Pierre G. *A travers les Anciens Canadiens de Philippe Aubert de Gaspé* (Montréal, 1943).

Sanguinet. See Verreau.

Shea, John Gilmary. "Why is Canada not a part of the U.S.?" *United States Catholic Historical Magazine* (1890), III. *Life and Times of the Most Rev. John Carroll, Bishop and first Archbishop of Baltimore* (New York, 1888).

Sherwood. "Letters from Captain Sherwood on secret service, 1780-1781," *Canadian Archives Report,* 1882-83.
Sister Mary Rita, S.C. "The Failure of a Mission," *Rapport de la Société canadienne d'histoire de l'Eglise catholique* (1957-58).
Smith, Justin H. *Arnold's March from Cambridge to Quebec. A Critical Study with a Reprint of Arnold's Journal* (New York and London, 1903) . *Our Struggle for the Fourteenth Colony, Canada and the American Revolution* (New York and London, 1907), 2 vols.
Smith, William. "First Days of British Rule," *Queen's University Bulletin.* No. 42.
South Carolina Historical Magazine. VII.
Stocking. "Interesting Journal," *Historical Collection of the Mahoning Valley.* I.
Stone, E. M. *The Invasion of Canada in 1775* (Providence, 1867).
Têtu, Mgr. Henri. *Les Evêques de Québec* (Québec, 1889).
Thayer. "The Journal of Captain Thayer," *The Invasion of Canada* by E. M. Stone.
Tower, Charlemagne. *The Marquis de La Fayette in the American Revolution* (Phil., 1901), 2 vols.
Treaties of 1778 and allied documents. Ed. by Gilbert Chinard, with an introduction and notes by James Brown Scott (Baltimore, 1928).
Trudel, Marcel, *Louis XVI, le Congrès américain et le Canada, 1774-1789* (Québec, 1949).
Turcotte, Louis Philippe. *Invasion du Canada et siège de Québec en 1775-1776* (Québec, 1876).
United States of America, Statutes at Large (1845), I.
Van Doren, Carl C. *Benjamin Franklin* (New York, 1938).   *Secret History of the American Revolution* (New York, 1941).
Van Tyne, Claude Halstead. *The Causes of the War of Independence* (Boston and New York, 1922).
Verreau, H. A. *Invasion du Canada, collection de mémoires recueillis et annotés par M. l'abbé Verreau, prêtre* (Montréal, 1873). The collection includes the following documents: "Extraits d'un mémoire de M. A. Berthelot sur l'invasion du Canada en 1775"; "Invasion du Canada par les Américains en 1775," Journal de J. Bte. Badeaux;   "Lettres écrites pendant l'invasion américaine en 1775 et 1776";   "Mes services pendant la guerre américaine de 1775," Mémoire de M. de Lorimier;   "Témoin oculaire de l'invasion du Canada par les Bastonnais," Journal de M. Sanguinet.
Washington, George. *The Writings of George Washington.* Ed. by Worthington Chauncey Ford (New York and London, 1889-93), 14 vols.
Wells, William V. *The Life and public services of Samuel Adams* (Boston, 1865).
Wrong, George M. *Canada and the American Revolution* (Toronto, 1935).

287

NOTES

CHAPTER I

1.) Cf. Franklin, Benjamin, *The Interest of Great Britain considered with regard to her Colonies and the Acquisition of Canada and Guadeloupe* (London, 1760).
2.) Lichtenberger, André, *Montcalm et la tragédie canadienne* (Paris, 1934), 130.
3.) *Documents relating to the Constitutional History of Canada*, "General Murray's Report, 6 June, 1762," ed. by Adam Shortt and Arthur Doughty (Ottawa, 1918), 71. *Bulletin des recherches historiques*, "Chanoine de Lorme à son frère, ler juillet, 1737," XIV, 39.
4.) Catalogne, Gédéon de, *Bulletin des recherches historiques*, "Mémoire sur les plans des seigneuries et habitations des gouvernements de Québec, des Trois-Rivières, et de Montréal" (1915), 334.
5.) $C^{11}A$, *Beauharnois et Hocquart au ministre, 15 octobre, 1730*, LII, 59.
6.) *R.A.Q.*, "Relation de M. Poulariès," 1931-32, 67.
7.) *Collection de mémoires et de relations sur l'histoire ancienne du Canada, d'après des manuscrits recemment obtenus des archives et bureaux publics en France* (Québec, 1840), 1-2.
8.) Montcalm, Louis Joseph de, *Journal du marquis de Montcalm* (Québec, 1894), 323.
9.) Kalm, Per, *Voyage de Kalm en Amèrique* (Montreal, 1880), 194. *Collection de mémoires*, 2-3.
10.) Montcalm, *Journal de Montcalm*, 63.
11.) *Relation par lettres de l'Amérique Septentrionale*, ed. by Father C. de Rochemonteix, 4.
12.) Montcalm, Louis Joseph de, *Lettres du marquis de Montcalm*, "Letter of July, 1757" (Quebec, 1894). 2 vols.
13.) Anburey, Thomas, *With Burgoyne from Quebec. . .*, first published in 1789 as vol. I of *Travels through the Interior parts of North America*, ed. with introduction and notes by Sydney Jackman (Toronto, 1963), 46.
14.) Q. 8, *Cramahé to Hillsborough, 25 July, 1772*, 161.
15.) *Const. Docts.*, "Carleton to Gage, 4 Feb., 1775," 661.
16.) *Ibid*, "General Murray's Report, 6 June, 1762," 79.
17.) Q. 2, *Murray to Lords of Trade, 29 Oct., 1764*, 233.
18.) Kalm, *Voyage de Kalm*, 237.
19.) Evêché de Joliette, cartable Lavaltrie, *Mgr. Briand à St.-Germain, 20 septembre, 1775*, I.
20.) Public Archives of Canada, Documents St.-Sulpice, *Ordonnance pour remédier à certain abus, 16 février, 1691*.
21.) Archêveché de Québec, Lettres, V, 105-08, 113-15.
22.) *Mémoires de la Société historique de Montréal*, "Règne militaire en Canada," ed. by J. Viger (Montréal, 1872). A collection of official documents.
23.) *Const. Docts.*, "Treaty of Paris," 97-108.

24.) *Ibid*, "Proclamation, 7 Oct., 1763," 163-68; "Instructions to Governor Murray, 7 Dec., 1763," 181-205; "Ordinance, 17 Sept., 1764," 205-10.

25.) Q. 2, *Murray to Halifax, 21 Aug., 1764*, 170.   *Const. Docts.*, "Col. Burton's Report of the State of the Government of Three Rivers, April, 1762," 81-7; "General Gage's Report of the State of the Government of Montreal, 20 March, 1762," 91-6.   Cf. Baby, Louis-François, *L'Exode des classes dirigeantes à la cession du Canada* (Montréal, 1899).   Q. 2, *Murray to Halifax, 21 Aug., 1764*, 170.

26.) *Memoirs and Letters and Journals of Major General Riedesel*, trans. by W. L. Stone (Albany, 1868), I, 60.

27.) Q. 1, *Adresse des habitants de Montréal, 23 mai, 1763*, 94; *Adresse des habitants de Québec, 10 juin, 1763*, 100.

28.) Dartmouth Papers, M. 383, *Lévesque, Lemoine et Porlier à Guimond, 27 septembre, 1765*, 126-32.

29.) *Mandements, lettres pastorales et circulaires des Evêques de Québec*, II, 165, 173.

30.) Cf. *Mémoires de la Société historique de Montréal*, "Règne militaire en Canada."

31.) Têtu, Mgr. Henri, *Les Evêques de Québec*, "Castelli à l'Isle-Dieu, 17 décembre, 1766," (Québec, 1889), 279-80.

32.) Archevêché de Québec, Adresses, Députations, Mémoires etc. au Gouvernement, *Requête des Vicaires Généraux à Murray, 1776*, IV.

33.) *Mandements des Evêques de Québec*, "Mandement de Mgr. Briand, 14 mars, 1772," II, 255-56.

34.) Archevêché de Québec, Lettres, *Mgr. Briand à M. de la Corne, 6 juin, 1774*, IV, 543.

35.) Dartmouth Papers, M. 383, *Mr. Cramahé's account of Quebec, 24 Aug., 1765*," 84.

36.) *Const. Docts.*, "Address of French Citizens to the King regarding the legal system" (1764), 223-29.

37.) Q. 6, *Carleton to Hillsborough, 25 Oct., 1769*, 164.

38.) Q. 1, *Gage to Egremont, 12 Feb., 1763*, 65.   B. 2, Pt. 1, *Haldimand to Gage, 20 June, 1765*, 160.   *Const. Docts.*, "General Gage's Report of the State of the Gov't of Montreal, 20 March, 1762," 91-6.

39.) Q. 1, *Suppliques des Bourgeois, citoyens et habitants . . . de Québec, 7 juin, 1762*, 31.

40.) Q. 2, *A sa Majesté le Roy de la Grande Bretagne* (1764), 352-56.

41.) *Documents relating to Canadian Currency, Exchange and Finance during the French Period*, ed. by Adam Shortt (Ottawa, 1925), 1004-10, 1012-18, 1054-60.

42.) Dartmouth Papers, M. 383, *Mr. Cramahé's Account of Quebec, 24 Aug., 1765*, 83.   *Const. Docts.*, "Presentments of the Grand Jury of Quebec, 15 Oct., 1764," 212-16.   Baby Papers, *Saint-Georges Dupré à Baby, 6 octobre, 1774*, fol. 44.   B. 8, *Adresse au roi des habitants de Montréal, 10 mars, 1765*, 11a.

43.) Dartmouth Papers, M. 383, *Lévesque, Lemoine et Porlier à Guimond, 27 septembre, 1765*, 126-32.

44.) Murray Papers, *Murray to Halifax, 23 April, 1764*, II, 129.

45.) Dartmouth Papers, M. 383, *Gage à Rigauville, 4 février, 1765*, 68.

46.) Canadian Archives, British Museum Additional Manuscripts, 35915, *Considerations on the present state of the Province of Quebec by Fowler, 1 March, 1766*, fol. 28.

47.) C.O. 5, *Circular letter from General Amherst to the Governors of New Hampshire, Massachusetts Bay, and New York, 13 Sept., 1760*, LIX, 174-75; *Gov'r Bernard to Amherst, 27 Sept., 1760*, 361.   C.O. 5, *Amherst to Pitt, 8 Dec., 1760*, LX, 89.

48.) Brit. Mus. Add. Mss., 35915, *Considerations . . . by Fowler, 1 March, 1766*, fol. 28.   *Const. Docts.*, "Carleton to Shelburne, 25 Nov., 1767," 281-88.

289

49.) In a note appended to the "Ordinance establishing Civil Courts" *(Const. Docts.*, p. 206, n.2), Murray estimates the number of Protestants in Quebec at 200. About the same time he countersigned two lists of English subjects in Montreal and Quebec, containing respectively 56 and 144 names Q. 2, *A List of Protestant House-Keepers in Quebec, 26 Oct., 1764*, 333-34; *A List of Protestant House-Keepers in Montreal, 26 Oct., 1764*, 335. A list drawn up in 1765, and signed by Murray, records the presence of 136 Protestants in Montreal, of whom 14 were immigrants from the American colonies. (See R. A. Ramsay, *Canada from the Conquest to the Quebec Act, 1760-75*, 130-31.)

50.) Q. 13, *List of the principal persons settled in the Province, 9 May, 1777*, 105-06. From a total of 29 colonial sympathizers, the list identifies 21 who were born in the British colonies, and 7 native Englishmen who had lived there. See *Report of the Public Archives of Canada, 1888*, 14.

51.) Ramsay, *Canada from the Conquest . . .* , 130-31.

52.) Murray Papers, *Murray to Halifax, 28 June, 1764*, II.

53.) Q. 2, *Murray to Lords of Trade, 3 March, 1765*, 378.

54.) C.O. 42, *Burton to Lords of Trade, 1 Feb., 1764*, I, 180.

55.) Q. 5, *Carleton to Shelburne, 25 Nov., 1767*, 265.

56.) Q. 3, *Mémoire des Seigneurs du district de Québec, avril, 1766*, 20.

57.) Brit. Mus. Add. Mss., 35915, *Considerations . . . by Fowler, 1 March, 1766*, fol. 28.

58.) Q. 3, *Carleton to Shelburne, 26 Oct., 1766*, 259.

59.) Q. 3, *Au Roy (Les Seigneurs du district de Québec) 1766*, 19.

60.) C.O. 42, *Burton to Lords of Trade, 1 Feb. 1764*, I, 180.

61.) Murray Papers, *Murray to Halifax, 26 June, 1764*, II.

62.) *Const. Docts.*, "Presentments of the Grand Jury of Quebec, 16 Oct., 1764," 212-13.

63.) Brit. Mus. Add. Mss., 35915, *Considerations . . . by Fowler, 1 March, 1766*, 20.

64.) *Const. Docts.*, "Statement by French Jurors, 26 Oct., 1764," 216-23.

65.) *Ibid*, "Address of French citizens to the King, 1764," 223-26.

66.) *Ibid*, "Petition of the Quebec Traders, 1764," 232-34.

67.) B. 8, *Murray to Shelburne, 20 Aug., 1766*, 6.

68.) Q. 3, *Carleton to Shelburne, 26 Oct., 1766*, 259.

69.) *Const. Docts.*, "Carleton to Shelburne, 24 Dec., 1767," 288.

70.) Q. 5-1, *The Memorial of the Subscribing Merchants, 17 March, 1767*, 249.

71.) Q. 7, *The Memorial of the Merchants and other Inhabitants of the City of Quebec, 10 April, 1770*, 99, 101, 104.

72.) *Const. Docts.*, "Petition of the Quebec Traders (1764)," 232;   "Petition of the London Merchants (1764)," 235;   "Representations of the Board of Trade (1765)," 247.

73.) *Const. Docts.*, "Carleton to Shelburne, 25 Nov., 1767," 281.

74.) *Ibid*, "Carleton to Shelburne, 24 Dec., 1767," 288-91.

75.) *Ibid*, "Carleton to Hillsborough, 20 Nov., 1768," 325-27.

76.) *Ibid*, "Carleton to Shelburne, 20 Jan., 1768," 294.

77.) *Ibid*, "Masères to Dartmouth, 4 Jan., 1774," 486.

78.) *Ibid*, 495-504.

79.) *Ibid*, "Petition for the restoration of French law and Custom, 1770," 419-22.

80.) *Ibid*, 492.

81.) *Ibid*, "Petition of French Subjects," 504-08.

CHAPTER II

1.) Archevêché de Québec, Lettres, *Mgr. Briand au Nonce à Paris, 10 mars, 1775*, IV.

2.) *Const. Docts.*, "The Quebec Act," 570-76. See appendices.

3.) Q. 11, *Adresse des citoyens de Montréal, 22 september;   Bal au Château de*

Ramezay, 6 octobre; Adresse de Montréal, 192;   *Adresse de Québec,* 23-4; *Adresse de Trois-Rivières,* 109.   *Quebec Gazette,* 17 Nov., 1774, "Addresse à Carleton par le Sieur Lausier."

4.) *Const. Docts.,* "Carleton to Shelburne, 20 Jan., 1768," 294.
5.) *Ibid,* "Carleton to Dartmouth, 23 Sept., 1774," 583.
6.) *Ibid,* "Carleton to Dartmouth, 11 Nov., 1774," 586.
7.) On 22 June, the day on which the Bill was to receive royal approval, the Lord Mayor of London, with several aldermen and more than 150 members of the council, petitioned the King not to approve the Act. See Cavendish, Henry, *Debates of the House of Commons, 1774, on the bill for making more effectual provision for the Government of the Province of Quebec* (London, 1839), 4.
8.) *Const. Docts.,* "Carleton to Dartmouth, 11 Nov., 1774," 586.
9.) Q. 11, *Jeffries to Minot, Boston, 10 Oct., 1774,* 105-07.
10.) *Collections of the Massachusetts Historical Society,* 4th series, IV, 234-35.
11.) *Const. Docts.,* "Gage to Carleton, 4 Sept., 1774," 583;   "Carleton to Gage, 20 Sept., 1774," 584.
12.) *Can. Archives Report,* 1904, "State of Two Companies, 5 June, 1775," 369.
13.) *Journals of the Continental Congress, 1784-1789,* ed. by W. C. Ford (Washington, 1904-1937), I, 31-40.
14.) *Ibid,* 40.
15.) *Ibid,* 66.
16.) *Ibid,* 72.
17.) *Ibid,* 76.
18.) *Ibid,* 88.
19.) *Const. Docts.,* 163.
20.) *The Grenville Papers* (London, 1852), II, 476-77.
21.) *Const. Docts.,* "Murray to the Lords of Trade, 29 Oct., 1764," 169.
22.) *Ibid,* "Shelburne to Carleton, 20 June, 1767," 196.
23.) Q. 5. See also *Const. Docts.,* p. 249, n. 2.
24.) *Report on the Laws of Quebec, 1767-1770,* ed. with an introduction and notes by W. P. M. Kennedy and Gustave Lanctot (Ottawa, 1931), 66-70.
25.) Explications de la coutume de Paris faite d'après les ordres du Très Hon. Guy Lord Dorchester (private collection).
26.) C.O. 42, *Dartmouth to Cramahé, 1 Dec., 1773,* XXXII, 93-4.
27.) *Ibid,* 99.
28.) *Ibid,* 101.
29.) *J.C.C.,* I, 105-13.
30.) *Ibid,* 117. According to Duane *(Canada and the Continental Congress,* 4), Dickenson, and not Lee, composed the Letter to the People of Canada.
31.) *Const. Docts.,* "Carleton to Shelburne, 20 Jan., 1768," 206.
32.) *J.C.C.,* I, 113.
33.) *Ibid,* 122.
34.) *Journals of Each Provincial Congress of Massachusetts in 1774 and 1775,* ed. by William Lincoln (Boston, 1838), 24.
35.) *Ibid,* 59.
36.) *Ibid,* 74.

CHAPTER III

1.) *Const. Docts.,* "Carleton to Dartmouth, 11 Nov., 1774," 586-88.   Q. 11, *Carleton to Dartmouth, 18 Nov., 1774,* 103.   Q. 13, *List of the principal persons* . . . , *1777,* 105-06.
2.) *Const. Docts.,* "Carleton to Dartmouth, 11 Nov., 1774," 588.
3.) *Ibid,* "Petitions for the repeal of the Quebec Act, 12 Nov., 1774," 589-92.
4.) *Ibid,* Baron Masères, "Considerations on the expediency of procuring an act of Parliament for the settlement of the Province of Quebec," 257-69.

5.) Masères, Francis, *An Account of the Proceedings of the British and other Protestant Inhabitants of the Province of Quebec in North America, in order to obtain an House of Assembly in that Province* (London, 1775), 238.
6.) *Const. Docts.*, "Carleton to Dartmouth, 11 Nov., 1774," 588.
7.) *Ibid.*
8.) *Ibid.*
9.) *Ibid*, "Chief Justice Hey to the Lord Chancellor, 28 Aug., 1775," 668.
10.) *J.C.C.*, I, 105-14.   Q. 11, *Copy of Intelligence, 2 April* 1775, 149.
11.) *Const. Docts.*, "Carleton to Dartmouth, 11 Nov., 1774," 588.
12.) Q. 11, *Carleton to Dartmouth, 12 Jan., 1775*, 110.
13.) Sanguinet, *Invasion du Canada*, "Témoin oculaire de l'invasion du Canada par les Bastonnais," ed. by H. A. Verreau (Montréal, 1873).
14.) *Const. Docts.*, "Chief Justice Hey to the Lord Chancellor, 28 Aug., 1775," 668.
15.) *Ibid*, 588.
16.) *Invasion* (S) 20.   Masères, *Account of Proceedings. . . ,* "Le Canadien Patriote." 265. In pre-revolutionary France, the typical *lettre de cachet* was the instrument through which a subject was condemned to banishment or detention in a state prison. The sentence was pronounced and could be revoked "at the King's pleasure." It did not emanate from any court of justice and it was not subject to appeal.
17.) *Ibid.*
18.) *Invasion* (S), 20.
19.) Masères, *Account of Proceedings. . . ,* 269.
20.) *Const. Docts.*, "Carleton to Gage, 4 Feb., 1775," 660.
21.) *Invasion* (S), 20; *Ibid*, "Journal de Badeaux," 164.
22.) Dartmouth originals, *A.V. to Mr. Tolver, 9 Dec., 1775*, IV, fol. 1607.
23.) *Const. Docts.*, "Carleton to Dartmouth, 11 Nov., 1774," 588.
24.) E Series, Quebec Council, C. II, 281.
25.) Masères, *Accounts of the Proceedings. . . ,* 265-70.
26.) *Ibid*, 168-69.
27.) *New York Gazette and Weekly Mercury*, 10 April, 1775, "Extract of a letter from Canada, Montreal, 24 March, 1775."
28.) *Const. Docts.*, "Carleton to Gage, 4 Feb., 1775," 660.
30.) Smith, J. H., *Our Struggle for the Fourteenth Colony* (New York and London, 1907), I, 91-5.
31.) *Ibid*, 91-5. *The Writings of Samuel Adams*, ed. by H. A. Cushing (New York, 1904-07), 182-84. Two men from the New Hampshire grants, Peleg Sunderland and Winthrop Hyot, accompanied Brown.
32.) Chittenden, Lucius Eugène, *The Capture of Ticonderoga*, "The Letter of John Brown to the Committee of Correspondence in Boston" (Montpelier, 1879), 97-9.
33.) Q.11, *Copy of Intelligence, 2 April, 1775*, 151.
34.) Q.11, *Extract of a letter from Montreal, 7 April, 1775*, 167-68.
35.) *Invasion* (S), 21.
36.) Q.11, *Extract of a letter from Montreal, 7 April, 1775*, 167-68.
37.) *Const. Docts.*, "Instructions to Governor Carleton, 1775," 594.
38.) *Journals of . . . Congress of Mass. . . . ,* 751-52.
39.) Chittenden, "The Letter of John Brown . . . ," *loc. cit.*
40.) Q.11, *Copy of Intelligence from Montreal, 2 April, 1775*, 149; *3 April, 1775*, 165.
41.) *Ibid, 10 April, 1775*, 169.
42.) Chittenden, "The Letter of John Brown . . . ," *loc. cit.*
43.) B.200-01, *H. Finlay to Haldimand, 30 Jan., 1781*, 266.
44.) Q.11, *Extract of a letter from Montreal, 7 April, 1775*, 168.
45.) *Ibid*, 165.
46.) *Ibid, Carleton to Dartmouth, 13 March, 1775*, 129;   *Carleton to Dartmouth, 15 May, 1775*, 161.

47.) *Invasion* (S), 22-4. *Quebec Gazette, 26 April,* 1775.
48.) Q.11, *Letter from Montreal, 1 May, 1775,* 170.
49.) Walker, Mrs. Thomas, *Shurtleff Manuscript, 153, Being a narrative of certain events which transpired in Canada during the invasion of that province by the American Army in 1775,* printed from the original with notes and introduction by the Rev. Silas Ketchum (Coll. of the New Hampshire Antiquarian Society: Cantoncook, 1876), 35.
50.) Q.11, *Extract of a letter from Montreal, 4 May, 1775,* 171-72.
51.) *Const. Docts.,* "Instructions to Carleton, 3 Jan., 1775," 594.
52.) *Invasion,* "François Baby à Pierre Guy, Québec, 17 avril, 1775," 304.
53.) Dartmouth Originals, *Hey to Dartmouth, 20 July, 1775,* III.

CHAPTER IV

1.) Smith, J. H., *Our Struggle for the Fourteenth Colony,* I, 140, 144. *Invasion* (S), 27.
2.) Smith, *op. cit.,* I, 156-57. *Invasion* (S), 29-33. *Const. Docts.,* "Carleton to Dartmouth, 7 June, 1775," 663.
3.) *Invasion* (S), 29-33. *Continental Congress Papers,* II, 134. *Const. Docts.,* "Carleton to Dartmouth, 7 June, 1775," 663-66.
4.) Q.11, *Ethan Allen to the Merchants of Montreal, 18 May, 1775,* 190-91.
5.) Q.11, *Arnold to Walker, Crown Point, 24 May, 1775,* 196.
6.) *Ibid.*
7.) *Journals of . . . Congress of Mass. . . . ,* 707.
8.) *American Archives,* Fourth series, II, 1254.
9.) Q.11, 233-34.
10.) *Am. Arch.,* Fourth series, II, 623-24.
11.) *Remembrancer,* "Letter from Philadelphia, 24 May, 1775," 84.
12.) *J.C.C.,* "18 May, 1775," II, 55-6.
13.) *Ibid,* 64, 69, 70. *Invasion* (S), 39.
14.) *J.C.C.,* II, 69-76.
15.) *Journals of . . . Congress of Mass. . . . ,* "Allen and Easton to Canadians, 4 June, 1775," 715-16.
16.) *Ibid,* note 307-08.
17.) *Ibid,* 307-08, 322.
18.) *Am. Arch.,* Fourth series, II, 1294.
19.) *Am. Arch.,* "Brown to Governor Trumbull, 14., Aug., 1775," Fourth series, III, 136.
20.) *Journals of . . . Congress of Mass. . . . ,* "25 June, 1775," 394.
21.) *Ibid,* "8 July, 1775," 474.
22.) *Const. Docts.,* "Chief Justice Hey to Lord Chancellor, 28 Aug., 1775," 668.
23.) *Ibid,* "Carleton to Dartmouth, 7 June, 1775," 663.
24.) *Invasion* (S), 33.
25.) Ferland, J.B.A., *Mgr. J. O. Duplessis* (Québec, 1878), 38.
26.) *Mandements des Évêques de Québec,* "Lettre circulaire, 15 octobre, 1768," II, 213-15.
27.) Archevêché de Québec, Lettres, *Briand au Nonce à Paris, 10 mars, 1775,* IV.
28.) *Ibid, Briand à St.-Onge, mai, 1775.*
29.) *Ibid, Briand au Nonce, 10 mars, 1775.*
30.) *Ibid, Briand à St.-Onge, mai, 1775.*
31.) *Mandements des Évêques . . . ,* "Mandement de Mgr. Briand, 22 mai, 1775," II, 264-65.
32.) Archevêché de Québec, Lettres, *Briand à St.-Onge, mai, 1775,* IV.
33.) *Ibid, Briand à St.-Onge, 4 juin, 1775.*
34.) Can. Archives, Documents du Séminaire de St.-Sulpice, *Serment prêché pour expliquer le mandement du 22 mai, 1775.* The Acadians had requested a modification in the form of the oath of allegiance which would have ex-

Canada and the American Revolution

emped them from the obligation to bear arms in the event of war between
England and France. The request was refused, and the expulsion came
about as a consequence of their refusal to take the oath in its unmodified
form.

35.) *Invasion* (S), 33-4.
36.) *Const. Docts.*, "Carleton to Gage, 4 Feb., 1775," 660.
37.) In similar circumstances, Haldimand proved to be more prompt to act and
more skilful in action.
38.) *Const. Docts.*, "Chief Justice Hey to Lord Chancellor, 28 Aug., 1775," 669.
39.) *Ibid*, "Carleton to Dartmouth, 7 June, 1775," 664.
40.) *Ibid.* B.20, *Capt. Gamble to Capt. Sheriff, 20 July, 1775*, 8.
41.) *Can. Archives Reports*, 1904, "State of two Companies, 5 June, 1775," 369.
Q.11, *State of His Majesty's Troops, 24 June, 1775*, 264.
42.) *Invasion* (S), 35-7.   *Quebec Gazette*, 15 June, 1775.
43.) Beaujeu, Monongahela de, *Documents inédits sur le Colonel de Longueuil*,
"Ordre de Carleton à M. de Longueuil, Montréal, 29 juin, 1775" (Montréal,
1891).
44.) *Mandements des Evêques* . . . , "Lettre circulaire, 13 juin, 1775," II, 265-66.
See appendices to this book.
45.) Masères, Francis, *Additional Papers concerning the Province of Quebec*
(London, 1776), 125.
46.) *Invasion, passim.*
47.) *Quebec Gazette*, 6 and 13 July, 1775.
48.) *Ibid*, 20 July, 1775.
49.) *Ibid*, 10 Aug., 1775.
50.) *Invasion* (S), 37.
51.) *Am. Arch.*, "Arnold to Continental Congress, Crown Point, 13 June, 1775,"
Fourth series, II, 976;   "Albany Comtee to Cont. Congress, 21 June, 1775,"
1048.
52.) *Invasion* (S), 38.   *Am. Arch.*, "Letter from Montreal, 10 July, 1775," Fourth
series, II, 1623.
53.) *Quebec Gazette*, 9 July, 1775.
54.) Baby Papers, *P. Guy à Frs. Baby, 19 juin, 1775*.
55.) *Quebec Gazette*, 13 July, 1775.
56.) Dartmouth Originals, *Hey to Dartmouth, Quebec, 20 July, 1775*, III.
57.) *Invasion* (S), 38-9.
58.) *Const. Docts.*, "Carleton to Dartmouth, 7 June, 1775," 664.
59.) Q.11, *Carleton to Dartmouth, 14 Aug., 1775*, 222.
60.) *Invasion* (B), 166.
61.) *R.A.Q.*, "Journal de MM. François Baby, Gabriel Taschereau, et Jenkins
Wilkins," 1927-28, 435-99; 1929-30, 138-40.
62.) M. 833, *Letter from Quebec, 1 Oct., 1775*, 61.
63.) *R.A.Q.*, (BTW), 1927-28, 471-72.
64.) Archevêché de Québec, Lettres, *Briand à Verreau, 4 juin, 1775*.
65.) *Quebec Gazette*, 6 July, 1775.
66.) Q.11, *Carleton to Dartmouth, 11 Aug., 1775*, 222.
67.) *Invasion* (S), 41.
68.) *Const. Docts.*, "Carleton to Dartmouth, 7 June, 1775," 664.
69.) Dartmouth Originals, *Hey to Barré, 19 Sept., 1775*.
70.) *Ibid.*
71.) *Const. Docts.*, "Carleton to Dartmouth, 7 June, 1775," 664.
72.) *Invasion* (S), 38-40.
73.) Dartmouth Originals, *Hey to Barré, 10 Sept., 1775*, III.
74.) Q.11, Carleton to Dartmouth, 26 June, 1775, 201.
75.) *Const. Docts.*, "Chief Justice Hey to the Lord Chancellor, 28 Aug., 1775,"
669.
76.) *Invasion* (S), 42.
77.) *Const. Docts.*, "Hey to Lord Chancellor, 28 Aug., 1775," 670.

CHAPTER V

1.) *J.C.C.*, II, 75.
2.) Q.11, *Déposition de Pierre Charlan, 6 août, 1775*, 242.
3.) *J.C.C.*, "12 July, 1775," II, 174.
4.) *Continental Congress Papers*, "2 Aug., 1775," I, 95-6.
5.) *Am. Arch.*, "Brown to Trumbull, 14 Aug., 1775," Fourth series, III, 136.
6.) *Ibid*, 109-10.
7.) Q.11, *Déposition de Pierre Charlan, 6 août, 1775*, 242. *Am. Arch.*, "Schuyler to Washington, Ticonderoga, 31 Aug., 1775," Fourth series, III, 467.
8.) Q.11, *Copy of a paper . . .* , 235.
9.) *Am. Arch.*, "Livingston to Schuyler, Aug., 1775," Fourth series, III, 468.
10.) *Ibid*, "Schuyler to Trumbull, 31 Aug., 1775," 470.
11.) *Const. Docts.*, "Cramahé to Dartmouth, Quebec, 21 Sept., 1775," 667.
12.) *Ibid*.
13.) *Invasion* (S), 43. Beaujeu, *Documents sur le colonel de Longueuil*, "Ordre de Prescott à Longueuil, 5 septembre, 1775."
14.) *Ibid*, "Ordre de Carleton à Longueuil, 6 septembre, 1775."
15.) Baby Papers, *Pierre Guy à Baby, 7 septembre, 1775*, fol. 40.
16.) *Const. Docts.*, "Cramahé to Dartmouth, Quebec, 21 Sept., 1775," 667.
17.) *Invasion* (S), 43. Beaujeu, *op. cit.*, "Ordre de Prescott . . . , 7 septembre, 1775."
18.) *Invasion* (S), 43-4.
19.) Washington Papers, 8925, *Schuyler's address to the Inhabitants of Canada, 5 Sept., 1775*. French text in Q.11, 258-60.
20.) *Ethan Allen's Narrative of the Capture of Ticonderoga and of his Captivity* (Burlington, 1849), 7. *Am. Arch.*, "Allen to Schuyler, 14 Sept., 1775," Fourth series, III, 742-43. *Const. Docts.*, "Cramahé to Dartmouth, 21 Sept., 1775," 667; "Chief Justice Hey to Lord Chancellor, P.S., 11 Sept., 1775," 671.
21.) *Invasion* (S), 44.
22.) *Am. Arch.*, "Livingston to Schuyler, in Schuyler's letter of 19 Sept., 1775," Fourth series, III, 744.
23.) Q.11, *A Messieurs les capitaines des côtes jusqu'à Québec, La Pointe Olivier, 16 septembre, 1775*, 255.
24.) Q.11, *Copy of an intercepted letter, 18 Sept., 1775*, 252.
25.) Probably Chambly, Pointe-Olivier (St.-Mathias), Beloeil, St.-Charles, St.-Antoine, and St.-Denis.
26.) Archevêché de Québec, Lettres, *Montgolfier à Briand, 18 septembre, 1775*.
27.) *Invasion* (S), 44-6, *Can. Archives Reports, 1904*, "Tryon to Dartmouth, New York, 11 Nov., 1775," 375.
28.) *Invasion* (S), 45-6.
29.) Archevêché de Québec, Lettres, *Montgolfier à Briand, 18 septembre, 1775*.
30.) Evêché de Joliette, Lavaltrie, *St.-Germain à Mgr. Briand, 16 septembre, 1775*.
31.) *Ibid, Mgr. Briand à St.-Germain, Québec, 20 septembre, 1775*.
32.) *Invasion* (B), 166.
33.) *Ibid*, 168.
34.) *R.A.Q.*, (BTW), 1927-28, 440.
35.) *Ibid*, 464-87.
36.) *Ibid*, 489.
37.) *Ibid*, 490, 491, 495, 497.
38.) *Ibid*, 435-36, 481, 490.
39.) *Ibid*, 439, 440, 461, 463, 465, 483.
40.) *Ibid*, 448, 449.
41.) *Ibid*, 443, 445.

Canada and the American Revolution

42.) *Ibid*, 447, 443, 444, 446, 464.
43.) *Ibid*, 454, 494, 439.
44.) *Const. Docts.*, "Carleton to Dartmouth, 7 June, 1775," 663-66; "Chief Justice Hey to Lord Chancellor, P.S., 11 Sept., 1775," 671; "Cramahé to Dartmouth, 21 Sept., 1775," 667.
45.) *Ibid*, "Hey to Lord Chancellor," 672.
46.) *Ibid*, "Carleton to Dartmouth," 663. M.384, *Remarks on the Province of Quebec, by Lieut. Marr*, 97-8. Archevêché de Québec, Lettres, *Briand au Nonce, 10 mars, 1775*.
47.) *Const. Docts.*, "Carleton to Gage, 4 Feb., 1775," 660.
48.) Salone, Emile, *La Colonisation de la Nouvelle-France. Etude sur les origines de la nation canadienne française* (Paris, 1906), 360-61.
49.) *Const. Docts.*, "Chief Justice Hey to Lord Chancellor, 28 Aug., 1775," 663. Masères, *Additional Papers*, "Letter from Quebec, 20 July, 1775," 8-9.
50.) M.833, *Letter from Quebec, 1 Oct., 1775*, 61. Shelburne Papers, *Masères to Shelburne, 24 Aug., 1775*, LXVI, 54-5. B.20, *Capt. Gamble to Capt. Sheriff, Quebec, 20 July, 1775*, 8.
51.) *Const. Docts.*, "Carleton to Gage, 4 Feb., 1775," 660.
52.) *Ibid*, "Chief Justice Hey to Lord Chancellor, 28 Aug., 1775, 668.
53.) *Ibid*.
54.) Dartmouth Originals, *Hey to Dartmouth, 20 July, 1775*, III.
55.) *Const. Docts.*, "Carleton to Dartmouth, 11 Nov., 1774," 586.
56.) Baby Papers. *Pierre Guy à François Baby, 19 juin, 1775*. Documents du Séminaire de St.-Sulpice, *Sermon préparé pour expliquer le mandement du 22 mai, 1775*.
57.) *Continental Congress Papers*, "Deposition of John Duguid, Aug., 1775," 153, I, 96.
58.) *Mandements des Evêques. . . ,* "Mandement aux sujets rebelles," II, 272-73. See appendices.
59.) Dartmouth Originals, *Hey to Dartmouth, 20 July, 1775*, III.
60.) *Const. Docts.*, "Chief Justice Hey to Lord Chancellor, 28 Aug., 1775," 668.
61.) *Ibid*, "Carleton to Gage, 7 June, 1775," 663.
62.) Q.11, *State of His Majesty's Troops, 24 June, 1775*, 265.
63.) *Const. Docts.*, "Hey to Dartmouth, 11 Sept., 1775," 672.
64.) *Ibid*, "Cramahé to Dartmouth, 21 Sept., 1775," 667.
65.) *Ibid*, "Carleton to Dartmouth, 7 June, 1775," 664.
66.) Q.31, *Memorandum of the Rebel Invasion of Canada in 1775, by Col. Claus*, 49.
67.) *Can. Archives Reports*, "Gage to Secretary of State, 20 Aug., 1775," 1904, 358.
68.) *Const. Docts.*, "Cramahé to Dartmouth, 21 Sept., 1775," 665.

CHAPTER VI

1.) Dartmouth Originals, *Hey to Barré, 19 Sept., 1775*, III.
2.) *Invasion* (S), 47-9.
3.) *Am. Arch.*, "Montgomery to Brown, 6 Oct., 1775," Fourth series, III, 1098.
4.) Q.11, *Carleton to Dartmouth, 25 Oct., 1775*, 267.
5.) *Am. Arch.*, "Allen's Narrative," Fourth series, III, 799.
6.) *Invasion* (S), 49-50. The *Quebec Gazette*, 5 Oct., 1775, gives the following figures: 34 soldiers, 80 English and 120 Canadian volunteers. A letter from Montreal, 25 Sept., 1775 (Dartmouth Originals, III), gives 300 citizens and 60 soldiers. Sanguinet, as an eye witness, is the best authority on the effective strength of the force.
7.) Q.11, *Carleton to Dartmouth, 25 Oct., 1775*, 268. *Am. Arch.*, Allen's Narrative," Fourth series, III, 799, note; "Letter from Philadelphia, 20 Oct., 1775," 800; "Letter from Quebec, 30 Sept., 1775," 845.

296

8.) M.833, *Letters relating to American Invasion*, 38.
9.) *Bulletin des recherches historiques*, "Mémoire de M. Porlier," VI, 134.
10.) Dartmouth Originals, *Extract of a letter from Montreal, 25 Sept., 1775*, III.
 Q.11, *List of the Rebel Prisoners . . . , Quebec, 9 Nov., 1775*, 313. *Quebec Gazette*, 29 Oct., 1775. The Canadians captured included: 3 from St.-Denis, 1 from Longueuil, 3 from Beloeil, 1 from St.-Ours, 1 from St.-Jean d'Eschaillons, and 1 from Chambly.
11.) *Invasion* (S), 51.
12.) *Ibid*, 51-2 *Am. Arch.*, "Montgomery to Schuyler, 9 Oct., 1775," Fourth series, III, 1096.
13.) M.99, *Lettres de M. de Montgolfier à Mgr. Briand, 28 septembre et 2 octobre, 1775.*
14.) *Ibid*, 2 octobre, 1775. *Invasion* (S), 49.
15.) *Am. Arch.*, "Montgomery to Schuyler, 24 Sept., 1775," Fourth series, III, 840.
16.) *Invasion* (S), 53-4. *R.A.Q.*, 1927-28, 455.
17.) *Quebec Gazette*, 5 Oct., 1775.
18.) *Memorial Book of Brown*, "11 Oct., 1775." *Quebec Gazette*, 12 Oct., 1775.
19.) *Remembrancer*, 1776, Pt. 2, 244-47. Q.11, *Dépositions de Deschamps, Bruyère, Guillette, et Leroux, octobre, 1775*, 301-12.
20.) Archevêché de Québec, Lettres, *Montgolfier à Briand, 9 octobre, 1775.*
21.) *Ibid, Montgolfier à Briand, 23 et 27 octobre, 1775.*
22.) *Invasion* (B), 170.
23.) *Ibid*, 170-71.
24.) Archevêché de Québec, Lettres, *Montgolfier à Briand, 23 octobre, 1775.*
25.) *Ibid, Montgolfier à Briand, novembre, 1775.*
26.) *Invasion* (S), 54.
27.) M.99, *Montgolfier à Briand, 23 octobre, 1775.* *Invasion* (S), 63-4. Q.11, *Déposition de Michel Guillette, 9 octobre, 1775,* 309.
28.) Archevêché de Québec, Lettres, *Montgolfier à Briand, 30 octobre, 1775.*
29.) *Ibid, Briand à Montgolfier, 5 novembre, 1775.*
30.) St.-Charles and St.-Vallier.
31.) Archevêché de Québec, Lettres, *Mgr. Briand à M. Lagroix, 1 octobre, 1775.*
32.) *Ibid, M. Maisonbasse à Mgr. Briand, 22 octobre, 1775.*
33.) *Ibid, Briand à Montgolfier, 5 novembre, 1775.*
34.) *Ibid, Montgolfier à Briand, 9 octobre, 1775.*
35.) *Ibid, Briand à Maisonbasse, 25 octobre, 1775.*
36.) *Invasion* (S), 54-5, 57-60.
37.) *Ibid*, 76-7. Q.11, *List of the troops . . . ,* 282-84.
38.) *Invasion* (S), 54-60.
39.) Archevêché de Québec, Lettres, *Montgolfier à Briand, 30 octobre, 1775.*
40.) *Invasion* (S), 56.
41.) *Ibid*, 58.
42.) *Ibid*, 62.
43.) Q.11, *Carleton to Dartmouth, 5 Nov., 1775,* 274.
44.) *Ibid, Carleton to Dartmouth, 25 Oct., 1775,* 270.
45.) Archevêché de Québec, Lettres, *Montgolfier à Briand, 30 octobre, 1775.*
46.) *Invasion* (S), 64-6.
47.) Archevêché de Québec, Lettres, *Montgolfier à Briand, novembre, 1775* (early in the month).
48.) *Am. Arch.*, "Schuyler to Congress, Ticonderoga, 29 Sept., 1775," Fourth series, III, 839.
49.) *Ibid*, "Montgomery to Schuyler, Camp South Side, St. Johns, 6 Oct., 1775," 1095.
50.) *Ibid*, 1096.
51.) *Ibid*, 1096.
52.) *Ibid*, "Livingston to Montgomery, Ft. Chambly, 26 Oct., 1775," 1196.
53.) *Ibid*, "Montgomery to Schuyler, St. Johns, 20 Oct., 1775," 1132.

54.) *Am. Arch.*, "Montgomery to Schuyler, Holland-House, 5 Dec., 1775," Fourth series, IV, 189.
55.) Hadden, James Murray, *Hadden's Journal and Orderly Books,* ed. by Horatio Rogers (Albany, 1884), 3.
56.) Q.11, *Return of His Majesty's Garrison of Chambly, made prisoners by the Rebels, 17 Oct., 1775,* 227.   *Am. Arch.*, "An Account of Stores taken at Chambly," Fourth series, III, 1133-34.
57.) *Invasion* (B), 171-74.
58.) Q.11, *List of the troops taken Prisoners at St. Johns, 2 Nov., 1775,* 282. *Liste de Messieurs les Officiers et Gentilshommes Canadiens,* 284.   *Invasion* (S), 76-7.
59.) *Am. Arch.*, "Letter from La Prairie, 3 Nov., 1775," Fourth series, III, 1342. This letter reports that 1,000 Canadians were serving in the American army, but in the light of available documentary evidence, the number should be reduced to half this figure.

CHAPTER VII

1.) Q.11, *Messieurs les habitants de Montréal, 9 novembre, 1775,* 321-23.
B.147, *Letters, of Clinton,* "6 juillet, 1780," 186;   "11 juillet, 1780," 206.
2.) *J.C.C.*, III, 477.
3.) Q.11, *Carleton to Dartmouth,* 318-19.
4.) *Literary and Historical Society of Quebec, Historical Documents,* "The Invasion of Canada," Letter attributed to Major Henry Caldwell, Second series, D5, 4.
5.) *Am. Arch.*, "Arnold to Wooster, Holland-House, 4 Jan., 1776," Fourth series, IV, 854.
6.) *Invasion* (S), 81-2.
7.) *Ibid,* 80-4.
8.) *Ibid,* 85-6.
9.) *Invasion* (B), 174-89.
10.) *Ibid,* 181.
11.) *Am. Arch.*, "Montgomery to Schuyler, Montreal, 19 Nov., 1775," Fourth series, III, 1682.
12.) *Ibid.*
13.) *Ibid,* "Montgomery to Schuyler, Montreal, 24 Nov., 1775," 1695.
14.) Stocking, *Historical Collection of the Mahoning Valley,* "Interesting Journal," I, 6.
15.) *Ibid.*
16.) *Ibid,* 20.
17.) *Historical Collection of the Mahoning Valley,* "Simon Fobes' Narrative," I, 353.
18.) *The Writings of George Washington,* ed. by W.C. Ford (New York and London, 1889-1893), III, 126-27.
19.) *Hist. Coll. of the Mahoning Valley,* I, 353.
20.) *The Writings of George Washington,* III, 122-23.
21.) *R.A.Q.*, 1927-28, 470.
22.) Masères, Francis, *Additional Papers concerning the Province of Quebec* (London, 1776).   Roy, Joseph Edouard, *Histoire de la Seigneurie de Lauzon* (Lévis, 1897-1901), II, 49.
23.) *Hist. Coll. of the Mahoning Valley,* I, 354.
24.) Q.11, *Arnold to Montgomery, 8 Nov., 1775,* 331-32.
25.) *Quebec Gazette,* 6 July, 1776.
26.) B.20, *Capt. Gamble to Capt. Sheriff, Quebec, 20 July, 1775,* 9.
27.) *Quebec Gazette.*
28.) *Ibid,* 14 Sept., 1775.

29.) *Ibid*, 21 Sept., 1775.
30.) Q.11, *Cramahé to Dartmouth, 30 Sept., 1775*, 256-57.
31.) Ainslie, Charles, "Journal . . . ," *Literary and Historical Society of Quebec, Historical Documents, Blockade of Quebec in 1775-76 by the American Revolutionists (Les Bastonnais)* (Quebec, 1905), D10, Seventh series, 15.
32.) *Blockade*, "Nouveau rôle de la milice canadienne qui a fait le service pendant le blocus de Québec . . . ," 292.
33.) *Quebec Gazette*, 2 Nov., 1775.
34.) B.200-01, 3.
35.) Q.11, *Arnold to John Mercer, Dead-River, 3 Oct.*, 297.
36.) *Ibid, Howe to Carleton, Boston, 13 Oct., 1775*, 288.
37.) *Ibid, Council of War, 6 Nov., 1775*, 342-44.
38.) Q.11, *Cramahé to Dartmouth, 9 Nov., 1775*, 286.
39.) *Blockade* (A), 16. *Am. Arch.*, "Arnold to Montgomery, Pointe-aux-Trembles, 30 Nov., 1775," Fourth series, III, 1697. *Historical Collection of the Mahoning Valley*, "Fobes' Narrative," I, 356.
40.) Quoted by Roy, in *Histoire de la Seigneurie de Lauzon*, II, 57.
41.) Q.11, *Cramahé to Dartmouth, Quebec, 19 Nov., 1775*, 324-26.
42.) *Am. Arch.*, "Arnold to Washington, Quebec, 5 Dec., 1775," Fourth series, IV, 190. *Blockade* (A), I, 18.
43.) *Am. Arch.*, "Montgomery to Schuyler, Holland-House, 5 Dec., 1775," Fourth series, IV, 189.
44.) *Ibid*, "Montgomery to Schuyler, 18 Dec., 1775," 310.
45.) Q.12, *22 Nov., 1775*, 24-6.
46.) *Am. Arch.*, "Letter from camp before Quebec, 6 Dec., 1775," Fourth series, IV, 204.
47.) Bradley, Arthur Grenville, *Lord Dorchester* (Toronto, 1907), 114.
48.) *Am. Arch.*, "Montgomery to Schuyler, Holland-House, 5 Dec., 1775," Fourth series, IV, 189.
49.) *Literary and Historical Society of Quebec, Historical Documents*, "The Invasion of Canada," Letter attributed to Major Henry Caldwell, D5, Second series, 7.
50.) Q.13, *List of the Principal Persons . . . who served the Rebels*, 105-06.
51.) *J.C.C.*, "10 and 16 Oct., 1775," III, 287, 296, 318.
52.) *Ibid*, 320.
53.) *Ibid*, 317, 339-41.
54.) *Ibid*, 353, 389, 418.
55.) *Ibid*, 446-51.
56.) *Invasion* (S), 89-93.
57.) B.185-1, *Order of Wooster to Bourdon, Montreal, 20 Dec., 1775*, 69.
58.) Q.12, *Montgomery to Carleton, 6 Dec., 1775*, 16-17.
59). *Ibid, Order of Mr. Montgomery, 15 Dec., 1775*, 20-1. *Am. Arch.*, "Montgomery to Schuyler, Quebec, 26 Dec., 1775," Fourth series, IV, 464.
60.) *Ibid*, 465; *Ibid*, "Schuyler to President of Congress, 13 Jan., 1776," 666; *Ibid*, "Arnold to Wooster, 2 Jan., 1776," 670. Schuyler wrote that Col. Livingston had only 160 Canadians at Quebec, and Arnold estimated the number of Canadians in Livingston's regiment at 200 in round figures.
61.) Morrison's "Journal," in Roberts, Kenneth, *March to Quebec*.
62.) *Invasion* (S), 117-22; *Blockade* (A), 27-32.

CHAPTER VIII

1.) *Blockade* (A), 32-3.
2.) Caldwell in *Literary and Historical Society of Quebec, Historical Documents*, D5, Second series, 13.

3.) *Am. Arch.*, "Arnold to Washington, Quebec, 14 Jan., 1776," Fourth series, IV, 674.
4.) *Ibid*, "Lettre de M. Pelissier, 8 janvier, 1776," 596.
5.) *Ibid*, 598-99.
6.) B.184-1, *Ordre de Wooster, 6 janvier, 1776*, 21-2.
7.) *Invasion* (B), 183.
8.) *Ibid*, (S), 94.   Daniel, François, *Histoire des grandes familles françaises du Canada* (Montréal, 1867).
9.) *Ibid*.
10.) B184-1, *Tètard à Dudevens, 13 janvier, 1776*, 23-4.
11.) *R.A.Q.* (BTW), 1927-28, 451.
12.) *Ibid*.
13.) *Ibid*, 494, 477-78.
14.) *J.C.C.*, IV, 38.
15.) *Ibid*, 71-5.
16.) *Ibid*, 78.
17.) *Ibid*, 85-6.
18.) *Invasion* (S), 96.
19.) *Blockade* (A), 32.   *R.A.Q.*, 1927-28, 450.
20.) *Blockade* (A), 34.
21.) *Invasion* (B), 183.
22.) *Invasion* (S), 98.
23.) *Ibid*, 101.
24.) Caldwell's letter in *Literary and Historical Society of Quebec, Historical Documents*, D5, Second series, 19.
25.) *J.C.C.*, "10 Aug., 1776," V.   Archevêché de Québec, *Lettre de Mgr. Briand, 8 novembre 1774.*
26.) *Blockade* (A), "Journal of the most remarkable occurrences in Quebec since Arnold appeared on the 14th Nov., 1775," 35.
27.) *Remembrancer*, 1776, "Letter from an officer of the Continental Army, Three Rivers, 24 March, 1776," 248.   *Invasion* (S), 96.   *R.A.Q.* (BTW), 1927-28, 461.
28.) *Invasion* (S), 96-8.
29.) *Remembrancer*, 1776, 248.   *Invasion* (B), 183.   *R.A.Q.* (BTW), 1927-28, 453-64.
30.) *Ibid*, 452, 474-92.
31.) *Ibid*, 435-99, *passim*.
32.) *Invasion* (S), 97.
33.) *American State Papers*, "Claims of François Cazeau," 516.
34.) *Invasion* (S), 100. Sanguinet's date, 28 Feb., for Hazen's arrival should probably be corrected to 8 Feb., since Hazen signed a proclamation in Montreal on 10 February.
35.) B.27, *Proclamation de Hazen, Montréal, 10 février, 1776*, 385-86.
36.) *Ibid, Hazen to Anctill, Montreal, 10 March, 1776*, 387.
37.) *Blockade* (A), 54.
38.) B.27, *Hazen to Anctill, Montreal, 26 March, 1776*, 302.
39.) Archevêché de Québec, Lettres, *Montgolfier à Briand, 17 juin, 1776.*
40.) *Invasion* (S), 94.   *Blockade* (A), 54.
41.) B.205, *Receipt of Du Calvet as ensign, 29 April, 1776*, 1.
42.) B.27, *Hazen to Anctill, 20 April, 1776*, 398-400.
43.) *Ibid*, 397.
44.) *R.A.Q.* (BTW), 1927-28, 496, 486.   *Bulletin des recherches historiques*, "Mémoire de M. Porlier," VI, 135.
45.) B.27, *Hazen to Anctill, Montreal, 10 March 1776*, 387;   *Ibid, 26 March, 1776*, 392-93.
46.) *Blockade* (A), 58.
47.) *Ibid*, 62.
48.) The following list indicates the number of recruits from each parish:

Beauport-10, St.-Joachim-1, St.-Pierre d'Orléans-3, Bécancour-2, Gentilly-2, Pointe-Lévy-10, St.-Charles-4, St.-Pierre-du-Sud-14, St.-Thomas-6, Islets-7, St.-Jean-Port-Joli-3, St.-Roch-3, Ste.-Anne-de-la-Pocatière-19, Rivière-Ou-elle-14, Kamouraska-14, Total-112.

49.) *R.A.Q.* (BTW), 1927-28, 436-98; 1929-30, 138-40.
50.) *Blockade* (A), 58.
51.) *Bulletin des recherches historiques*, VI, 135-36.
52.) Archives des Jésuites, *Mgr. Briand, 26 septembre, 1776*, fol. B, I.
53.) *Remembrancer*, 1776, "Letter from an officer of the Continental Army, Three Rivers, 2 March, 1776," 248-49.
54.) *Am. Arch.*, "Hazen to Schuyler, Montreal, 1 April, 1776." Fourth series, V, 870.
55.) Arch. Jesuites, *Mgr. Briand, 26 septembre, 1776*, fol. B, I.
56.) *Pennsylvania Archives, selected and arranged from original Documents in the Office of the Secretary of the Commonwealth*, "The Memorial of Col. Moses Hazen to Gen. Washington, 1779" (Philadelphia, 1853), Sixth series, VIII, 17-19. The total of 477 for 1779 represents enlistments in the Colonies, rather than in Canada, at a date ulterior to the siege of Quebec.
57.) *Blockade* (A), 95.
58.) *Am. Arch.*, "Arnold to Chase, 15 May, 1776," Fourth series, VI, 580.
59.) *Invasion* (S), 94.
60.) *Ibid*, 101.
61.) *Ibid*, 107.
62.) *Ibid*, 93, 95, 96.
63.) *Ibid, passim. R.A.Q.* (BTW), 1927-28, 452-72, 478, 481, 484.
64.) *Ibid*, 467, 480, 482, 496.
65.) *Ibid*, 496, 446, 449, 450, 463, 471-72, 477, 486, 490, 497, 440.
66.) *Ibid, passim.*
67.) *Ibid*, 488.
68.) *Ibid*, 490.
69.) *Ibid*, 496.
70.) *Ibid*, 447.
71.) *Ibid*, 450.
72.) *Ibid*, 470.
73.) *Ibid*, 480.
74.) *Ibid*, 496.
75.) *R.A.Q.* (BTW), 1929-30, 139.
76.) Archevêché de Québec, Lettres, *Briand à Montgolfier, 25 octobre, 1775.* Arch. Jésuites, *Mgr. Briand, 26 septembre, 1776*, fol. B, I.
77.) *Invasion* (S), 57-60.
78.) *Am. Arch.*, "Arnold to Chase, 15 May, 1776," 580.
79.) *R.A.Q.* (BTW), 1927-28, 438-41.
80.) *Ibid*, 445-47.
81.) *Ibid*, 450-52, 455, 467, 480.
82.) *Ibid*, 466, 468, 491.
83.) *R.A.Q.* (BTW), 1928-30, 139-40.
84.) *Bulletin des recherches historiques*, VI, 134-37, 140.
85.) *Invasion* (S), 95.
86.) Canadian Archives, Bibliothèque Sainte-Geneviève, 2088, La Valinière, Huet de, Mémoires sur l'état actuel du Canada, 4. According to La Valinière, the two priests were the Abbé Robert, curé of St.-Sulpice, and the Abbé St.-Germain, curé of Lavaltrie. As the name St.-Germain is not listed in Allaire's *Dictionnaire du clergé canadien*, it is possible that the priest in question was Father Germain, curé of St.-François-du-Lac from 1767 to 1779.
87.) *R.A.Q.* (BTW), 1927-28, 437.
88.) *Ibid*, 441.
89.) *Ibid*, 447.

90.) *Ibid*, 458-59.
91.) *Ibid*, 463.
92.) *Ibid*, 468.
93.) *Bulletin des recherches historiques*, "Note par Mgr. H. Têtu," VII, 178.
94.) *Am. Arch.*, "Mott to Goforth, Quebec, 26 March, 1776," Fourth series, V, 869.
95.) Archevêché de Québec, Lettres, *M. Sarault à Mgr. Briand, 8 mai, 1776*.
96.) *Blockade* (A), 67.
97.) Têtu, Mgr. Henri, *Les Evêques de Québec* (Québec, 1889), 334, note.
98.) Roy, Joseph Edouard, *Histoire de la Seigneurie de Lauzon* (Lévis, 1897-1901), III, 53, note.
99.) Carayon, Auguste, *Bannissement des Jésuites de la Louisiane*, "Floquet à Briand, 15 juin, 1776," 107.
100.) *Ibid*, 107-09.   Archevêché de Québec, Lettres, *Montgolfier à Briand, 17 juin, 1776*.
101.) *Ibid, Montgolfier à Briand, 21 octobre, 1776*.
102.) *Ibid, Briand à Meurin, 21 avril, 1777*.
103.) *Ibid, Montgolfier à Briand, 10 février, 1777.   Q. 16, Haldimand to Germain*, 24 Oct., 1779, 690.
104.) Archevêché de Québec, Lettres, *Montgolfier à Briand, 12 août, 1776; Ibid, Montgolfier à Briand, 12 juin, 1777*.

CHAPTER IX

1.) *Am. Arch.*, "Wooster to Schuyler, Montreal, 5 Jan., 1776," Fourth series, IV, 669.
2.) *Ibid*.
3.) *Blockade* (A), 54, 58, 73.
4.) *Invasion* (B), 187.
5.) *R.A.Q.* (BTW), 1927-28, 441, 447, 469, 475, 485.
6.) *Blockade* (A), 70.
7.) *Am. Arch.*, "Montgomery to Schuyler, Quebec, 25 Dec., 1775," Fourth series, IV, 464.
8.) *J.C.C.*, "14 Feb., 1776," IV, 149.
9.) *Am. Arch.*, "Schuyler to Washington, Albany, 9 March, 1776," Fourth series, V, 147-48.
10.) *Invasion* (B), 192.
11.) B. 27, *Pierre Hayot, 16 mars, 1776*, 391.
12.) *Ibid*, 389-90.
13.) B. 27, *Hazen to Anctill, Montreal, 10 March, 1776*, 387.
14.) *Am. Arch.*, "Wooster to Schuyler, 5 Jan., 1776," Fourth series, IV, 669.
15.) *Ibid*, "Arnold to Wooster, 14 Jan., 674.
16.) *Am. Arch.*, "Arnold to Wooster, 2 Jan., 1775," Fourth series, III, 670. *Blockade* (A), 54;   *Ibid*, "Journal by a Garrison Officer," 207.
17.) *Am. Arch.*, "Wooster to Schuyler, 14 Jan., 1776," Fourth series, IV, 853.
18.) *Invasion* (S), 101-02.   *Remembrancer*, "1776," 249.
19.) *Invasion* (S), 95-7.
20.) *R.A.Q.* (BTW), 1927-28, 496, and *passim*.
21.) *J.C.C.*, "14 Feb., 1776," IV, 148-49.
22.) *Ibid*, "15 Feb., 1776," 151-52.
23.) *Ibid*, 157-59.
24.) *Ibid*, 168, 173.
25.) *Ibid*, 186, 191.
26.) *Ibid*, "20 March, 1776," 215.
27.) *Ibid*, 216.
28.) *Ibid*, 216-17.
29.) *Ibid*, 217.

30.) *Ibid*, 217-19.
31.) *Ibid*, 218.
32.) *Ibid*.
33.) *Ibid*, 219.
34.) *Ibid*, 223.
35.) *Ibid*, 236.
36.) *Blockade* (A), "8 March," 54.   *Invasion* (S), 98.
37.) B.27, *Information by Jean Bte. Chasseur, 13 March, 1776*, 398.
38.) *Invasion* (L), 268.   B. 27, *Hazen to Anctill, Montreal, 20 April, 1776*, 398.
39.) *Am. Arch.*, "A return of the forces of the United Colonies, 18 Feb., 1776," Fourth series, V, 104.
40.) *Invasion* (S), 103.
41.) *Ibid*, 104.
42.) *Ibid*.
43.) *Ibid*, 105.
44.) *Am. Arch.*, "Arnold to Wooster, 5 Jan., 1776," Fourth series, IV, 854. Lanaudière, "4 janvier, 1776," 855.
45.) B. 27, *Déposition de Chasseur, 13 mars, 1776*, 501-03.
46.) *Bulletin des recherches historiques*, "Mémoire de M. Porlier," VI, 134-37, 140.
47.) *Ibid*, 137-38.
48.) *Ibid*, 138-39.
49.) The references in this and the following notes are to the BTW "Journal" in *R.A.Q.*, 1927-28, 435-99; and 1929-30, 138-40. The men were drawn from the following parishes: St.-François-du-Sud-1, St.-Pierre-du-Sud-9, St.-Thomas-11, Islets-9, St.-Jean-Port-Joli-14, St.-Roch-des-Aulnaies-29, Ste.-Anne-de-la-Pocatière-24, Rivière-Ouelle-7, Kamouraska-36, 486-99, 139-40.
50.) From the following parishes: St.-Pierre-du-Sud-9, St.-Thomas-11, St.-Roch-8, Ste.-Anne-de-la-Pocatière-10, Rivière-Ouelle-7. Pages 486-99, 139-40.
51.) The Canadians belonged to the following parishes: St.-Henri-9, Pointe-Lévis-14, Beaumont-2, St.-Vallier-21, Berthier-11, St.-François-du-Sud-41, St.-Pierre-du-Sud-40, St.-Thomas-5, Ste.-Anne-de-la-Pocatière-7. Pages 469-97.
52.) Joseph and François Morin from St.-Roch were killed. A young Janot from St.-Thomas, Joseph Boucher from Rivière-Ouelle, and the Abbé Bailly were wounded. Pages 482, 488, 494, 499.
53.) *Am. Arch.*, "Arnold to Deane, Quebec, 30 March, 1776," Fourth series, V, 550;   *Ibid*, "Arnold to Wooster, 28 March, 1776," 512.   *Bulletin des recherches historiques*, "Mémoire de M. Porlier," VI, 140. *Invasion* (S), 105-06; *Ibid*, (B), 197;   *Ibid*, "Le capitaine Michel Blais," 375-76.
54.) *Bulletin des recherches historiques*, VI, 139.   *R.A.Q.* (BTW), 1928-29, 482.
55.) *Am. Arch.*, "Hazen to Schuyler, Montreal, 1 April, 1776," Fourth series, V, 870.
56.) *Ibid*, "Arnold to Schuyler, Montreal, 20 April, 1776," 1099-1100.   *Invasion* (S), 123.
57.) *Am. Arch.*, Fourth series, V, 869-70.
58.) *Ibid*, "Letter of Capt. Goforth," 871.
59.) *Invasion* (S), 101-02.
60.) *Am. Arch.*, "Return of the forces which passed Fort George between the 12th and 26th April, 1776," Fourth series, V, 1098. Sanguinet's figure is 1213.
61.) *J.C.C.*, IV, 250-51, 301.
62.) *Ibid*, 302.
63.) *Ibid*, 304, 308-09.
64.) Mgr. Carroll to his mother, 1 May, 1776 in Shea, *Life and Times of the Most Reverend John Carroll . . .* , 149.
65.) Carayon, *Bannissement des Jésuites de la Louisiane*, "Floquet à Briand, 15 juin, 1776," 107-19.
66.) B. 205, *Déposition de Jolybois, 26 octobre, 1784*, 301.

67.) Unfinished draft of a report by Father Carroll, quoted in Griffin, *Catholics and the American Revolution*, III, 303-04.
68.) "General Lee to Congress, 27 Feb., 1776," in Griffin, 262.
69.) *Am. Arch.*, "Commissioners to Congress, 1 May, 1776," Fourth series, V, 1166.
70.) *Ibid*, "Commissioners to Congress, 6 May, 1776," 1214.
71.) *J.C.C.*, IV, 250-51.   *Am. Arch.*, "Commissioners to Congress, 8 May, 1776," Fourth series, V, 1237.
72.) Q. 12, *Copy of Intelligence, 14 May, 1776*, 23.

CHAPTER X

1.) Q. 12, *Germain to Carleton, 17 Feb., 1776*, 1-3;   *Ibid*, 28 March, 1776, 4-7.
2.) *Invasion* (S), 125-26.   Q. 12, *Carleton to Germain, Quebec, 14 May, 1776*, 8-9.
3.) *Invasion* (S), 127.   Q. 12, *Carleton to Germain, Quebec, 14 May, 1776*, 7; *Ibid, MacLean to Germain, 10 May, 1776*, 69-70.
4.) *Invasion* (S), 127-28.
5.) *Quebec Gazette*, 10 May, 1776.
6.) *Ibid*, 12 May, 1776.
7.) *Invasion* (S), 129.
8.) Q. 12, *General Return of the British Army . . . June, 1776*, 106.
9.) *Invasion* (S), 107.
10.) *Ibid*.   Q. 12, *Copy of Intelligence, Montreal, 14 May, 1776*, 22-3.
11.) *J.C.C.*, IV, 376-78.
12.) *Ibid*, 383-84, 389-96.
13.) *Ibid*, 410-12.
14.) *Invasion* (de Lorimier), "Mes Services pendant la guerre américaine de 1776," 265.
15.) *Invasion* (S), 106.   *Am. Arch.*, "Arnold to Schuyler, 20 April, 1776," Fourth series, V, 1099.
16.) *Am. Arch.*, "Arnold to Washington, Montreal, 8 May, 1776," Fourth series, VI, 389.
17.) *Invasion* (L), 276.   *Am. Arch.*, "Accounts," Fourth series, VI, 598-99.   Q. 12, *Carleton to Germain, 12 May, 1776*, 49.
18.) *Invasion* (L), 278-81.   *Am. Arch.*, "Letter from Major Henry Sherburne, 18 June, 1776," Fourth series, VI, 598-99.
19.) Ethier, Marcel, *Narration authentique de l'échange des prisonniers aux Cèdres* (Montréal, 1873).   *Invasion* (L), 281-83.   *Am. Arch.*, "Arnold to the Commissioners, 27 May, 1776," Fourth series, VI, 595-97;   *Ibid*, "Accounts," 598-99.
20.) *Ibid*, "Thomas to Commissioners, Three Rivers, 15 May, 1776," 588-89.
21.) *Ibid*, "Commissioners to President of Congress, Montreal, 17 May, 1776," 587-88.
22.) *Ibid*, "Commissioners to President of Congress, Sorel, 20 May, 1776," 592.
23.) *Ibid*, "Commissioners to President of Congress, Montreal, 27 May, 1776," 412;   *Ibid*, "Dr. Morgan to Adams, New York, 25 June, 1776," 1070.
24.) *Ibid*, "Council of War, 30 May, 1776," 628.
25.) *Ibid*, "Thompson to Washington, 2 June, 1776," 684.
26.) *Ibid*, "Letter from Sorel, 12 June, 1776," 826-28;   *Ibid*, "Sullivan to Washington, Sorel, 5 June, 1776," 921-22;   *Ibid*, "Instructions for General Sullivan, Sorel, 6 June, 1776," 923.   Q. 12, *Carleton to Germain, Montreal, 20 June, 1776*, 65.   *Invasion*, 133-34, 219, 238.
27.) *Ibid*.
28.) B. 39, *Carleton to Douglas, Three Rivers, 13 June, 1776*, 7-8.
29.) *The British Invasion from the North. The campaigns of Generals Carleton and Burgoyne from Canada, 1776-77, with the Journal of Lieutenant William Digby*, ed. by J. P. Baxter (Albany, 1887), 111.   *Ibid*, 4.

30.) Q. 12, *Carleton to Germain, Montreal, 20 June, 1776,* 65-6.   *Invasion* (S), 132-33.   Archevêché de Québec, Lettres, *Montgolfier to Briand, 17 June, 1776.   Am. Arch.,* "Arnold to Washington, Albany, 25 June, 1776," Fourth series, VI, 1107-08;   *Ibid,* "Arnold to Washington, Crown Point, 2 July, 1776," 1219.
31.) Q. 12, *Carleton to Germain, 10 Aug., 1776,* 135.
32.) B. 39, *Carleton to Howe, 8 Aug., 1776,* 93.
33.) *Ibid, Foy to M. de Bonvouloir, 12 juillet, 1776,* 69.   Hamon, Joseph, *Le Chevalier de Bonvouloir, Premier Emissaire secret de la France auprès du Congrès de Philadelphie avant l'Indépendance américaine* (Paris, 1953). *Despatches and Instructions of Conrad Alexandre Gérard, 1778-1780,* ed. by John J. Meng (Paris, 1939), 45. With an historical introduction and notes.
34.) *Affaires étrangères, Correspondance politique; Angleterre,* "Garnier à de Rayneval, Londres, 27 septembre, 1776," DXVIII, fol. 174.
35.) *Invasion* (S), 134.
36.) *J.C.C.,* V, 431-53.
37.) *Ibid,* 472.
38.) *Ibid,* 535-39.
39.) *Ibid,* 617-23.
40.) *Ibid,* 642-46.
41.) Q. 12, *Copy of Intelligence, 14 May, 1776,* 23.
42.) Baby Papers, fol. 3, 205.   Séminaire de Québec, Fonds Verreau, Boîte 9, *The Court of Enquiry of Damages occasioned by the Invasion of the Rebels,* 34-5.
43.) Wilkinson, *Mémoires,* I, 58.
44.) Woedtke's Orderly Book, *7 June, 1776.*
45.) Sém. de Québec, Fonds Verreau, Boîte 9, *The Court of Enquiry . . . ,* 1-35.
46.) *Am. Arch.,* "Arnold to Chase, 15 May, 1776," Fourth series, VI, 581.
47.) *Invasion* (B), 211.
48.) *Ibid,* 212.
49.) *Ibid.*
50.) *Ibid* (S), 133.
51.) *Remembrancer,* 1776, "Letter from Quebec to Halifax, 11 July, 1776," 17-19.
52). *Pennsylvania Archives,* "The Memorial of Col. Moses Hazen," Sixth series, 1779, 17-19.
53.) *Bulletin des recherches historiques,* III, 209-13. Forty-two men from the Montreal district left the province: 22, including Jeremiah Duggen, from St.-Ours, 5 from St.-Denis, 6, including Pierre Boileau and François Monty, from Pointe-Olivier, 2 from Berthier, and 10 from Rivière-du-Loup.   B. 171, *List of the Inhabitants of the different Parishes in the district of Montreal which are now amongst the Rebels sent by Justice Fraser,* 134-37. (This list was drawn up by the captains of militia. Mention is also made of five others from St.-Denis who left the country in 1778.)
54.) *Public Papers of George Clinton,* I, 453.
55.) *J.C.C.,* "10 Oct., 1776," VI, 865.

CHAPTER XI

1.) *Invasion* (S), 127-28.
2.) *Am. Arch.,* "Thompson to Commissioners, Sorel, 25 May, 1776," Fourth series, VI, 594-95.
3.) *Invasion* (L), 276, 278;   *Ibid* (S), 133.
4.) Q. 12, *Carleton to Germain, Quebec, 2 June, 1776,* 57.   *Am. Arch.,* "Sullivan to Washington, Sorel, 5 June, 1776," Fourth series, VI, 922.
5.) *Invasion* (B), 219.
6.) *Memoirs and Letters and Journals of Major General Riedesel,* "Quebec, June, 1776," trans. by W. L. Stone (Albany, 1869), 342.

7.) Q. 12, *Carleton to Germain, Montreal, 20 June, 1776,* 67.   The British Invasion from the North, "Journal of the Campaign in Canada under Sir Guy Carleton," 10.
8.) *Invasion* (L), 285.
9.) B. 19, *Carleton to Burgoyne, La Prairie, 20 June, 1776,* 26.
10.) *The British Invasion from the North,* "Digby's Journal," 105.
11.) *Remembrancer,* "Letter from an army officer, 20 June, 1776," 26.
12.) Archevêché de Québec, Lettres, *Montgolfier à Briand, 12 août, 1776.*
13.) *Memoirs of General Riedesel,* "Letter from Quebec," 242.   Mandements des Evêques de Québec, "Mandement aux sujets rebelles," II, 270. See appendices.
14.) Series S, Lower Canada, *Commission to St.-Georges Dupré, E. W. Gray, and Pierre Panet, 25 June, 1776.*
15.) *R.A.Q.* (BTW), 1927-28, 435-99; 1929-30, 138-40.
16.) B. 39, *Au curé de la Baye St.-Antoine, Québec, 6 février, 1777,* 351.
17.) Q. 12, *Commission to Mabane, Dunne, and Panet, 30 July, 1776,* 127-30. *Quebec Gazette,* 12, 19, 26 Dec., 1776 and 2, 9, 16, 23, 30 Jan., 1777.
18.) Séminaire de Québec, Fonds Verreau, Boîte 9, 1-35.
19.) B. 83, *General Order, 5 June, 1776,* 4.
20.) *Ibid, General Order, Chambly, 22 July, 1776,* 23-4.
21.) Archevêché de Québec, Lettres, *Montgolfier à Briand, 12 août, 1776.*
22.) *Hadden's Journal and Orderly Books; a Journal kept in Canada upon Burgoyne's Campaign in 1776 and 1777,* "Chambly, 25 June, 1776," ed. by Horatio Rogers (Albany, 1884), 235.
23.) *The British Invasion from the North,* "Digby's Journal, Chambly, 18 June," 120.
24.) *Invasion* (S), 134.
25.) B. 39, *Carleton to Cramahé, 25 July, 1776,* 112.
26.) B. 83, *General Order, Chambly, 8 Aug., 1776.*
27.) B. 39, *Foy to Lachine priest, Chambly, 15 July, 1776,* 70-1.
28.) Archevêché de Québec, Lettres, *Bédard à Briand, St.-François, 26 août, 1776.*
29.) B. 39, *Carleton to Powell, Chambly, 24 Aug., 1776,* 110.
30.) *Ibid, Carleton to Phillips, 20 Nov., 1776,* 269-70.
31.) M. 834, *Ordre de Carleton, 7 septembre, 1776.*
32.) B. 39, *Foy à Dufy, Tonnancourt et Voyer, 23 septembre, 1776,* 180.
33.) *Invasion* (S), 134-35.
34.) B. 39, *Foy à Tonnancourt, Chambly, 4 octobre, 1776,* 195.
35.) *Const. Docts.,* "Carleton to Germain, Chambly, 28 Sept., 1776," 675.
36.) B.39, *Foy à Tonnancourt, Chambly, 4 octobre, 1776,* 195.
37.) *Ibid, Foy à Riedesel, Québec, 20 décembre, 1776,* 314.
38.) Séminaire de Québec, Fonds Verreau, Boîte 9, *Reçu 2 décembre, 1776.* B.39, *Foy à Dupré, Québec, 20 décembre, 1776,* 315.
39.) *Invasion* (S), 135.
40.) Séminaire de Québec, Fonds Verreau, Boîte 9, *Liasse 5-27.*   B. 39. *Lettre à Gall, 15 mars, 1777,* 383;   *Ibid, Lettre à Riedesel, 15 mars, 1777,* 351-52; *Ibid, Lettre au Commissaire de la Milice, 15 mars, 1777,* 384.
41.) *Mandements des Evêques de Québec,* "12 mai, 1776," II, 207-08.
42.) Archevêché de Québec, Lettres, *M. Sarault à Mgr. Briand, St.-Charles, 8 mai, 1776.*
43.) *Ibid, Montgolfier à Briand, 12 mai, 1776.*
44.) *Ibid, Briand à Sarault, 11 mai, 1776.*
45.) *Ibid, Porlier à Briand, 14 octobre, 1776.*
46.) *Ibid, Briand à Porlier, 19 novembre, 1776.*
47.) *Ibid, Acte dressè par M. Bèdard, 9 juillet, 1776; Ibid, Bèdard à Briand, 26 août, 1776; Ibid, Briand à Bèdard, 30 août, 1776.*
48.) Carayon, Auguste, *Première Mission des Jésuites au Canada, Lettres et documents inédits,* "Floquet à Briand, Québec, 29 novembre, 1776" (Paris,

1864), 104.   Gosselin, Auguste, *L'Eglise du Canada depuis Mgr. de Laval jusqu'à la conquête* (Québec, 1914), 229. Note.

49.) Archevêché de Québec, Lettres, *Montgolfier à Briand, 12 août, 1776.*   Allaire, J.B.A., *Dictionnaire biographique du clergé canadien-français, Les Anciens* (Montréal, 1910), I, 99.

50.) Can. Archives, Bibliothèque Ste.-Geneviève, 2088, La Valinière, *Mémoires sur l'ètat actuel du Canada; Ibid, La Valinière, Vraie histoire, ou simple précis des infortunes, pour ne pas dire des persécutions qu'a souffert et que souffre encore le Rev. P. H. de La Valinière, mis en vers par lui-même en juillet, 1792* (Albany, 1792).

51.) Archevêché de Québec, Lettres, *Montgolfier à Briand, 12 août, 1776.*

52.) *Mandements des Evêques . . .* , "Mandement aux sujets rebelles, 1776," II, 269-72. See appendices.

53.) *Ibid*, 271-72.
54.) *Ibid*, 272-73.
55.) *Ibid*, 273-74.
56.) *Ibid*, 275.
57.) *Ibid*, 275-76.
58.) *Ibid*, 276.
59.) *Ibid*, 277.
60.) *Ibid*, 278-79.
61.) Archives des Jésuites, *Mgr. Briand, Québec, 26 septembre, 1776*, fol. B.I.B.
62.) *Mandements des Evêques . . .* , "20 décembre, 1776," II.
63.) Letter from Mère Marie Catherine Duchesnay de St.-Ignace of the General Hospital. Quoted in Têtu, *Les Evêques de Québec*, 345-46.
64.) Archevêché de Québec, Lettres, *Mgr. Briand aux habitants de St.-Joseph de Chambly, 19 janvier, 1777.*
65.) *Ibid, Corbin à Briand, St.-Joachim, 28 février, 1777.*
66.) *Ibid, Gatien à Briand, 18 octobre, 1777.*
67.) Gaspé, Philippe Aubert de, *Les Anciens Canadiens* (1934), 270. In the single parish of St.-Michel de Bellechasse five persons were buried on their own farms. See Roy, P. G., *A travers les Anciens Canadiens de Philippe Aubert de Gaspé* (Montréal, 1943), 156-57.

CHAPTER XII

1.) Q. 12, 124-25.
2.) State Book, Quebec Legislative Council, vol. D, *passim*.
3.) Q. 12, *Carleton to Germain, 14 Oct., 1776*, 225.
4.) *Remembrancer*, "Letter from an officer, 16 May, 1777," 225.
5.) State Book, Quebec Legislative Council, vol. D, 7.   *Const. Docts.*, "Ordinances passed . . . 1777," 678.
6.) *Ibid*, "Carleton to Germain, Quebec, 9 May, 1777," 677.
7.) Q. 13, *Carleton to Burgoyne, Quebec, 29 May, 1777*, 222.   Quoted in *Const. Docts.*, 677, Note 1.
8.) *Quebec Ordinances*, 1777-86, 33-40.
9.) *Invasion* (S), 143-44. Q. 13, *Carleton to Germain, 10 July, 1777*, 333.
10.) Q. 13, *Carleton to Germain, 29 May, 1777*, 222-24.
11.) *Invasion* (S), 143-44.
12.) B. 39, *Foy to Mackay, 19 May, 1777*, 498; *Ibid, 18 June, 1777*, 532. Archevêché de Québec, Lettres, *Montgolfier à Briand, 12 juin, 1777.*   Q. 23, *Letter of Haldimand, 19 Nov., 1783*, 363.
13.) Q. 13, *Burgoyne to Carleton, 26 May, 1777*, 213.
14.) *Ibid, Carleton to Germain, 10 July, 1777*, 334-35.   B. 39, *Carleton to Cramahé, 16 1777*, 528.
15.) Q. 13, *Burgoyne to Germain, 22 June, 1777*, 282; *Ibid*, 284.   B. 39, *Foy to Day, 25 Aug., 1777*, 689-70.

Canada and the American Revolution

16.) *Invasion* (S), 145-46. M. 689, Memorial of Peter Livius, *23 Sept., 1778*, 17.
17.) B. 39, *Foy to Maclean, 4 July, 1779*, 267.
18.) *Ibid, Carleton to Longueuil, 11 Aug. 1777*, 655.   Q. 13, *Burgoyne to Germain, 22 June, 1777*, 284.
19.) Q. 14, *Powell to Carleton, Mt. Independence, 5 Oct., 1777*, 288.
20.) Q. 13, *Carleton to Burgoyne, 29 May, 1777*, 224.
21.) B. 39, *Foy to Maclean, 25 July, 1777*, 625;   *Ibid, Carleton to Marr, 18 Aug., 1777*, 679.
22.) B. 39 *Carleton to Burgoyne, 17 June, 1777*, 529;   *Ibid, Foy to Maclean, 24 July, 1777*, 627.
23.) Beaujeu, Monongahela de, *Documents inédits sur le Colonel de Longueuil*, "Maclean à Longueuil, Montréal, 2 juillet, 1777."
24.) B. 39, *Foy to Lieut.-Col. Chrencrook, 30 June, 1777*, 560-61.
25.) *Invasion* (S), 146.
26.) M. 689, Memorial of Peter Livius, *23 Sept., 1778*, 17.
27.) State Book, Quebec Lesgislative Council, *Finlay's opinion*, 1785, vol. D, 219-221;   *Ibid, Caldwell's reasons of dissent*, 1785, 278.
28.) *Remembrancer*, 1778, "Letter from Quebec, 14 June, 1778," 183.
29.) B. 39, *Foy to Maclean, Quebec, 31 July, 1777*, 637.
30.) *Ibid, Foy to Maclean, 24 July, 1777*, 625.
31.) *Ibid, Carleton to Marr, 18 Aug., 1777*, 679.
32.) *Ibid, Foy to Maclean, 10 July, 1777*, 574.
33.) *Ibid, Carleton to Maclean, 11 Aug., 1777*, 655.
34.) *Ibid, Carleton to Burgoyne, 2 July, 1777*, 564.
35.) *Ibid, Foy to Maclean, 10 July, 1777*, 575.
36.) *Ibid, Foy to Officer at Pt. Levy, 9 July, 1777*, 569.
37.) *Ibid, Allowances to the Inhabitants for transporting provisions, artillery, etc.* . . . , 576-77.   Q. 24-2, *Representation of a number of the inhabitants of Montreal . . . 11 April, 1785*, 357-62; *Ibid, Tableau des prix des corvées* . . . , 362a.
38.) B. 39, *Carleton to Burgoyne, 13 June, 1777*, 526.   B. 40, *Carleton to Powell, 29 Sept., 1777*, 67.
39.) In considering the system of corvées, we must be careful to avoid exaggerated criticism. In the memorandum which he drew up after he had quarrelled with Carleton, Judge Livius presents a very one-sided picture.   M. 689, Memorial of Peter Livius, *23 Sept., 1778*, 20.
40.) *J.C.C.*, "22 July, 1777," VIII, 585.
41.) *Ibid*, "4 Nov., 1777," IX, 870.
42.) Q. 14, *Capitulation* . . . , 390.   *Remembrancer*, 1778, "Gates to President, Council of the State of Massachusetts, 19 Oct., 1777," 477. The list of prisoners reads: "Canadians, volunteers, etc. . . 1,100." This total was made up of "volunteers," American loyalists, "sailors, workmen, carters, women, and children" (*Invasion* (S), 150); it also included servants and camp followers. The strength of both companies of militia was reduced to a minimum, and Monnin's alone remained to the end of the campaign. The men assigned to corvée duty deserted "in dozens," or refused to cross the frontier.
43.) *J.C.C.*, IX, 924.
44.) *Ibid*, 921.
45.) Chastellux, François Jean, *Voyages dans l'Amérique septentrionale dans les années 1780, 1781, 1782* (Paris, 1786), I, 300.
46.) *J.C.C.*, "2 Dec., 1777," IX, 986-88.
47.) *Ibid*, 999-1000.
48.) *South Carolina Historical Magazine*, "La Fayette to Henry Laurens, 14 Dec., 1777," VII, 1906, 63.
49.) *J.C.C.*, X, 85, 87.
50.) *The Writings of George Washington*, "Washington to T. Nelson, 18 Feb., 1778," ed. by W. C. Ford, VI, 361.
51.) *J.C.C.*, X, 87, 96, 107, 142.

308

52.) *S.C. Hist. Mag.*, "La Fayette to Laurens, 26 Jan., 1778," VII, 126.
53.) *Ibid*, 181.
54.) *Ibid*, "31 Jan., 1778," 184.
55.) *Ibid*, "La Fayette to Laurens, 19 Feb., 1778," 192-98.   Tower, Charlemagne, *The Marquis de La Fayette in the American Revolution*, "La Fayette to Washington, 17 Feb., 1778" (New York, 1941), I, 283-85.
56.) *Ibid*, 274-75.
57.) *Ibid*, 274.
58.) *J.C.C.*, X, 216-17.
59.) *Invasion* (S), 150.
60.) Q. 15, *Carleton to Germain, 10 June, 1778*, 36-7.   B. 117, *De Rouville à Carleton, St.-François, 1 décembre, 1777*, 5;   *Ibid, 7 février, 1778*, 13-14.
61.) *Invasion* (S), 151.
62.) *Ibid*, 151-53.
63.) *Ibid*, 153-54.
64.) Q.15, *Carleton to Germain, 24 June, 1778*, 38-9.
65.) *Ibid*, 39.
66.) *Invasion* (S), 155.
67.) B. 129, *Powell to Carleton, 2 March, 1778*, 5.   Série S 17, Inter-Corr. Que., 1778, "Fraser to Gray, 5 April, 1777," 21-3.

CHAPTER XIII

1.) Q. 14, *Germain to Haldimand, 19 Sept., 1777*, 3-4.
2.) Q. 15, *Haldimand to Germain, 30 June, 1778*, 34.
3.) Doniol, Henri, *Histoire de la participation de la France à l'établissement des Etats-Unis d'Amérique* (Paris, 1886-92), I, 129.   *Despatches and Instructions of Conrad Alexandre Gérard, 1778-1780* (Paris, 1939), 45. With an introduction and notes by John J. Meng.
4.) *J.C.C.*, "18 July, 1776," V, 579.
5.) Affaires Etrangères, Correspondance Politique, Etats-Unis, *Remis par les trois députés des colonies unies (janvier, 1777)*, 6-7.
6.) *J.C.C.*, 4 May, 1778, XI, 450.
7.) B. 229, *Memorandum*, 110-14.
8.) Q. 15, *(Returns) June, 1778*, 40-4.
9.) *Ibid, Haldimand to Germain, 25 July, 1778*, 170;   *Ibid, 15 Oct., 1778*, 269-70.
10.) *Ibid, 25 July, 1778*, 170-71.
11.) B. 181, *Letter of John Prebly, 1 June, 1778*, 305.
12.) B. 66, *Haldimand to Budé, 24 Oct., 1778*, 93.
13.) Q. 15, *Haldimand to Germain, 15 Oct., 1778*, 279.
14.) *Ibid*.
15.) B. 66, *Haldimand to Budé, 24 Oct., 1778*, 93.
16.) B. 117, *passim*.
17.) *Quebec Gazette*, 23 July, 1778.
18.) B. 129, *Powell to Haldimand, 25 July, 1778*, 12.   B. 131, *Haldimand to Powell, 18 Sept., 1778*, 6.
19.) B. 89, 73-6.
20.) *Ibid*, 19-22.
21.) B. 114, 68-9.
22.) S. 17, Int. Corr. Que. 1778-79, "9 April," 21-3.
23.) B. 170, *Tonnancourt à Haldimand, Trois-Rivières, 3 octobre, 1778*.
24.) B. 188, *T. Carleton to Haldimand, 10 Sept., 1778*.
25.) *Ibid, Carleton to Haldimand, 20 Dec., 1778*, 27.
26.) B. 156, *MacBean to Haldimand, 15 Sept., 1778*, 84.
27.) B. 188, *Carleton to Haldimand, 3 May, 1778*, 40.
28.) *Despatches . . . of Gérard*, 129.   Affaires Etrangères, Corr. Pol., Etats-

Unis, *Vergennes à M. Gérard, 29 mars, 1778,* III, 7-8. On France's policy, see Doniol's *Histoire de la participation de la France.* . . . The Canadian aspect of the question is thoroughly explored in Marcel Trudel's solidly documented study: *Louis XVI, le Congrès américain et le Canada* (Québec, 1949).

29.) Aff. Etr., Corr. Pol., E-U., *Gérard à Vergennes, 16 juillet, 1778,* IV, 22.
30.) *Writings of George Washington,* "Washington to President of Congress, White Plains, 12 Sept., 1778," VII, 192, 191 (Note).
31.) *J.C.C.,* "16 Sept., 1778," XII.
32.) For the text of the instructions, see Doniol, *Histoire de la participation* . . . , I, 237-38.
33.) *Writings of George Washington,* "Laurens to Washington, 20 Nov., 1778," VII, 265. *Despatches* . . . *of Gérard,* "Gérard à Vergennes, 4 janvier, 1779," 461.
34.) Aff. Etr., Corr. Pol., E-U, *Gérard à Vergennes, 20 octobre, 1778,* V, 23-4.
35.) *Journals (secret) of the Acts and Proceedings of Congress from the first meeting thereof to the dissolution of the Confederation by the adoption of the Constitution of the United States,* "22 Oct., 1778 (Boston, 1820), II, 107-24.
36.) *Mémoires, correspondances et manuscrits du général La Fayette, publiés par sa famille,* "Lettre à Vergennes, 14 février, 1779," (Paris, 1837-38), 286. $C^{ue}E, Le Sr. Cebet, Projet pour faire rentrer le Canada sous la domination de la France, 12 janvier, 1777,* IX, 211-13; *Ibid, Mèmoire sur le Canada, 12 juillet, 1777,* 215 ff.
37.) Aff. Etr., Corr. Pol., E-U, *Gérard à Vergennes, 20 octobre, 1778,* V, 40-1.
38.) *Writings of George Washington,* "Washington to Scott, 14 Nov., 1778," VII, 260, Note. Q. 16, 297-303.
39.) *Journals (secret)* . . . *of Congress,* "22 Oct., 1778," II, 111-18.
40.) *J.C.C.,* XII, 1053.
41.) *Writings of George Washington,* "Washington to Pres. Congress, 11 Nov., 1778," VII, 239-58.
42.) *Ibid,* 261-64.
43.) Aff. Etr., Corr. Pol., E-U, V, 65-6.
44.) *Journals (secret)* . . . *of Congress,* II, 125-26.
45.) *Ibid,* 127-30.
46.) *Ibid,* 133-34.
47.) *Ibid,* 226-27.
48.) B. 171, *Déposition d'Athanase Boudreau, 27 septembre, 1780,* 44-5.   Q. 15, *Haldimand to Germain, 15 Oct., 1778,* 269-78.
49.) B. 170, *Haldimand à Tonnancourt, 17 février, 1779,* 16-17.
50.) B. 184-91, *Enquête faite par F. de Tonnancourt, 12 mars, 1778,* 46-9.
51.) *Writings of George Washington,* "Washington to Scott, 14 Nov., 1778," VII, 260, Note.
52.) *J.C.C.,* XII, 1190.
53.) Q. 16, *Boston, 20 décembre, 1779,* 105-10.
54.) B. 184-91, *Déclaration de Marie Louise Emond, 23 mars, 1779,* 50.
55.) Q. 16, *Haldimand to Germain, 12 June, 1779,* 242.
56.) B. 184-91, *Papier remis par l'évêque, le 5 mars, 1779,* 148-49.
57.) B. 72-1, 177.   Q. 16, *Haldimand to Germain, 7 June, 1779,* 128-29.
58.) *Ibid, Haldimand to Germain, 18 June, 1779,* 292-93.   B. 135, *St.-Léger to Haldimand, 7 May, 1779,* 24.
59.) B. 150, *Haldimand to MacLean, 26 May, 1778,* 7.   B. 170, *Tonnancourt à Haldimand, Trois Rivières, 14 juin, 1779,* 58-61. $C^{ue}E$, *Lettre de Cazeau, Paris, 12 décembre, 1790,* II, 232.
60.) B. 170, *Tonnancourt à Haldimand, 14 juin, 1779,* 60.
61.) Q. 16, 298.
62.) *Ibid,* 299.
63.) *Ibid,* 300.

64.) *Ibid, 301.*
65.) Q. 16, *Déclaration adressée au nom du roi, 28 octobre, 1779,* 302.
66.) B. 150, *Haldimand to MacLean, 26 May, 1779,* 7.
67.) *Ibid, Haldimand to Hughes, 29 May, 1779,* 10.
68.) B. 66, *Haldimand to Budé, 17 June, 1779,* 137-38.
69.) *Ibid, Haldimand à Montgolfier, Québec, 15 février, 1779,* 593.
70.) Q. 16, *Haldimand to Germain, 14 sept., 1779,* 593.
71.) *Ibid, Haldimand to Germain, 18 Feb., 1779,* 292-93.
72.) B. 72, *LeMaistre à Haldimand, Montréal, 14 juin, 1779,* 17.
73.) B. 171, *Memorandum concerning priest of Lotbinière,* 37-8.
74.) Q. 16, *Haldimand to Germain, 24 Oct., 1779,* 689-91.
75.) B. 182, *Report by T. Sherwood and party, St. Johns, 12 Dec., 1779,* 129-32.
76.) Q. 16, *Haldimand to Germain, 14 Sept., 1779,* 598-99.
77.) *Ibid,* 594.
78.) B. 72, *LeMaistre à Haldimand, Montréal, 14 juin, 1779,* 17.
79.) B. 181, *Intelligence from Claremont, St. Johns, 18 Sept., 1779,* 241.
80.) Q. 16, *Haldimand to Germain, 18 June, 1779,* 594.
81.) *Ibid, Haldimand to Germain, 18 June, 1779,* 292-93.
82.) B. 181, *Intelligence from Claremont, St. Johns, 18 Sept., 1779,* 241-42.
83.) Q. 16, *Haldimand to Germain, 7 June, 1779,* 123-28.
84.) B. 171, *Déclaration d'Athanase Boudreau, 27 septembre, 1780,* 44-5.
85.) B. 182, 484-85.   Griffin, M. I. J., *Catholics and the American Revolution,* "Papers of Washington," 135-39.
86.) B. 100, *Bolton to Haldimand, Niagara, 21 Oct., 1779,* 302.
87.) B. 182, *Sherwood to Powell, St. Johns, 26 Dec., 1779,* 133-34.
88.) B. 181, *Intelligence from Claremont, St. Johns, 18 Sept., 1779,* 241-42.
89.) Q. 16, *Germain to Haldimand, 6 April, 1779,* 30-1.
90.) B. 176, *Gosselin à sa femme, 29 octobre, 1779,* 7-9.
91.) B. 139, *Haldimand à St.-Léger, 5 juin, 1779,* 12.   B.170, *Haldimand à Tonnancourt, 11 mars, 1779,* 23.
92.) B. 61, *Mathews to Gray, 5 Aug., 1779,* 13.
93.) B. 16, *Haldimand to Germain, 7 June, 1779,* 128-29.
94.) B. 182, *St. Johns, 12 Oct., 1779,* 112-13.
95.) B. 170, *Tonnancourt à Haldimand, 14 décembre, 1779,* 91-2.

CHAPTER XIV

1.) Q. 16, *Haldimand to Germain, 18 June, 1779,* 292;   *Ibid, Tonnancourt à Haldimand, 6 mars, 1779,* 20.
2.) B. 184-2, *Examination of William Flood, 18 March, 1780,* 526-27.
3.) B. 185-1, *Tonnancourt à Haldimand, 19 septembre, 1780,* 286-88.
4.) B. 135, *Haldimand to Powell, 10 April, 1780,* 102.
5.) Q. 20, *Deposition of William Flood, 18 April, 1780,* 172.
6.) Q. 20, *Examination of James Kenny, 1 Sept., 1780; Ibid, Confession of Mr. James Kenny, 11 April, 1781,* 23-4; *Ibid, Haldimand to Germain, 16 July, 1782,* 1-6.
7.) Aff. Etr., Corr. Pol., E-U, *Réclamation du sieur Cazeau à la Cour de France, 20 mai, 1780,* XII.   B. 131, *Mathews to MacLean, 30 March, 1780,* 44.
8.) Aff. Etr., Corr. Pol., E-U, *La Luzerne à Vergennes, Philadelphie, 20 mars, 1780,* XII.
9.) *Ibid, La Luzerne à Vergennes, 7 juillet, 1780,* XIII.
10.) *Writings of George Washington,* "Washington to La Fayette, Morristown, 19 May, 1780," VIII, 280-81.
11.) Q. 17, *La Fayette, Proclamation,* 175-80. See appendices.   *Ibid, Haldimand to Germain, 25 Oct., 1780,* 152.
12.) *American Historical Review,* "Lettres from La Fayette to Luzerne, 25 May, 1780," 1914-15, XX, 349.

13.) *Writings of George Washington*, VIII, 281.
14.) B. 147, *Clinton à Haldimand, 6 juillet, 1780.*
15.) *Am. Hist. Rev.*, "La Fayette à La Luzerne, 2 juillet, 1780," XX, 361.
16.) Aff. Etr., Corr. Pol., E-U, *La Luzerne à Vergennes, 20 mai, 1780,* XII.
17.) *Ibid, La Luzerne à La Fayette, 30 mai, 1780.*
18.) *Ibid, La Luzerne à Vergennes, 24 juin, 1780.*
19.) Aff. Etr., Corr. Pol., E-U, *La Luzerne à Vergennes, 7 juillet, 1780,* XIII.
20.) Sparks, J., *Diplomatic Correspondence of the American Revolution*, "Petition to Washington, 30 Aug., 1780," III, 68-70.
21.) Q. 17, *Réponse de M. le Comte de Rochambeau, 30 août, 1780,* 181-82.
22.) *Ibid, Haldimand to Germain, 25 Oct., 1780,* 152.
23.) Aff. Etr., Corr. Pol., E-U, *La Luzerne à Vergennes, 3 septembre, 1780,* XIV.
24.) *Ibid, Vergennes à La Luzerne, 22 octobre, 1780.*
25.) B. 133, *Carleton to Haldimand, 21 June, 1780,* 192;   *Ibid, 28 June, 1780,* 192-99.
26.) B. 182, *Carleton to Haldimand, 14 June, 1780,* 230-31.
27.) B. 133, *Carleton to Haldimand, 21 June, 1780,* 198.
28.) Q. 20, *Carleton to Haldimand, Chambly, 18 July, 1780,* 40-1.
29.) *Ibid, Carleton to Haldimand, 30 July, 1780,* 42.
30.) *Ibid, Lettre de Pilon,* 80.
31.) *Ibid, Examination of Joseph Dufort, 14 Nov., 1780,* 66.
32.) B. 205, *Marsell to Haldimand, 13 Aug., 1780,* 68-9.
33.) Q. 20, *Deposition of Joseph Gilson, 21 Feb., 1781,* 173.
34.) Q. 20, *Examination of William Ferris, 21 Feb., 1781,* 181-85.
35.) Q. 20, *To General Washington, Montreal, 7 Sept., 1780,* 81-3;   *Ibid, A La Fayette, 8 septembre, 1780,* 84-5;   *Ibid, A Messrs. les principaux sujets du Congrès, 8 septembre, 1780,* 78-9;   *Ibid, Examination of Michel Hamel, 13 Nov., 1780,* 71-7.
36.) Q. 20, *Carleton to Mathews, 24 Sept., 1780,* 44.
37.) *Ibid, Deposition of Stephen Ducoulon, St. Johns, 21 Feb., 1781,* 181-85.
38.) Q. 20, *MacLean to Mathews, 26 Sept., 1780,* 36-9.
39.) B. 205, *Examination of Pilon, 20 Oct., 1780,* 118-20.
40.) Q. 20, *Du Calvet à Haldimand, 30 septembre, 1780,* 95.
41.) B. 205, *Cramahé to Provost Marshal Prentice, 14 Nov., 1780,* 159.
42.) B. 113, *Mathews to Campbell, Montreal, 7 Dec., 1780,* 118.
43.) Q. 20, *Washington to William Osborne, 17 Aug., 1780; Ibid, Reçus de Nadeau et Charland, 8 septembre, 1780; Ibid, Examination of Pierre Charland, 15 Nov., 1780,* 62-70.
44.) B. 185-1, *Déposition de François Breton, 5 septembre, 1780,* 282.
45.) *Ibid,* 283-84.
46.) B. 205, *LeMaistre to Haldimand, 27 Oct., 1780,* 128-29.
47.) Baby Papers, *St.-Georges-Dupré to Baby, 22 juin, 1780,* fol. 44.
48.) B.147, *Haldimand to Clinton, 13 Aug., 1780,* 222-23.
49.) B. 133, *Carleton to Haldimand, 21 June, 1780,* 192.
50.) Q.20, *Examination of Pierre Charland, 15 Nov., 1780,* 70.
51.) B.205, *Hurtubise Gagné à Cazeau, Québec, 9 septembre, 1780,* 7.
52.) B. 133, *Carleton to Haldimand, 9 July, 1780,* 203-04.
53.) B. 184-2, *Examination of William Flood, 18 March, 1780,* 526-27.   Q. 20, *Examination to Joseph Dufort, 14 Nov., 1780,* 46-61.   B. 184-2, 521-22; *Ibid, Journal of Capt. Breakenridge, 24 March, 1780,* 528-34.   B. 205, *Examination of Pilon, 20 Oct., 1780,* 120.   B.133, *Carleton to Haldimand, 28 June, 1780,* 525.   B. 170, *De Tonnancourt à Haldimand, 3 octobre, 1780,* 181-82.   Q. 20, *Pilon à Washington, 7 septembre, 1780,* 81-3.   B. 135, *Haldimand to Carleton, 13 July, 1780,* 120.   B. 170. *Tonnancourt à Haldimand, 12 août, 1780,* 159-60.
54.) B. 136, *Hamilton to Carleton, 10 April, 1780,* 102.
55.) B. 205, *Capt. Schmidt à Haldimand, 14 octobre, 1780,* 109-11.
56.) Q. 17, *Haldimand to Germain, 25 Oct., 1780,* 152-60.

57.) B. 205, *Pilon à Pilon fils, Montréal, 2 septembre, 1780,* 77.
58.) *Ibid, Carleton to Haldimand, 18 July, 1780,* 79-80.
59.) B. 205, *Pritchard to Carleton, Chambly, 16 Sept., 1780,* 79-80.
60.) Q. 20, *Message de Pilon, septembre, 1780,* 80.
61.) *Ibid, Examination of Pierre Charland, 15 Nov., 1780,* 64-7.
62.) B. 65, *Haldimand to Germain, 28 Nov., 1780,* 49-52.
63.) B. 204, *Mabane to Haldimand, 8 March, 1780,* 49-52.
64.) *Ibid.*
65.) Baby Papers, *Magnan to Baby, Kamouraska, 20 février, 1780.*
66.) B. 170. *Tonnancourt à Haldimand, 22 mars, 1780,* 106.
67.) Q. 17, *Haldimand to Germain, 12 July, 1780,* 118-24.
68.) B. 204, *Mabane to Haldimand, 8 March, 1780,* 49-52.
69.) Q. 17, *Haldimand to Germain, 25 Oct., 1780,* 152-60.
70.) B. 184-2, *Deposition of William Flood, 10 March, 1780,* 523-24.
71.) B. 55, *Haldimand to Germain, 28 Nov., 1780,* 30-1.
72.) B. 66, *Haldimand à Briand, 13 juin, 1780,* 181.
73.) B. 129, *St.-Georges-Dupré à MacLean, 23 décembre, 1780,* 194-95. Pouchet's father tried to overpower his son and to have the sacrament administered to him by force. Pouchet died the next day, having persisted to the end in his refusal to retract, and the curé refused to allow his body to be buried in consecrated ground.
74.) *Mandements des Evêques . . . ,* "Lettre circulaire au sujet des blés, 17 janvier, 1781," II, 303.

CHAPTER XV

1.) B. 182, *Hudibras (Smyth) to Haldimand, 31 Jan., 1781,* 306.
2.) B. 200-1, *Finlay to Haldimand, 30 Jan., 1781,* 249.
3.) B. 201, *Finlay to Haldimand, Quebec, 17 Feb., 1781,* 255-57;   *Ibid,* 289.
4.) B. 200-2, *Finlay to Mabane, 7 Feb., 1781,* 281.
5.) Q. 19, *Haldimand to Germain, 23 Nov., 1781,* 270.
6.) B. 200-1, *Finlay to Haldimand, 30 Jan., 1781.* Finlay names the following parishes: Autray—p. 250, La Prairie—p. 255, Chambly—pp. 256-57, St.-Charles—p. 257, and St.-Ours—pp. 250, 255, 256, 261.
7.) *Ibid,* 255, 257, 263.   B. 74, *Lanaudière à Haldimand, 23 janvier, 1781,* 8.
8.) B. 220, *29 janvier, 1781,* 91-6.
9.) *Ibid, 6 février, 1781,* 103-06.
10.) *Ibid, 20 février, 1781,* 109.
11.) Q. 18, *Haldimand to Germain, 6 July, 1781,* 107.
12.) B. 200-1, *Finlay à Haldimand, 30 janvier, 1781,* 252-53.
13.) *Ibid,* 255.
14.) *Ibid,* 267.
15.) B. 117, *Haldimand to Schmidt, 6 Aug., 1781,* 299-300;   *Ibid, Schmidt to Haldimand, 16 Aug., 1781,* 302-03.   Baby Papers, *Louis Demers, missionnaire, à Baby, St.-Pierre-les-Becquets, 17 novembre, 1781,* fol. 39.
16.) B. 74, *Le curé à St.-Léger, 18 janvier, 1781,* 6.
17.) B. 185-1, *Déposition du caporal George, février, 1781,* 297-98.
18.) B. 180, *Sherwood to Mathews, 10 March, 1781,* 12.
19.) B. 133, *Deposition of Benjamin Patterson, 23 Sept., 1781,* 146.
20.) B. 176, *Smith to Mathews, 13 Oct., 1781,* 322.   B. 131, *Haldimand to Brig. Gen. Speth, 22 Nov., 1781,* 136.
21.) B. 61, *Mathews to John Fraser, 23 Dec., 1781,* 84.
22.) B. 131, *Haldimand to Speth, 22 Nov., 1781,* 136.
23.) B. 61, *Mathews to Fraser, 23 Dec., 1781,* 84.
24.) B. 185-1, *Obligation de François Breton, 27 juin, 1781,* 291-92.   B. 170, *Haldimand à Tonnancourt, 26 juillet, 1781,* 239.

25.) Q. 19, *Haldimand to Germain, 23 Nov., 1781,* 269-74.
26.) B. 200-2, *Mabane to Finlay, Feb., 1781,* 516.
27.) B. 138, *Riedesel to Haldimand, Sorel, 13 Feb. 1781,* 84.
28.) *Mandements des Evêques* ..., "Circulaire au sujet des blés, 17 janvier, 1781," II, 303.
29.) Q. 18, *Haldimand to Germain, 6 July, 1781,* 106-09.
30.) Baby Papers, fol. 39, *passim.* B. 74, *Porlier à St.-Léger, 18 janvier, 1781,* 6. B. 133, *St.-Léger à Haldimand, 17 janvier, 1781,* 5.
31.) Archevêché de Québec, Lettres, *1782, Briand à Hubert, 25 février, 1782,* V.
32.) B. 147, *Haldimand's Memo, 1781,* 408-09.
33.) Q. 18, *Germain to Haldimand, 4 May, 1781,* 49.
34.) Doniol, *Histoire de la Participation* ..., IV, 565-66.
35.) *J.C.C.,* XXI, 1062.
36.) B. 148, *Haldimand to Clinton, 5 March, 1782,* 17.
37.) Q. 19, *Haldimand to Germain, 5 March, 1782,* 285-88.
38.) B. 177-2, *T.S. 26 July, 1782,* 394-95. B. 178, *Sherwood to Mathews, 13 Feb., 1783,* 78. B. 137, *Riedesel to Haldimand, 1 Aug., 1782,* 208.
39.) S. Series, Lower Canada, Justice, *1770-1783.*
40.) B. 188, *Montréal, 17 juin, 1782,* 172-73; *Ibid, Maurer to Geneway, 24 June, 1782,* 175-78.
41.) B. 177-2, *George Smith to Mathews, 17 Aug., 1782,* 447-48.
42.) Q. 20, *Haldimand to Shelburne, 15 Aug., 1782,* 10-12.
43.) *Ibid, Haldimand to Shelburne, 15 Aug. 1782,* 169-71.
44.) *Writings of George Washington,* "Plan of Campaign, 1 May, 1782," IX, 497-505.
45.) Q. 20, *Haldimand to Shelburne, 17 July, 1782,* 110-11.
46.) B. 50, *Shelburne to Haldimand, 20 April, 1782,* 164-67.
47.) Q. 20, *Haldimand to Shelburne, 17 Aug., 1782,* 199.
48.) *Ibid, Haldimand to Townsend, 25 Oct., 1782,* 320-25.
49.) Griffin, M. I. J., *Catholics and the American Revolution* (Ridley Park, 1907), I, 114, 118.
50.) *United States of America, Statutes at Large,* I, 547-49.
51.) Q. 22, *Haldimand to North, 12 Oct., 1783,* 87.
52.) *Laws of the State of New York,* 735.
53.) Q. 21, *Townsend to Haldimand, 28 Feb., 1783,* 72-3.
54.) B. 205, *Mathews to Mr. Prentice, Provost Marshall, 2 May, 1783,* 260.
55.) Du Calvet, Pierre, *The Case of Peter Du Calvet, esq., of Montreal in the province of Quebeck. Containing an account of the long and severe imprisonment he suffered in the said province by the order of General Haldimand, the present governor of the same, without the least offence or other lawful cause whatever* (London, 1784).

INDEX